Devolution:

The End of Britain?

D1334883

Devolution:
The End of Britain?

Tam Dalyell

JONATHAN CAPE
THIRTY BEDFORD SQUARE LONDON

First Published 1977
© 1977 By Tam Dalyell

Jonathan Cape Ltd, 30 Bedford Square, London WC1

British Library Cataloguing in Publication Data
Dalyell, Tam
Devolution.
1. Decentralization in government – Great
Britain
I. Title
354′.41′082 JN329. D43

ISBN 0–224–01559–1
ISBN 0–224–01560–5 Pbk

Printed in Great Britain by
R. and R. Clark Ltd. Edinburgh

For Kathleen
and the forty-three Labour Members of Parliament
who by vote or abstention
refused to support the Guillotine Motion
on the 22nd February 1977

Contents

Foreword

Hugh Trevor-Roper
Regius Professor of Modern History, Oxford

All those who believe in Great Britain and its continued existence, now threatened, should be grateful to Mr Tam Dalyell, Labour Member of Parliament for West Lothian, the author of this book. Many others in our country — the vast majority, I believe — wish to preserve its unity; but too many of that majority either do not think at all about the essential nature and conditions of such unity, or do not think clearly, or lack either the basis of factual knowledge on which to reason or the courage to resist an apparently irresistible tide. If Great Britain should be dismantled, posterity will know where to lay the blame. If that sorry fate should be avoided, and the tide turned, it should know whom to thank. In particular, it should thank Mr Dalyell.

I say this in full knowledge that hundreds of British people have spoken up, rationally and clearly, against the folly of the present Government's Bill for the devolution of legislation in Scotland and Wales. They have shown how that project was hatched out of electoral expediency, fed by the irresponsible publicity of the media, allowed to grow through public in- difference to what seems, and is, an irrelevant exercise, and nearly carried through by ordinary Parliamentary management. But the voices of these critics would all have been ineffective against the brute force of Parliamentary mathematics had not twenty-two Labour MPs had the courage to defy their whips and vote against their own party in a crucial debate. By that rebellion they denied to their own Government the power which it sought to curtail inconvenient debate and force its undigested bill through the House of Commons.

To oppose and defeat one's own party on a legislative programme declared by it to be of central importance is a very serious act of defiance, which no MP undertakes without an overwhelming conviction of its necessity. It also requires courage. I can think of no parallel to the action of those twenty-two MPs on 22 February 1977 since the debate, on 7 May 1940, which persuaded Neville Chamberlain to resign. But would all those twenty-two MPs have been willing to act as they did without the consistent well-informed speeches and incessant activity of Mr Dalyell?

Mr Dalyell's qualifications to speak on Scottish affairs are unquestionable. He is a Scotsman who for fifteen years has represented in Parliament a constituency in the industrial centre of Scotland. He was Chairman of the Scottish Labour Group of MPs between June 1974 and November 1975. When he speaks about Scottish nationalism, he has a right to be heard, for he has watched its politics at close quarters: he has regularly defeated the Chairman of the Scottish National Party for the Parliamentary seat which he holds. Equally, when he deals with external affairs — when he refutes the claim that an independent Scotland would wield more influence in the EEC than in the United Kingdom — he knows what he is talking about: for he has been for the last two years a member of the European as well as of the British Parliament.

No man, it can be said, has so deep an understanding of the Devolution project, in so far as it concerns Scotland, as Mr Dalyell. He can speak with equal authority on its political and its electoral history, on its Parliamentary fortunes, and on its administrative and economic consequences. This is more than can be said of any of those English politicians, both Labour and Tory, who invented the project, not because it was relevant to any of our real problems, but in order, as they thought, to steal the thunder of a vocal minority and thereby shore up their own failing electoral strength in the wayward constituencies of Scotland.

The proposed devolution of legislation in Scotland does not concern only the Scots: otherwise I would not be writing this foreword. It is not a mere matter of local government — although its advocates would like us to believe so, in order to lull the English into indifference. A cardinal belief of those who oppose

the project is that such devolution is not only pointless, in
that it will solve no real problem, and harmful, in that it will
increase the economic cost of Scottish administration, but also
unworkable and can only lead, through inevitable friction, to
the ultimate disintegration of the United Kingdom. This view
is shared by the Scottish National Party, which voted for the
Bill precisely because they believed that it would lead to that
result which the Government promised that it would prevent.
For the same reason, they will vote for the new and separate
Scotland and Wales Bills again.

When two opposed parties insist that the same measure will
lead to opposite results, one of them at least must be wrong, and
we and our posterity, who will be the victims of any mistake,
have a right to expect rational arguments, not merely un-
documented paternal assurances, from those who prophesy our
salvation. So far we have never heard, from the supporters
of the Devolution Bill, any rational demonstration that their
project, or any variant of it, will bring any administrative or
economic benefit to the people of Scotland or of Great Britain;
nor have we heard any rational reply to the specific and concrete objections which have already been made against it.
As Mr Dalyell points out, Ministers have shown consistent
unwillingness to discuss these questions. They have preferred
to rely on vague assurances and — as they hoped — docile
Parliamentary votes. Believing that, in politics, a week is a long
time, they have behaved as if, for the sake of a few more votes
in the immediately foreseeable future, a union of three centuries
can be lightly gambled away.

History takes terrible revenges on such short views. There is a
momentum in politics more powerful than the hands of those
who release it. Great states have been unmade by the un-
controllable consequences of ill-considered decisions made to
secure immediate petty gains or to postpone immediate petty
losses. The unity of Great Britain, its continuance as Great
Britain, is a matter which concerns all British people, English
as well as Scots and Welsh. The Devolution Bill, which the
courage of a few Parliamentary rebels stopped in its apparently
well-oiled tracks on 22 February 1977, will, we are told, be
presented to Parliament again; in the form of separate Bills for
Scotland and Wales with only cosmetic changes from the

original Bill fully described in Mr Dalyell's book; and this time,
with the aid of a little judicious horse-trading, Mr Michael
Foot may perhaps get his psephological sums to come out.
Therefore it is essential that the true facts about Scottish government and the Scottish economy, and the real implications of
the Bill, be fully ventilated and understood, before we are
carried away by what may prove an irreversible process. Mr
Dalyell's aim, in this book, is to set out those facts and those
implications. His arguments are, I believe, unanswerable.
If not, let them be answered.

Acknowledgments

I would like to thank David Machin and Graham Greene, directors of Jonathan Cape, for their encouragement over twelve months; Jeremy Lewis for help in clarity of presentation; Mrs Pat Newnham and the staff of Cape's; also, the ever helpful staff of the House of Commons Library. Many thanks are due to R. & R. Clark, the distinguished Edinburgh printers, for their speed, quality and helpfulness.

I would like to thank the members of the West Lothian Constituency Labour Party, some of whom share my views on Devolution, and others who, in varying degrees, do not, for their understanding and many kindnesses to me on the issue, over the years.

Above all, I would like to thank my wife Kathleen, not only for her many suggestions, and insights into the whole Devolution issue, but for her active support, without which I could not be a useful Member of one Parliament, let alone two.

T. D.

1

Dismantling the United Kingdom

On 25 March 1707, the Scottish Parliament met for the last time in Edinburgh: just over a month later, on 1 May, it was united with that of England to form the Parliament of Great Britain. Those who were responsible for the Act of Union rightly realised that, after centuries of futile feuding, this could only be to the benefit of both countries; and over the past 270 years the political, social, commercial and family ties between England and Scotland have grown steadily closer and closer. Like Wales — which was united with England as far back as the early Middle Ages — Scotland has successfully retained her own very distinctive identity while enjoying the benefits of a wider political association; and Scottish politicians, soldiers, scientists, artists and businessmen have made an outstanding contribution to the well-being of the United Kingdom as a whole. To suggest that England, Scotland and Wales might once again be parted from one another has always seemed absurd, impractical and entirely undesirable.

Yet in the past couple of years the dismantling of the United Kingdom has suddenly become all-too-real a possibility; and the tragedy is that it could well be brought about by well-meaning politicians who fail to realise the full implications of what they are doing in their feverish — and quite unnecessary — anxiety to appease small yet vociferous nationalist minorities in Scotland and Wales. Earlier this year, the House of Commons came close to taking the penultimate step towards the creation of separate Scottish and Welsh states. The ill-conceived Scotland and Wales Bill was mercifully defeated following a dogged resistance by forty-three Labour back-benchers: but it would be over-optimistic to assume that devolution is now a dead duck, and it is in order to fortify the opposition to any future schemes of this kind that this book has been written.

For reasons which we will examine in a later chapter, Scottish and Welsh nationalism flowered in the late 1960s and 1970s — sustained in the case of Scotland by visions of Scots hogging the North Sea oil revenues. Many of those who voted for the Scottish National Party and Plaid Cymru did so as a form of protest against the apparent incompetence and mismanagement of the economy by both Labour and Conservative Governments, rather than because they wanted to see the breakup of the United Kingdom: yet politicians in all the major political parties were so rattled by nationalist successes in local government and in by-elections that instead of devoting their energies to the fundamental issues facing the country, the Government have preferred to waste invaluable time and energies, Parliamentary, Ministerial and Civil Service, elaborating dangerous and impractical schemes with which to try to appease the nationalists. In their anxiety to do so, they have put the future of the United Kingdom at risk, for — as the SNP fully realises — devolving power to a Scottish legislative assembly could only be a temporary staging-post on the way to full independence. Devolution has been resorted to by baffled, frightened politicians from a mixture of vague idealism — the belief that the appearance of bringing government closer to the people concerned must, almost by definition, be a good thing — and political expediency: yet few of those who so blithely advocate the devolutionary cause seem to have a realistic idea of where it must, inevitably, lead us.

Nor is it entirely surprising that the cause of devolution has made such progress under Labour administrations. Scotland and Wales have traditionally returned many Labour MPs to the House of Commons, particularly from industrial areas, and we Labour politicians are only too aware of how potentially vulnerable we are to the nationalist challenge in our Welsh and Scottish constituencies. Yet instead of standing up to the nationalists, many Labour MPs have preferred to try to win back erstwhile supporters by stealing some of the nationalists' clothes and promising the essentially unstable half-way house of devolution. Sad to say, some members of the Labour Government have apparently been prepared to put the continued unity of Britain at risk in the mistaken belief that, by so doing, they could improve their chances of remaining in office. As we shall see, devolution would bring no benefits to the people of Scotland: how absurd, and how unworthy, if it were to be introduced for reasons of short-term expediency by jittery politicians who have little real belief in it, and know only too well how irrelevant it is to the real problems confronting the United Kingdom and its constituent countries.

It may be helpful to the reader if I indicate the broad structure of the book at this stage. A good deal of power is already devolved to Scotland, and in Chapter 2 I shall examine the existing situation in some detail. I then go on to discuss the Government's most recent proposals, as set out in the Scotland and Wales Bill: although this particular Bill has been defeated, it seems highly likely that any future Bills will incorporate many of its proposals. From there we examine the very broad reasons for the rise of nationalism and the success of the SNP, before going on to describe the process by which both the major political parties took up the cause of devolution in order to 'dish the Nats'. Chapters 9 and 10 examine the attitudes of various institutions and pressure groups in Scotland towards devolution (most of them are firmly opposed to it, and their reasons for so doing are explained), while the following two chapters suggest some of the more general arguments against the SNP and their fellow-travellers. The devolution debate has been conducted against the background of the Ulster troubles, and Chapter 13 examines the haunting — if extremely misleading — parallels between the Irish and Scottish situations. In the penultimate Chapter I offer some constructive — if, of necessity, somewhat marginal — suggestions of my own, both positive and negative, as guidelines for Governmental action; in the final chapter I return to my basic argument that devolution is a moving escalator to an independent Scotland, and that the only way to contain the SNP is to confront the Scottish people with the harsh reality of what a separate Scottish state would mean to them.

Comparatively little will be said about devolution as far as it affects Wales: partly because I am not as fully qualified to discuss the situation there, and partly because it is fundamentally different from that in Scotland. The fact that Wales and Scotland were — in defiance of all reason — lumped together in the same Bill earlier this year is, alas, symptomatic of the heedless haste with which the Bill was cobbled together in the hope that it could be rushed through Parliament before anyone (and not least the English, to whom the whole subject has been a matter of profound indifference) could have an opportunity of working out its full implications. Nevertheless, many of the arguments put forward here apply equally well to Wales; and if my book weakens the cause of devolution in Wales as well as in Scotland, I shall regard that as a very welcome bonus.

2

The Status Quo

When people make the deceptively vague and seemingly unexceptionable claim that the Scots ought to have more say in their own affairs, they often fail to realise the large extent to which administrative devolution in Scotland already exists. Later on, we will come to the argument — so often and eloquently deployed by Professor John Mackintosh, MP — that it is precisely the extent of the Scottish Office's administrative authority which makes it so necessary for a democratic element to be added in the shape of an Assembly in Edinburgh. In the meantime it is important to outline the current position, both in the interests of clarity and because — as we shall be arguing in a later chapter — the real answer to demands that the Scots should have a greater say in their own affairs is to build on *existing* institutions rather than burden the country with an impractical and expensive additional layer of government, the political implications of which would be far more wide-ranging and disruptive than well-intentioned devolutionists care to imagine.

The Secretary of State for Scotland

Apart from a modest and skeleton staff, based on the elegant Dover House in Whitehall, which deals with the needs of Scottish Office Ministers attending Parliament, Cabinet and Ministerial Committees in London, the Civil Service in Scotland operates from New St Andrew's House and St Andrew's House in Edinburgh. In so far as they affect Scotland, the work of eleven United Kingdom Departments is carried out on an administrative basis by civil servants in Edinburgh.

The Civil Service in Scotland is an integral part of the United Kingdom Civil Service, and there is a good deal of cross-fertilisation of personnel between Government departments. Civil servants are recruited through the normal processes of the United Kingdom Civil Service Commission. Since the Stafford Northcote Reforms of 1853, many Scots have achieved positions of eminence within the British Civil Service.

What so many enthusiasts for devolution fail to realise — or conveniently choose to forget — is that some of the most sensitive areas of government in Scotland are, in fact, the direct responsibility of the Secretary of State for Scotland rather than the relevant Ministry in London. Accepting one's own shortcomings is always an uncomfortable business, yet however hard the SNP may try to blame Scottish grievances in such areas as education, health and housing — the real gut issues of politics — on to faceless, bigoted Englishmen in Whitehall, the truth of the matter is that they are the direct responsibility of a fellow-Scot, to whom very considerable powers have already been devolved.

The post of Secretary of State for Scotland was established in 1887, but his power increased considerably in 1939, when the Scottish Office was moved from London to St Andrew's House in Edinburgh. The Secretary of State has a seat in the Cabinet — where his influence inevitably depends to some extent on his own personality and his relationship with the Prime Minister of the day. As we shall see, he is responsible for many areas of government which are the responsibility of individual Ministers in England, and he represents the interests of Scotland in general to the Cabinet — often with considerable success.

AGRICULTURE

Apart from certain aspects of agricultural research, the Secretary of State for Scotland is Minister of Agriculture in Scotland. Although the June 1975 Agricultural Census recorded 32,000 full-time farm workers in Scotland, barely one-third of the numbers employed in 1939, Scottish farming is in a basically healthy state, and the decline in numbers working on the land has been caused largely by factors which have affected agriculture throughout the world: increasing mechanisation and improved technology, and rationalisation of the size of agricultural holdings. The Secretary of State for Scotland is represented at the Price Review policy formulation, and in Brussels during the European Farm Price annual negotiations, often by a Junior Scottish Office Minister with specific responsibility for agricultural problems.

About 40 per cent of Britain's 2 million hectares of woodland is in Scotland. Well over half — 432,000 hectares — of the 809,000 hectares of Forestry Commission plantations are in Scotland, employing 2,400 full- and part-time industrial workers. The Secretary of State has Ministerial responsibility for an industry which is selling timber worth about £9 million a year.

FISHING

At the end of 1976, there were just over 7,000 full-time fishermen in Scotland, and about another 18,000 were employed in processing, net-making, boat-building and repairing, and other occupations related to the fishing industry. The value of fish landed is about £70 million per year, or about a quarter of the United Kingdom catch. During 1976 and 1977, in the course of the difficult negotiations with EEC countries and Iceland on the almost intractable problem of North Sea fishing, the Secretary of State or his representative has been present to explain the problems and argue the case of the Scottish fishermen. And occasionally Britain has been represented in such negotiations by a Scottish Office Minister, speaking on behalf of the fishing interests of the whole of the United Kingdom.

INDUSTRY

The Secretary of State for Scotland is expected to play an important role in the promotion and support of a strong Scottish industrial base. He has Governmental responsibility for stimulating expansion and new industrial investment in Scotland. He is the final arbiter when it comes to granting selective financial assistance under Section 7 of the 1972 Industrial Act — the pivotal piece of legislation through which industries with what appear to be temporary difficulties can be helped. He has to guide the Scottish Development Agency, and accept ultimate political responsibility for its actions. Through the Scottish Economic Planning Department, he has to exercise certain statutory functions concerning electricity generation and distribution by the South of Scotland Electricity Generating Board, and the North of Scotland Hydro-Electricity Board. He has statutory functions concerning Highland Development, new town development and tourism. He has to liaise with the UK Departments concerned as far as Scottish aspects of the steel industry, aircraft construction and coal mining are concerned. He is directly concerned with EEC Regional and Industrial Policy, and must try to co-ordinate any EEC assistance to Scotland through the important Regional Development Grant which is paid automatically towards capital expenditure in qualifying industries, and is administered in Scotland by the Department of Industry office in Glasgow.

The Secretary of State for Scotland and the Scottish Office are playing an increasingly large part in the United Kingdom's work as a Member of the European Community. Quite apart from their interest in the EEC's Regional and Industrial Policy, they are particularly involved in the operation of the European Regional Development Fund, the European Social Fund, the European Coal and Steel Community and the European Investment Bank. Assistance is available from the Regional Development Fund towards the cost of infrastructure provided by public authorities to assist economic development and towards industrial projects. In co-ordination with the Secretary of State for Scotland, more than £28 million had been committed by the Fund by January 1977 for a variety of projects in Scotland, including water, roads, sewerage, industrial estate schemes, major port and airport improvement works, and a large number of industrial ventures. Assistance from the European Social Fund for training and resettlement schemes in Scotland has totalled more than £19 million. The Secretary of State also deals with loans approved by the European Investment Bank for Scottish Projects; these totalled around £170 million in 1977, including £48 million for the development of the Frigg Gas field.

He also exercises co-ordinating functions as far as a number of aspects of on-shore development in support of North Sea oil are concerned, and has a continuing role in co-operating with the Department of Energy over platform construction. The development of land in connection with North Sea Oil is controlled by him under the Town and Country Planning (Scotland) Acts; and although considerable planning powers were delegated in 1976 to the Orkney and Shetland Authorities and to the Grampian and Highland Regional Authorities, any decisions they make are subject to appeal to the Secretary of State. If a proposed development does not accord with the development plan, the planning authority must inform the Secretary of State, who has to decide whether or not to intervene within twenty-eight days, by 'calling in' the application for his own decision.

He may call in an application on one of four grounds: if it is on a significant scale in relation to the development plan as a whole; if it is of more than local importance; if it raises a new issue of general policy; or if it is the kind of development over which he is generally exercising control at the time. If he decides to call in an application, he has to give both the planning authority and the applicant the opportunity to ask for a public local enquiry — or he may decide himself that an enquiry is needed. As the development of North Sea resources enters a new stage, moving from production to processing, new demands are being made on the land and on planning applications, especially in relation to delicate issues of industrial zoning. Furthermore, under the Offshore Petroleum Development (Scotland) Act 1975, the Secretary of State is given the power to acquire land either by agreement or compulsorily if it is required for one of a number of defined oil-related purposes. Where such land is urgently required, and planning permission has been given, the Secretary of State may acquire it by an expedited acquisition order. However, a statutory instrument containing such an order cannot be made, unless a draft of it has been laid before, and approved by resolution of, both Houses of Parliament.

If I have gone into the powers of the Secretary of State for Scotland in relation to North Sea oil development in some detail, this is partly because it is frequently implied that decisions affecting Scotland with regard to the on-shore problems of North Sea oil are made in London; on the contrary, they are almost always made in Edinburgh, Aberdeen or Glasgow.

EDUCATION

With the exception of the universities in Scotland, which are ultimately responsible to the Department of Education and Science in London through the University Grants Committee, public sector education in Scotland is the responsibility of the Secretary of State rather than of the Minister of Education. In turn, he is responsible to Parliament for the overall control and development of the education system. As in England, public sector education is run jointly by national local authorities, and the actual provision of education is the duty of nine regional and three islands councils, which educate more than 1 millon pupils in 3,200 schools, most of them comprehensive and co-educational. Though most Scottish schools are non-denominational, there are separate Roman Catholic schools within the public system, in which under an important settlement between Church and State in a 1918 Act of Parliament, the Catholic Church approves teachers as regards belief and character, and religious instruction is an integral part of the curriculum. The Scottish Education Department is also responsible for informal education, including youth and community service, and adult Education. Ten Colleges of Education, providing courses of professional training for teachers, are under the day-to-day management of independent boards of governors, but are supported by direct grant from the Secretary of State for Scotland's vote (allocation of public funds) and therefore major decisions are his. He is also responsible for fourteen institutions of further education, and over sixty further education day colleges. An Under-Secretary of State for Scotland has direct responsibility for the work of the Scottish Education Department.

HEALTH

The Secretary of State for Scotland is responsible to Parliament for the administration of the National Health Service in Scotland, and all aspects of the health of the population. For a quarter of a century following the establishment of the National Health Service, in July 1948, the organisation of the NHS in Scotland remained substantially unchanged. There were 5 Regional Hospital Boards for planning hospital services, 65 boards of management for day-to-day management of the hospitals and 25 Executive Councils for general medical, dental, pharmaceutical and ophthalmic services; 56 local Health Authorities provided services for mothers, young children and the elderly.

In April 1974, a new structure was introduced. Fifteen Health

Boards, charged with the administration of the health services in their respective areas, are now directly accountable to the Secretary of State. Some services, like the ambulance service, blood transfusion and legal advice, are provided centrally for the whole NHS by an organisation called the Common Services Agency. However, the fifteen Health Boards administer all aspects of the Health Service in their respective areas on the Secretary of State's behalf. They take major policy decisions on such matters as the broad allocation of resources and the long-term planning of services. Many day-to-day decisions, however, are taken by the chief officers of each Health Board, working together as an executive group. In addition to the chairmen of the Boards, 276 members are appointed to the Boards by the Secretary of State. Members are appointed primarily for their potential contribution as individuals from names submitted by over 180 organisations, representing a wide range of interests. Other criteria, such as geographical distribution, are also taken into account. It should not be overlooked that these appointments, like a host of other appointments in his gift, make the Secretary of State and the Scottish Office a source of a great volume of patronage. However, the patronage stems from Edinburgh, and not London.

HOUSING

As in England, public sector housing is the responsibility of the local authorities, but ultimate responsibility resides with the Secretary of State for Scotland, in the same way as it resides with the Secretary of State for the Environment in England. Successive Governments have pursued somewhat divergent policies in Scotland, where the proportion of public sector to private sector housing has been significantly higher than south of the Border, and they have acquiesced in a policy of low rents, possibly to the detriment of housing standards and maintenance.

Unique to Scotland is a direct government-run housing authority, called the Scottish Special Housing Association, the management of which is responsible to the Secretary of State. Its function is to build and let houses in areas of need throughout Scotland. Over the years, the SSHA have been heavily subsidised by central government, tempting Dame Evelyn Sharp — while Permanent Secretary to the Ministry of Housing and

Local Government in Whitehall — to remark that when she surveyed the finances of the SSHA, she felt like becoming an English nationalist.

The Scottish Grand Committee

On most Tuesday and Thursday mornings when the House of Commons is in session, Scottish MPs meet in the largest Committee Room at Westminster to form the Scottish Grand Committee, which transacts exclusively Scottish business. In order that the United Kingdom party balance may be reflected in the Committee, a number of English MPs are added to make up numbers. (In recent times, because the Labour majority in Scotland has been higher than the proportionate majority in the whole of the United Kingdom, the additional MPs have been Conservatives — often Members who have incurred the displeasure of the Conservative whips are banished to do a stint on the Scottish Grand Committee, and accordingly they only register a token appearance, if they find it convenient.)

The Grand Committee deals with the general Second Reading discussion on Scottish Bills, after they have been referred to it by a purely formal Resolution on the Floor of the House. During the year, there are also six to eight 'Matter Days' when subjects of topical interest can be raised by the Opposition parties, usually in June and July.

The Grand Committee is much more than a 'talking shop' or a piece of window-dressing. It really does tackle the nuts and bolts of Scottish legislation. If Governments tend to get their way in the Scottish Grand Committee, this is equally true on the floor of the House of Commons. The very existence of the Grand Committee is proof that the views of Scotland already receive closer attention than those of the regions of England, many of which have very similar needs and problems.

The Royal Commission on Local Government Reform

Throughout the early 1960s, there was mounting dissatisfaction both in Scotland and in England with the many anomalies of the system of local government, which had grown like the proverbial Topsy, and in particular with its mounting costs, which were making the rate support grant one of the major items of public expenditure.

As a result the Labour Government decided to set up two Royal Commissions, to look into local government in England and Scotland under Sir John Maud (later Lord Redcliffe-Maud) and Lord Wheatley respectively. Both produced heavyweight reports in 1971 — it is fair to say that Wheatley was better received than Maud — and their findings formed the basis of the Local Government Reform Acts of the 1970s.

Wheatley produced a carefully balanced package, based on the philosophy of regionalisation, geared where appropriate to the idea that the 'estuary', such as the Forth or the Tay, ought to be a major determining factor. (In the event, Fife won a battle in the House of Commons to remain as a single unit, so upsetting the balance in the East of Scotland.)

In spite of the teething troubles, which are inevitable in any major shake-up of the machinery of government, I am convinced that the basic belief of the Royal Commission that major functions such as planning, education and social work should be carried out on a Regional scale, with housing and certain other functions going to a second tier of District authorities, was correct. Of the Regions established following the Report's recommendations, — Borders, Dumfries and Galloway, Central, Fife, Grampian, Highland, Lothian, Strathclyde, Tayside, Orkney and Shetland, and Western Isles — five can be said to be working well, the rest are likely to work well. Contrary to popular belief, considerable savings have been made as a result of their being set up.

If the Regions have been brought into a measure of public disrepute, it is largely because of golden handshakes to a smallish number of senior employees. Naturally enough, the press has wallowed in such cases. However, since such a system is inevitable in any reorganisation — unless men and women with years of loyal service are to be summarily dismissed in a style which would simply not be acceptable in this day and age — it is difficult to avoid certain high compensation payments.

Two other points should be made here about the Royal Commission. First of all, the recommendations were put forward along with proposals that certain councillors — and particularly chairmen of Council committees — should be paid.

Had both Conservative and Labour Governments not funked doing this, I believe the whole image of local government, now so tarnished by corruption, would have been different. In Scotland there has been a very high incidence of what one can call 'petty corruption' in local government. There is no question of huge sums being involved — the amount of money passing through local government hands which is misappropriated is infinitesimally small. None the less, the stink of corruption has a habit of hanging around and of course this makes the Labour Party, some of whose members are largely responsible, open to attack by a young and aggressive Scottish National Party, which remains untainted simply because it has not been in a position of power.

Second, the Districts have been extremely dilatory about implementing the Wheatley recommendation that Community Councils should be set up to deal with the most local grassroots matters — even though not much public money was involved. Failure to have done this as speedily as it ought to have been done has given credence to the accusation that local government is now less in touch than it used to be. In fact, at the root of such accusations is a certain nostalgia among some Scots people for the days when the local councillor used to spend his life hearing grievances and fixing 'wee things' for his electors. The failure to press ahead with community councils demonstrates once again the difficulties of accepting most, but not all, the recommendations of a carefully balanced report. Had the reluctance to set up community councils been clear to Lord Wheatley and his colleagues on the Royal Commission, their recommendations on other matters might well have been different. As it is, the alleged and exaggerated remoteness of local government has benefited the SNP.

The Convention of Scottish Local Authorities

The Convention was formed following the reform of local government in Scotland in May 1975 to represent the interests of the new Regional, District and Island authorities in Scotland.

In the former system of local government there were four associations to represent the interests of the local authorities then established. These were the Association of County Councils in

Scotland, the Scottish Counties of Cities Association, the Convention of Royal Burghs and the District Councils' Association of Scotland. The Convention of Royal Burghs was by far the oldest local authority association in the United Kingdom, dating from before the Union of the Crowns, and accordingly it was decided to maintain the historical tradition by incorporating the word 'Convention' in the title of the new body.

The Convention was formed specifically to protect the interests of the new local authorities in matters of national concern. Thus, the Convention considers legislation before Parliament on topics which are of interest to local government and, indeed, in many cases when a Bill is presented into Parliament it has been the subject of prior consultation with the Convention. The Convention also engages in negotiations and discussions with other bodies of national significance whose functions impinge upon those of local authorities or who look towards local government for a measure of financial support. The most significant negotiations are those with civil servants and Ministers on levels of public expenditure and on the amount of Exchequer grant payable to local authorities in each financial year. The Convention also submits evidence on behalf of local authorities to Royal Commissions and Committees of Enquiry and it is available to offer guidance to its member Councils in relation to any matter where uniformity of approach by the individual authorities is desirable. It therefore tries to ensure that the voice of Scottish local government is heard in every matter of major significance which has some bearing upon local government.

The Convention as such meets only four times per year, one of these meetings taking the form of a Conference. All member Councils are represented at Convention meetings but in view of the great disparity in size and resources between the local authorities who make up the membership of the Convention it carries out most of its executive work through committees. It is thus in the main a deliberative body which cannot overturn the decisions reached by its executive committees but may merely remit back for further consideration any matter not acted upon by the time it meets.

The Convention endeavours to speak with one voice as often as possible. It is acknowledged, however, that there may be occasions when the interests of the Regions and Districts may differ on a particular issue. The structure of the Convention therefore provides for three types of committee. Some deal only with District functions and on such committees District councils and Islands Councils only are represented. Because there are fifty-six District and Islands Councils, it is obviously impossible to give each member Council a place on every committee, but each District and Islands Council is represented on at least one. In respect of the smaller Districts places on committees are allocated by balloting from authorities within certain population bands. Each District authority with a population in excess of 100,000 has at least one representative on every District committee.

There are also certain committees dealing with Regional functions only and here the membership is drawn from the Regional and Islands Councils. Because there are only nine Regions and three Islands Councils, it is possible for each of the Regional Councils to be represented on such committees. The basis of representation is such that Strathclyde and the other large Regions have more places than the smaller Regions but their representation is not proportionate to their size.

The third category of committee is that which covers the joint or concurrent functions. Representation on such committees is arranged in such a way that Regional Councils and District Councils each have the same number of representatives, thus ensuring that one tier of local government cannot override the wishes of the other. This is reinforced by a provision in the Constitution of the Convention to the effect that, if a major dispute should arise between Region or District, it shall be possible for separate viewpoints to be expressed to the Government or any other interested party.

The Convention is a voluntary body in that member Councils are free to withdraw from membership if they so choose. It is financed by way of subscriptions received from the member Councils. Each year a budget is drawn up and, having regard to the functions which they respectively exercise, three-quarters of the budget is allocated against Regional Councils and one-quarter against District and Islands Councils. Having thus established the total sum of money to be paid by the respective tiers of local government, the individual contributions are determined by reference to population.

The Courts

Under the Act of Union, Scotland retained her own system of law, which is derived from Roman Law, and is more akin to Continental than to Anglo-Saxon Law. The Courts which exercise criminal jurisdiction in Scotland are the High Court of Justiciary, the Sheriff Court and the District Court. The two main civil courts are the Court of Session — the supreme central court, subject only to the House of Lords — and the Sheriff Court.

There are two types of criminal procedure, solemn and summary. In solemn procedure, in both the High Court of Justiciary and the Sheriff Court, trial is before a judge sitting with a jury of fifteen laymen, and the alleged offence is set out in a document known as an indictment. The judge decides questions of law, the jury questions of fact; they may reach a decision by a simple majority. In summary procedure in the Sheriff and District Courts, the judge sits without a jury and decides questions of both law and fact. The offence charged is set out in a document called a summary complaint.

In Scotland, unlike England, proceedings in the criminal court are never initiated by the police, and only in a small number of special cases by individuals or officials of public bodies. Responsibility for prosecutions in criminal causes in Scotland rests with the Lord Advocate — as Senior Scottish Law Officer and the equivalent of the Attorney-General — acting on behalf of the Crown. The Government Department which handles criminal matters on behalf of the Lord Advocate is the Crown Office. In practice, most prosecutions are taken on behalf of the Crown by the Solicitor-General, the second Law Officer, by seven advocates-depute, and a staff of local prosecutors called procurators-fiscal. The procurators-fiscal are civil servants, with a training either as advocates or solicitors. The police report details of an alleged crime to the local procurator-fiscal, who has discretion whether to prosecute subject to the direction and control of the Lord Advocate and the Crown Office. There are forty-four full- and part-time procurators-fiscal.

The supreme criminal court in Scotland is the High Court of Justiciary, which sits in Edinburgh and also goes on circuit in several major towns and cities. It only hears cases taken on indictment, presided over by a judge sitting with a jury of fifteen, and has exclusive jurisdiction over certain serious crimes including murder, treason and rape. The High Court of Justiciary also sits, in a court of at least three judges, as the Court of Criminal Appeal, hearing appeals from the High Court as the court of first instance, and from the Sheriff and District Courts. The Sheriff Court deals with offences committed in the area within which it has jurisdiction in both summary and criminal cases. Under solemn procedure, a sheriff may sentence offenders for up to two years, and has an additional power of remit to the High Court of Justiciary if he thinks a heavier sentence should be imposed. District Courts, set up by an Act in 1975, are the administrative responsibility of the local authority. They preserve some of the traditional features of the former burgh and Justice of the Peace (JP) Courts. The maximum fine they can impose is £100, and the longest prison sentence sixty days. The bench of a District Court may be constituted by one or more lay judges or by a stipendiary magistrate, who is a professional lawyer of at least five years' standing, and has the same summary criminal jurisdiction and powers as the Sheriff. Three stipendiary magistrates sit in the Glasgow District Court.

The supreme civil court in Scotland is the Court of Session, which sits in Edinburgh and may hear cases transferred to it and appealed from the Sheriff Courts. Only the Court of Session can hear certain categories of cases, especially those relating to personal status such as divorce. There is a right of appeal from the Court of Session to the House of Lords. A major principle of the Court is that cases originating in it are both prepared for decision and decided by judges sitting singly, whose decisions are subject to review by several other judges. The total number of judges is twenty, of whom twelve, called Lords Ordinary, mainly prepare and decide cases in the first instance. This branch is called the Outer House. The eight other judges are divided into two divisions of four judges each, forming the Inner House. The First Division is presided over by the Lord President of the Court of Session, and the Second Division by the Lord Justice Clerk. The main business of each division is to review the decisions of the Lords Ordinary or inferior courts which have appealed to it.

In addition to its criminal jurisdiction, the Sheriff Court deals with most civil litigation in Scotland. Its jurisdiction is very wide. The value of the subject matter with which the court can deal has, with few exceptions, no upper limit, and a wide range of remedies can be granted. For example, actions can be entertained for debt, contract, reparation, rent restriction, possessory actions and actions affecting the use of property, actions affecting leases and tenancies and actions for alimony and the custody of children.

There are several other courts with particular functions, including: the Land Valuation Appeal Court; United Kingdom Courts of Special Jurisdiction, such as the Restrictive Practices Court; the Scottish Land Court, with jurisdiction on agricultural and crofting tenancies; Church Courts, which are technically civil courts of the realm, but have jurisdiction only over members of the Church of Scotland and include the General Assembly of the Kirk, synods, presbyteries and kirk sessions; and the Court of the Lord Lyon, King of Arms, which has historical jurisdiction in disputes over the rights to bear coats of arms (and is no mean dollar earner!).

By Act of Sederunt, the Court of Session regulates its own procedures and the procedure of civil proceedings in the Sheriff Courts, while by Act of Adjournal the High Court of Justiciary regulates its own procedure and that of criminal proceedings in the Sheriff Courts and District Courts. The Secretary of State for Scotland is responsible for the organisation and administration of the Sheriff Courts, and, to a lesser extent, the supreme courts. In exercising their judicial functions, the judges are not in any way subject to Ministerial control; however, Sheriff Principals have certain administrative functions, in the exercise of which they have a responsibility to the Secretary of State to ensure the speedy and efficient disposal of justice in their sheriffdoms.

It is against this background that any discussion about transferring responsibility for the Scottish courts to the Assembly should be judged.

3

The Scotland and Wales Bill

It is a myth that the 1977 Scotland and Wales Bill failed in the House of Commons because it was incompetently drafted, or because it was badly handled by the Ministers in charge of the legislation and responsible for steering it through Parliament. The truth is different. The Bill was the outcome of a huge volume of hard work by clever civil servants, and a succession of senior Ministers and able and inventive Junior Ministers, specially chosen for their suitability for the task. Ministers and civil servants, with the most skilful of Parliamentary draughtsmen working on their behalf, burnt a great deal of midnight oil devising the best possible scheme, as they saw it. Had it been possible to find some magic clause which would have made the Bill more workable and more acceptable, it would have been discovered many months before. Had there been acceptable ways of circumnavigating the reefs on which the Bill was to founder — such as the fact that Scottish MPs at Westminster would still be able to vote on English matters for which they were not responsible, or the failure to give the Assembly taxation powers — they would surely have been discovered.

The truth is that the Scotland and Wales Bill was probably the least unsatisfactory set of proposals which it was possible for pro-devolutionists to devise. Since it reflected in legislative form the pro-devolution argument in its strongest form, we must examine the Bill in some detail, and find out exactly what it sought to do.

This chapter presents a clear outline of the Government's proposals for the reader who comes to the subject for the first time.

The Government proposed that there should be Assemblies in Scotland and Wales, to be directly elected by the same basic method as the House of Commons. These Assemblies were to be responsible for those areas of government activity — known as 'devolved matters' — which concern the people of Scotland and Wales only. These would be more extensive in Scotland than in Wales, primarily on account of Scotland's distinctive law and legal system. In Wales, the Law of England operates.

The Government laid down a basic statement of constitutional principle, affirming the continuing unity of the United Kingdom and the unabated sovereignty of the House of Commons in Westminster. (Like many other Governmental statements, the right to make such a claim has been bitterly disputed by Members of Parliament. Reference to the unity of the United Kingdom implies the exclusion of separatism, while the 'unabated sovereignty of Parliament' implies the exclusion of federalism.)

Assembly Members — about 150 for Scotland and 80 for Wales — were to serve for four years. There was no provision for premature dissolution of the Scottish or Welsh Assembly for a period under four years, and a 'hung' Parliament was possible. Each Westminster constituency would have been divided into two or, if the electorate was very large, three Assembly constituencies. Because it would have taken time to make this division, for the first elections each Westminster constituency was to have been a single constituency, but with two or three members as the case may be. Although political parties might have laid down separate rules, there was at present nothing to stop someone from being an Assembly member and a Member of the House of Commons at the same time, or from being an Assembly member and a local authority councillor.

The Scottish Assembly would have had powers of primary legislation, but not powers of taxation, or the power to amend the Scotland and Wales Act itself. If the Government in Westminster thought that a Bill put forward in the Scottish Assembly exceeded that body's legal powers, they could not reject it outright; but Westminster could submit it to the Judicial Committee of the Privy Council, by whose finding both Westminster and the Assembly would then have to abide. If the Government in London regarded a Bill from the Scottish Assembly as being contrary to the United Kingdom's international obligations, as interpreted by the Government in London, they could reject the measure from Edinburgh.

The Government proposed a Scottish Executive, headed by a Chief Executive or Prime Minister of Scotland. In order to keep the necessary constitutional link with the Crown, the appointment of the Executive was to be made by the Secretary of State, which the Government claimed to be a formality — a point hotly disputed by Mr Enoch Powell. In this matter, the Secretary of State would be bound by the Assembly's and Chief Executive's wishes. Law officers but no one else could be appointed from outside the Assembly. (An arrangement of this kind has occasionally proved necessary for the Lord Advocate and Solicitor-General for Scotland.) Executive members could operate, in devolved matters, much as Ministers do now in the United Kingdom Cabinet.

In relation to devolved matters, the Scottish Executive would have been able to make subordinate legislation, and to create procedures of Parliamentary control over such legislation.

The list below summarises the devolved matters in simplified terms:

1 Education (other than the universities)
   The arts; libraries, museums and art galleries; crafts; social, cultural and recreational activities, including sport

2 Health

3 Social work

4 Water services

5 Local government, including:
   i   constitution, area, general powers and duties of local authorities;
   ii rating and valuation for rating, rate support grant for all services and specific grant for devolved services;
   iii rate rebates (provided that they met specified minimum standards)

6 Ancient monuments and historic buildings

7 Various matters including:
    i parks and open spaces
   ii betting, gaming and lotteries
  iii licensing
  iv charities
   v shop hours
  vi fire services and precautions
 vii registration services
viii public holidays

8 Environment, including:
    i land use and development (subject to a procedure for call-in of certain planning issues by the Government when they involve wider United Kingdom interests)
   ii industrial sites
  iii building control
  iv new towns
   v countryside
  vi the environmental functions of the Scottish Development Agency

9 Development and industry, including:
    i the industrial investment functions of the Scottish Development Agency (in conformity with guidelines approved by Parliament)
   ii the functions of the Highlands and Islands Development Board (the economic development functions in conformity with guidelines)
  iii factory building by public bodies (the Government would continue to specify conditions as to the disposal of premises or other land for industrial purposes)

10 Agricultural land, crofting, forestry, deer, marine works and salmon and freshwater fisheries.

11 Housing, including:
    i provision, improvement and management
   ii regulation of rents (subject to the reserve power to hold down rents to counter inflation — Clause 52)
  iii rent rebates (provided that they met specified minimum standards)

12 Transport and road traffic, including:
  i public passenger transport other than that pro-
     vided by the British Railways Board
  ii air and shipping services for the Highlands and
     Islands
  iii the Scottish Transport Group
  iv aerodromes
  v road traffic regulation
  vi inland waterways

13 Tourism

14 Pollution

15 Scottish Law functions, including:
  i   the courts (other than certain aspects)
  ii the general criminal law (but not the police or
      prosecutions)
  iii Scots private law
  iv legal aid
  v   regulation of the legal profession
  vi treatment of offenders (including responsibility
      for penal institutions)
  vii tribunals and enquiries in devolved fields.

The Assembly would have its own system of committees, on
subjects such as education, health and housing to monitor and
advise on what the Executive should do, including advice on
any proposed new primary or secondary legislation. There were
to be scrutiny committees composed of back-bench members of
the Assembly, and arrangements corresponding with the
scrutiny committee on Statutory Instruments at Westminster,
the composition of which would reflect the balance of the parties
in the Assembly. Scottish Assembly Bills involving expenditure
would not be passed without the concurrence of the Executive
in the Assembly.

Civil servants working for the Executive would be separate
from the Assembly staff and would be responsible to both the
Scottish Assembly and the Westminster Government.

The pay, allowances and pensions of Assembly Members,
including the Scottish Prime Minister and Members of the

Scottish Cabinet, would be settled by the Assemblies, though the Secretary of State would lay down initial levels for Assembly Members in order to get things started.

United Kingdom government Departments or other public bodies, and the devolved administrations, could arrange by agreement for one to undertake work or provide services on behalf of the other, where this seemed convenient. The Government were at pains to make clear that such an arrangement would not alter basic responsibilities. The Government in London or the House of Commons could require the Assembly to provide information — such as statistics — necessary for European Community purposes.

Though the Assembly's own borrowing powers were to be limited by Treasury control, the Treasury, if it wished, could extend the borrowing powers of any subordinate body set up by the Scottish Assembly if the Assembly so wished.

Westminster would retain other important reserve powers. If a Scottish Assembly Bill had repercussions which were judged to be unacceptably damaging to matters outside the Assembly's responsibility, London could ask for Parliament's approval to set it aside; and there would be similar powers in the executive field, whereby, if a devolved action, or indeed, omission, unacceptably affected non-devolved matters, subject to Parliament's specific approval the Government could issue the necessary directive to the devolved administration. Whitehall and Westminster could revoke a statutory instrument made by a devolved administration if it were thought to have unacceptably damaging effects on non-devolved matters.

The British Government would retain the power to prescribe a framework within which the devolved administrations must operate in supervising the industrial activities of certain public bodies, so as to ensure that these activities were not to the economic disadvantage of other parts of the United Kingdom. For example, London would lay down guidelines, subject to annulment by Parliament, governing the use of industrial investment powers of the Scottish Development Agency, which in most other respects would have been entirely under the control of the Edinburgh Assembly. There were to have been similar guidelines over the economic development powers of the Highlands and Islands Development Board, and over the whole

question of the disposal of land or buildings by a number of
public bodies.

Westminster could bar or restrict increases in housing rents,
where it considered this to be necessary for a counter-inflation
policy. While it would not have the power to increase rents in
Scotland, it could make sure that the rent rebate and allowance
schemes did not fall below a minimum standard. At first sight
this may look an odd requirement, but without it people not
otherwise needing supplementary benefit might have been
forced to seek support from the social security system, for which
the United Kingdom Government would have remained
responsible. It was for this reason, basically, that London could
also lay down minimum standards for systems of rate rebate.

The Government proposed to retain on a reserve basis in
London their existing powers with relation to the pay and conditions of various categories of people in public employment.
There would be a general provision requiring the Assemblies to
have regard, in pay matters, to any national pay policy considerations. In respect of the pay of specified groups of public
employees in devolved fields, London would have to consent to
any changes, unless it waived its right to do so. Although this
provision would not have affected local authority staff, it would
have concerned those in any similar groups established by
future Scottish Assembly legislation, as well as those whose pay
and conditions the Government now controls.

The Government proposed to convert the present non-
statutory system of control of teachers' pay into a statutory one.
While the system of teachers' pay was to be transferred to the
Assembly in Edinburgh, a requirement for United Kingdom
Government consent was attached to it.

Finance

Finance was both critical and complex. Scottish Consolidated
Funds and Loan Funds would be established, which would
take care of money for the Edinburgh Assembly Government's
day-to-day expenditure. Money could be appropriated from
the Consolidated Funds only by properly authorised procedures
and for specified purposes. Provision was made for the treatment
of receipts, in the hope that this would cover the problem of

what precisely the Treasury in London would do if the Assembly Executive seriously overspent in, let us say, hospital provision to the detriment of some other equally essential requirement, whose protagonists then demanded that it be brought up to United Kingdom standards. In certain political circumstances, it might have been difficult to refuse the Scots yet more money over and above that originally allocated to them. This is why the Bill also stressed the importance of proper procedures governing issues from the Loans Fund.

The celebrated and controversial Clause 62 of the Bill provided for an annual block grant or fund to be voted by Parliament for the Scottish Assembly. In seeking Parliament's approval, the Government would have to submit a statement explaining the proposed amount. The Scottish Assembly could make a short-term borrowing in sterling, within specified limits, to deal with any temporary cash-flow problem. In authorising borrowing from their own Loans Funds or elsewhere by public corporations or local authorities for capital expenditure on devolved matters, the Assembly would have to try to keep expenditure within the limits laid down by Westminster. This control was obviously needed in order to keep public expenditure in Scotland at levels compatible with the needs of the United Kingdom economy. Advances from the Scottish Loans Fund to bodies set up by Assembly legislation were not to be made at lower rates of interest than advances from the National Loans Fund. Accounting and audit arrangements — Controllers and Auditors-General, and Accounts Committees, including a Public Accounts Committee similar to the Public Accounts Committee in Westminster — were to be set up under the control of the Edinburgh Assembly.

The Government at Westminster had to account to the House of Commons for payments to and from the Scottish Loans Fund. Advances from those Funds were to be a matter for the Assemblies' own accounting systems.

Rate support grant to local authorities would be paid by the Assemblies at their discretion out of block funds.

An Ombudsman system covering the business of the Scottish Assembly was to be set up: he would be paid and his staff provided out of Assembly funds.

Further obscurities about the Government's position may be

cleared up by giving some of the Government's own replies to a variety of questions in a briefing to MPs at the time of the 1975 White Paper:

Q *Why have devolution at all?*
A Devolution will increase democratic control, bring government closer to the people, and recognise more fully the special national characteristics of Scotland and Wales. Although the Kilbrandon Commission expressed differing opinions on which kind of devolution is best they were in no doubt that devolution is needed.

Q *Will devolution not lead to complete separation?*
A No. The great majority of people in Scotland and Wales do not want complete separation. Even many of those who vote nationalist do not want it. What many people do want is a reasonable degree of devolution. If they have that, plus the benefits of continued membership of the United Kingdom, their wishes will be met. Unity is much more likely to be preserved by implementing devolution than by denying it. The status quo is not an option.

Q *Why deal with Scotland and Wales before the English regions?*
A There is a strong sense of separate national identity in Scotland and Wales. Their boundaries are clear; and they already have substantial institutions of government under the Secretaries of State for Scotland and Wales on which we can build. The interests of England will continually be borne in mind.

Q *Will Scottish and Welsh MPs continue to be able to vote at Westminster on English business in fields which are dealt with for Scotland and Wales by the Scottish and Welsh Assemblies?*
A The Kilbrandon Commission pointed out that it is impracticable to have MPs moving in and out of the voting according to the type of business being discussed. It is virtually impossible to define 'English' business satisfactorily. A Government's majority could be affected by changes in the numbers entitled to vote.

And in any case, whatever is decided for 83 per cent of the population (England) is almost bound to affect the remainder, who ought therefore to have a say in it.

Q Will the Assemblies not make Scotland and Wales over-governed?

A The proposals do not create a large new volume of government. The Assemblies will carry out functions which are at present largely carried out by the Secretaries of State, other Government Ministers and the Westminster Parliament. The functions of the United Kingdom authorities will therefore be correspondingly reduced.

Q Will the Assemblies have enough important work to do, sandwiched between the two tier local government structure and the higher government structures in Westminster and Brussels?

A It will not be a question of finding new work for the Assemblies to do. They will have their hands full with existing work which will be taken over from the overburdened central government.

Q What reduction in the size and cost of government in London will be achieved by devolution?

A Many of the subjects to be devolved are already largely administered in Scotland and to some extent in Wales. There may be economies in Parliament because of the transfer of much Scottish legislative business to Edinburgh and the making of statutory instruments in Wales; and in the case of Wales, in particular, there should be administrative savings in Whitehall as a result of transferring responsibilities to Cardiff.

Q Won't we need far more extra staff for devolution than the White Paper suggests?

A We are aiming to provide closer and more responsive government. There is no reason to expect a great increase in costs. The process of government is already well established in Scotland and to a lesser extent in Wales. It is largely a question of transferring responsibility for existing work.

Q *What will be the cost of the Assembly buildings, members'*
  salaries and the additional staff needed for the Scottish and
  Welsh administrations?

A This cannot yet be determined exactly, but in Scotland
  the capital outlay will be in the region of £2m to £3m,
  with additional annual running costs of about £10m.
  In Wales, where a relatively bigger build-up of staff is
  required, the corresponding figures are £1m to £2m
  and £5m rising to £12m.

Q *What advantages are expected to derive from a committee*
  system? Should it not be left to the Assemblies to determine
  their own procedures and working arrangements?

A Only a minimum structure in general terms will be laid
  down in the devolution Bill. The Assemblies will have
  considerable discretion to determine their own procedures and arrangements. But the Government think it
  worthwhile to prescribe enough in the devolution Bill to
  ensure a framework of procedure calculated to involve
  all Members actively in the work and decisions of their
  Assembly.

Q *Can a committee system effectively initiate primary legislation in*
  Scotland?

A The Scottish Executive itself will normally introduce
  Bills. The Executive member responsible for a new piece
  of legislation will have to consult the relevant committee of the Assembly (except in cases of special urgency or
  confidentiality). Before a Bill is introduced the committee may discuss its principles and report on it to the
  Assembly, as a prelude to general consideration of the
  Bill in plenary session. The Assembly may also use these
  or other committees for the detailed scrutiny stage of
  Bills (equivalent to the Committee Stage at Westminster).

Q *Would the Government allow the formation of separate civil*
  services for Scotland and Wales?

A That can be considered if and when the matter is raised
  by the Scottish and Welsh administrations, which cannot be before the Assemblies are established. The

Government have made clear their own view that advantages would be gained by maintaining a unified civil service, and they hope the new Scottish and Welsh Administrations will share this view.

Q *Why should there be oversight of the Scottish Assembly's legislation by the Secretary of State?*

A The Scottish Assembly will be constitutionally subordinate to Parliament; it will have been created by Parliament and will always remain subject to Parliament's laws. Complete freedom in legislation would imply separatism. But in the ordinary course Scottish legislation will go forward for Royal Assent without any trouble or delay. Difficulties can be expected to be resolved by informal consultation between London and Edinburgh before formal checks are made.

Q *What provisions will there be for private Members' Bills in the Scottish Assembly?*

A Individual members of the Assembly will be able to introduce Bills (though if the Bills entail expenditure they will be able to proceed only with the Executive's agreement). Any differences in handling between Members' Bills and Bills introduced by the Executive will be for the Assembly itself to settle. The devolution Bill will lay down in broad terms the various stages for handling of legislation by the Assembly.

Q *Instead of Westminster retaining the power of veto, would it not have been preferable to set up a system of judicial review in Scotland to decide whether the Assembly had exceeded its powers?*

A Judicial review of Assembly Acts is an open question, as explained in the White Paper. It should not be confused with the power of veto. It is concerned with whether, in a particular case, an Assembly Act exceeds the powers laid down in the devolution Act. Resolving that question is essentially a rather slow legal process which may be unsuitable for urgent questions of administration. These require some sort of last resort veto power in the hands of the United Kingdom.

Q *What is to be the relationship of the Scottish and Welsh admini-
      strations to the Crown?*

A Access to the Crown will be through the Secretary of
   State. In the ordinary course he may be expected to
   advise the Crown in accordance with the administration's wishes, but he will not be constitutionally obliged
   to do so.

Q *What will be the future role of the Secretaries of State for
      Scotland and Wales?*

A They will represent Scotland and Wales in the United
   Kingdom Government. They will have a valuable part
   to play in those functions which are not devolved, particularly in the economic field. They will be a channel
   of communication between the Assemblies and the
   Crown. They will develop arrangements for co-operation between the Government and the Assemblies by
   mutual agreement. Additionally, the Secretary of State
   for Wales will continue to be closely concerned with
   new United Kingdom legislation and policies affecting
   Wales in the devolved fields.

Q *What will be the future role of the Lord Advocate?*

A The Lord Advocate will retain his existing functions as
   the Senior Scottish Law Officer of the Crown which include giving advice to the United Kingdom Government and Parliament on questions of Scots law. Under
   the Government's proposals the Lord Advocate will
   also remain responsible for the system of public prosecutions in Scotland. In addition, he may be expected to
   play an important part in advising the Government on
   constitutional issues arising out of devolution — for
   example, on the question whether an Assembly Bill is
   within the scope of the devolved powers.

Q *If the Assemblies wish to improve/abolish the Ombudsman, will
      they be able to do so?*

A No. The Assemblies will administer complaints
   machinery in Scotland and Wales as required by existing legislation and the devolution Act. Any proposals
   to change this machinery will require new legislation by
   Parliament.

Q *Will diplomatic representation abroad be changed by setting up the two new Assemblies?*

A No. The United Kingdom will remain a single sovereign state and the United Kingdom Government will continue to be responsible for all international relations, including those concerned with our membership of the EEC. So far as international or EEC matters are of interest to the Scottish or Welsh administration, the Government will ensure that their views are fully taken into account. The best way of doing this will be worked out when the Assemblies come into being.

Q *Will the Scottish and Welsh administrations be free if they so wish to establish an office in Brussels in order to make direct contact with the Commission and other European organisations, i.e. for propaganda and pressure group purposes?*

A The Government foresee extensive and regular consultation between themselves and the Scottish and Welsh administrations on EEC matters. But the Government alone is responsible to the EEC for all parts of the United Kingdom and it cannot pass this responsibility to anyone else. The EEC itself will take cognizance of the views of particular areas and authorities in Britain only as far as they are expressed through the United Kingdom Government.

Q *Why cannot the Government leave the Assemblies to act on EEC requirements and use its powers of veto and countermanding if they do not comply?*

A The United Kingdom Government is the body responsible to the EEC. It cannot divest itself of that responsibility. It should not leave responsibility to the Scottish and Welsh administrations and take action only after something goes wrong. The proper and most practicable course is for the Government to consider EEC requirements in the devolved fields as they are promulgated, and to decide then whether they require action by the Government itself or whether (as will commonly be the case) implementation can be delegated to the Scottish and Welsh administrations.

Q *How will the Government's proposals affect the Scottish courts?*

A Judges of the High Court of Justiciary and the Court of
Session will continue to be appointed by the Queen on
the recommendation of the United Kingdom Government; and the right of appeal to the House of Lords in
civil matters will be retained. But whether the courts
themselves should be devolved has not yet been decided. The arguments for and against are set out in the
White Paper and the decision will be made in the light
of the ensuing debate.

Q *How will the Government's proposals affect Scots private law?*
A There will be extensive devolution in this field, e.g. in
relation to the law of persons, property, trusts, succession, delict and the like. There is a problem, however,
because private law interacts with fields such as company law, consumer protection and industrial relations
for which it is important to maintain a common or
compatible framework throughout Great Britain. The
Government are studying this problem and hope to be
assisted to a solution.

Q *Will the Scottish Assembly have power over the structure and
functions of bodies whose members are now nominated by the
Government?*
A Yes, if the nominated body operates wholly within
Scotland in a devolved field of activity. If the nominated body operates in the devolved fields but is
organised on a Great Britain or United Kingdom
basis there are three possibilities:

   (a) the body may continue to act, reflecting Scottish
       administration policy in its Scottish operations;
   (b) the Secretary of State can vary the Scottish
       arrangements for any particular body by agree-
       ment between himself, the Scottish administra-
       tion and the body concerned;
   (c) in default of agreement otherwise, the Scottish ad-
       ministration will be free to terminate a particular
       body's responsibility in Scotland and to make new
       arrangements (unless exceptionally the devolu-
       tion Act provides specially for the maintenance of
       a particular body, e.g. the Forestry Commission).

Q *Is there likely to be a restructuring of local government following establishment of the Scottish and Welsh Assemblies?*

A The Government feel it would be a mistake if early changes were made in the pattern of local government so recently introduced. Time is required to let the new local authorities settle down and create a working relationship with the Assemblies. Only then can a proper assessment be made as to whether any, and if so what, further changes are needed.

Q *Will the reservation of the universities not conflict with the ability of the Assemblies to organise higher education?*

A The Government believe that it is in the best interests of the United Kingdom and the universities that they should continue to be financed as part of a wider system, with free movement of staff and students, and by the University Grants Committee. But the Government attach great importance to the maintenance of close liaison between the Scottish and Welsh universities and those other parts of the higher education system which will become the responsibility of the Scottish and Welsh administrations.

Q *What economic powers will be devolved?*

A The administrations will acquire a major influence over the Scottish and Welsh economies because they will decide priorities between programmes and influence the location of spending of very large sums of public money (on last year's expenditures about £2,000 million in Scotland and about £900 million in Wales). Their responsibilities for roads, housing, land use and the environmental functions of the Development Agencies will enable them to provide an infrastructure attractive to incoming firms, and give them an important role in the industrial regeneration of Scotland and Wales. A wide measure of control over the whole range of activities of the Highlands and Islands Development Board will be transferred to the Scottish administration.

Q *Will the arrangements for the Highlands and Islands Development Board be the same as for the Development Agencies?*

A   No. The Scottish administration will assume full executive responsibility for the Board, and will appoint the
Chairman and all members of the Board. When the
Board acts in fields which elsewhere will be reserved
(e.g. assistance to industry, fishing and agriculture) the
Secretary of State will lay down guidelines and cash
limits for individual projects. He will be responsible for
determining the geographical area for the Board's
activities, and legislation to amend its powers will be
reserved.

Q   *Which nationalised industries will be devolved?*
A   Scottish Transport Group, British Waterways Board
activities in Scotland and Wales, the main forestry
activities of the Forestry Commission in Scotland and
Wales, and, at a later appointed day, the airport and
aerodrome activities in Scotland of the British Airports
Authority and the Civil Aviation Authority.

Q   *What powers will be devolved over agriculture and fisheries?*
A   The main economic and international functions will be
retained by the Government (e.g. financial support,
international fishing limits). But a number of matters
related to land and natural resources in Scotland and
Wales will be devolved, in addition to forestry. These
include estate management, crofting, smallholdings,
agricultural landlord/tenant relationships and freshwater fisheries.

Q   *Will the Forestry Commission/British Waterways Board/*
British Airports Authority remain accountable only to
United Kingdom Ministers and Parliament?
A   No. Where the Scottish and Welsh activities of a Great
Britain body have been devolved and are to be funded
from the block grants it will be required to produce
separate accounts for the administrations and will be
accountable for these activities to the Scottish and
Welsh Assemblies.

Q   *Will the administrations be able to give special advantages to*
attract industry to Scotland and Wales?
A   The Government will retain control of the preferential

arrangements for the assisted areas and for industrial support under its regional policies, and the industrial development certificate system. The administrations will not therefore be able to give incoming firms an unfair advantage. But they will be well equipped to provide an environment and infrastructure attractive to incoming firms, and they will be responsible for factory building functions not only of the Development Agencies (and the Highlands and Islands Development Board in Scotland) but also of new town corporations and local authorities.

Q *Will employment and training functions be devolved?*

A No, because despite local variations Great Britain forms a single labour market and labour is an important national economic resource. But responsibility for the activities in Scotland and Wales of the Manpower Services Commission and its Agencies will be transferred to the Scottish and Welsh Secretaries of State to ensure that full attention can be given to local problems within the national labour market.

Q *Will the Development Agencies be responsible to the Assemblies, or to the Secretaries of State?*

A Responsibility will be divided. The environmental and factory-building functions (subject to Government control of the terms of disposal of factories) will come under the Scottish or Welsh administration. Most industrial functions will come under the Secretary of State. The administration will appoint half the members of the Board, and will be consulted before the Secretary of State appoints the Chairman. The Secretary of State will appoint the other members.

Q *Will the Scottish and Welsh administrations be able to promote their tourist industries overseas?*

A Yes, but they will receive no funds from the Government for this purpose because the Government will provide funds for the British Tourist Authority for overseas promotion covering all parts of Great Britain. Tourism in Scotland and Wales will nevertheless be fully devolved.

Q *How will the devolved services be financed?*

A By a combination of block grant voted by Parliament, local authority taxation, and borrowing by local authorities and public corporations. In 1974/75 the proportions would have been:

	Scotland	Wales
	(£million, rounded)	
Block Grant	1,300	650
Local Authority Taxation	300	90
Borrowing	500	170
Total (including loan charges met by local authorities)	2,100	910

Q *Who will be responsible for discussions with the Government about the block grant?*

A It will be for the Scottish and Welsh administrations to decide who will represent them in these discussions. The Government will prescribe the general pattern and timetable of the talks.

Q *What part will the Secretaries of State play in determining the block grant?*

A It will be for the Government as a whole to decide finally the size of the block grant, but the Secretaries of State will naturally play a major role in the discussions.

Q *Will the block grant in Scotland be paid to the Scottish Executive or the Scottish Assembly?*

A The grant will be paid to the Scottish Consolidated Fund and will be appropriated by the Assembly to particular items of expenditure proposed by the Executive.

Q *How will the block grant be calculated?*

A On the basis of expenditure needs in the devolved services, after full consultation with the devolved administrations on their proposals. No account will be taken of the proportion of United Kingdom taxes produced in Scotland and Wales, and there will be no earmarking of particular taxes, including oil revenues, for Scottish or Welsh use. The block grant will be determined as an outcome of the annual United Kingdom public expenditure review.

Q *What proportion of public expenditure in Scotland and Wales will be under the control of the Assemblies?*

A More than half of identifiable public expenditure will be on devolved services in Scotland and Wales. The priorities for these expenditures will be settled by the Scottish and Welsh administrations, not by Whitehall.

Q *Will any part of the block grant be earmarked for particular programmes?*

A No. Once the block grant has been fixed by Parliament the Scottish and Welsh administrations will decide how it should be spent.

Q *What Parliamentary control will there be of the Scottish and Welsh administrations' accounts?*

A Responsibility for controlling issues from the Scottish and Welsh funds and for supervising the arrangements for monitoring and audit will rest squarely with the Scottish and Welsh authorities themselves. The Scottish Comptroller and Auditor General will report to the Scottish Accounts Committee, and it will be for the Scottish Assembly to decide what action should be taken on the Committee's reports. The situation will be the same in Wales. The devolution Act will, however, require the publication of these reports, so that devolved expenditure undergoes the same public scrutiny as the corresponding expenditures do now.

Q *Will the Scottish Executive get their fair share of North Sea oil revenues after devolution?*

A North Sea oil is a source of revenue for the whole of the United Kingdom. Through the block grant and the borrowing arrangements Scotland will receive a fair share of these revenues in accordance with her relative needs.

Q *Other countries devolve important taxes to regional administrations. Why not in Scotland and Wales?*

A In such a system the regions producing a low tax yield may have greater expenditure needs than richer regions; this can lead to wide differences in local services. Our tradition is for uniform taxes and reasonable comparability of services. Substantial differences in say income tax for those with similar incomes would not be acceptable in the United Kingdom. If only minor variations were permitted the yield of the regional tax would be low, and the cost of collecting it would take up much of the yield.

4

The Rise of Nationalism and the SNP

Two days before the publication of the Scotland and Wales Bill, in November 1976, Alan Watkins, the Political Correspondent of the *Observer*, complained:

> I have yet to meet a single Minister who actively and positively wants devolution at all. Instead a variety of justifications or explanations is produced; that the alternative is the complete loss of Scotland to the Labour Party, even to Britain; that it is useless to argue with the inevitable; that the Party entered into a rash commitment which cannot now be escaped; that events acquire their own momentum.

This feeling of helplessness and hopelessness, added Mr Watkins, 'is reflected in the ministerial appointments made by James Callaghan, and before him, by Sir Harold Wilson as well. The principle has been to exclude anyone who is either knowledgeable or enthusiastic about the subject.'

Mr Watkins's analysis was borne out by events after the publication of the Bill and when it embarked on its giddy passage in the House of Commons during January and February 1977. Cabinet Ministers normally devote weekend after weekend to delivering fulsome speeches in support of controversial Government legislation. Apart from anything else, by so doing they can ingratiate themselves both with their party and their Prime Minister. On devolution, however, the similar cascade of speeches was not to be heard. On the contrary, there was an uncharacteristic reluctance to say anything on the subject. Throughout the critical weeks before and after New Year 1977

only one Cabinet Minister with no direct responsibility for the
Scotland and Wales Bill made a public utterance in its defence.
Shortly before the fateful vote of 22 February 1977 on whether
or not to guillotine the Bill, William Rodgers, Secretary of
State for Transport, addressed a Labour Party dinner in the
North-East of England, during which Rodgers said it was his
opinion that although the Bill was unsatisfactory, none the less
Labour MPs should vote in its favour. Not to do so would under-
mine the authority of the Labour Government, and perhaps
help Mrs Thatcher to enter 10 Downing Street. Even so, Mr
Rodgers was careful not to underwrite any merits which the
Bill may have had. Never was a Government proposal so
damned by faint praise from a member of the Cabinet.

On the floor of the House of Commons itself, during the four
days of the Second Reading debate, and the eleven days of the
Committee stage, hardly a back-bench voice was heard in
favour of the Bill from either side of the House. Indeed, the
Ministers in charge of the Government's legislation could not
conceal their bitter feelings towards their own colleagues, who
had demanded legislative proposals on devolution, yet had
failed to turn up to speak in support of the Government. Even
during the critical Guillotine debate back-bench supporters of
the devolution proposals from England as well as from Scotland
and Wales were conspicuous by their absence, and even after the
Government's defeat on the Guillotine motion Professor John
Mackintosh, the ardent devolutionist, was prepared to admit in
Political Quarterly that the Scotland and Wales Bill 'contained so
many weaknesses that the most ardent decentralisers were not
prepared to fight hard for it'.

All this simply goes to show that the whole 'devolution
caper', to use the phrase of a senior civil servant, has been
considered primarily as an exercise in party politics. Such an
approach has ruled out any serious study of how our constitutional structures could be changed in such a way as to meet the
real needs of Britain in the 1980s. Trying to appease a minority
of voters in Scotland is hardly an elevated motive for putting
forward important constitutional proposals which would reverse
the whole trend of British history.

Indeed, the reader may be forgiven for asking where the
dynamic for devolution is coming from. One's first answer must

be a negative one: it does not come from the reasoned convictions of most members of Mr Callaghan's Cabinet. Most controversial measures which come before the House of Commons arise from the deeply held beliefs of the politicians and the party in office. This was not the case with devolution. However vehemently the Prime Minister, James Callaghan, the ex-Prime Minister, Harold Wilson, and other senior Cabinet Ministers may deny it, the Scotland and Wales Bill was hastily cobbled together in order to meet the electoral threat posed by the Scottish National Party. Nevertheless, merely to claim that politicians were panicked into devolution — however true that may be — is too incomplete an explanation. To understand why devolution has been taken up by all the major political parties it is necessary to examine political developments in Scotland over the last fifteen years or more, the English reaction — or lack of reaction — to them, and the haphazard, yet critical events which resulted from the General Elections of 1974. But before we embark on a detailed account of these events, it is essential to consider in very general terms the issues which have contributed to the demand for devolution in Scotland.

The United Kingdom Economy

Perhaps the most important factor which contributed to the rise of Scottish nationalism in the late 1960s and 1970s was a general feeling of dissatisfaction with the performance of the United Kingdom economy as a whole, and a belief that Scotland might well do better by itself. Although the British economy was said to be the strongest in Europe after the Second World War, it has made an unimpressive showing since then in comparison with the economies of some of our European neighbours, such as France and Western Germany. The fact that a number of smaller countries, such as Austria and Norway, appear to have managed their economies more successfully than Britain, and to enjoy a higher standard of living, gave rise to an admittedly rather nebulous feeling that perhaps a small country like Scotland might make a better go of it on its own; or that, at the very least, it could hardly do worse.

Dissatisfaction with the way in which a Government is handling the economy and the effect this has on the standard of living possibly has more influence than any other issue on marginal voters — those who sway from right to left, or left to right, and in effect decide the fate of General Elections. Many of them do not vote pro-Labour and anti-Tory, or vice versa; theirs is the classic protest vote. In Scotland, the protest vote was able to find an obvious alternative in the shape of the Scottish National Party; in England, such a vote can form the basis of a Liberal success in a by-election, as it did in Orpington in 1962 and Sutton and Cheam in 1973. Until very recently at any rate, the SNP has benefited from the protest vote; this will no longer be the case as soon as it becomes at all likely that there could be an SNP Government in Scotland. If it seems at all possible that an SNP Government could be formed, committed to dismantling the Union between Scotland and England, the protest vote will switch back to the Labour, Conservative or Liberal Party, depending on which one anti-SNP electors felt had the greatest chance in a given constituency. Thus the anti-SNP vote in rural areas would probably go to the Conservatives and in industrial areas to Labour. What concerns us here is that a significant protest vote, exaggerated by economic dissatisfaction, has been tapped by the Scottish National Party. Whether one can assume from this that such protest voters support the SNP's demands for constitutional change is open to question. At first sight, it is difficult to reconcile the fact that — according to public opinion polls — over 40 per cent of those who vote SNP also say that they do not want Scottish independence, since Scottish independence is the main aim of the SNP. On the other hand, what political party can claim that all its voters are agreed in demanding particular items of policy? Could Labour leaders have been certain that the overwhelming majority of Labour voters were ardently in favour of nationalising the aircraft and shipbuilding industries?

As we will see, economic discontent in Scotland was fuelled by the — mistaken — belief that the Scots were not given their rightful share of the cake. However, the combination of economic dissatisfactions and political protest was given its greatest boost by the discovery of oil in substantial quantities in the North Sea in the early 1970s; and it is to this highly vexed and emotive subject that we shall turn next.

The Impact of North Sea Oil

People in Wales who oppose a Welsh Assembly are fond oi saying that Plaid Cymru will never match the electoral success of the Scottish National Party until massive oil deposits have been discovered in Welsh territorial waters. They point out that whereas the SNP vote in Scotland has passed the 30 per cent mark, that of Plaid Cymru is less than 11 per cent. (In fairness, it should be mentioned that Welsh devolutionists hold that the distinct language and culture of parts of Wales and the sense of identity symbolised by the Eisteddfod, more than cancel out the electoral advantages of Scottish oil.) How great an impact has the discovery of oil reserves in the North Sea had on the political situation in Scotland?

The SNP themselves vehemently deny that their electoral success has been fuelled by North Sea oil. With a certain amount of justice, they point out that their fortunes were on the rise long before its significance was realised; yet before drilling in the North Sea began, the SNP were unable to sustain their electoral success over two Parliamentary elections in any constituency. Some of the SNP's Labour and Conservative opponents vehemently proclaim that their recent electoral achievements owe everything to instincts of greed and cupidity, aroused by the prospect of Scotland becoming an oil-rich North European sheikhdom. Neither of these extreme explanations is convincing: the truth is not to be found in the terms of a slanging match.

To understand the position, one must appreciate that only in the early 1970s did it become apparent that there was oil under the North Sea in commercial quantities. As a member of the Committee stage of the 1963 Continental Shelf Bill, I well remember that the best-informed geological opinion of the time tended to discount the possibility of there being substantial quantities of oil in the North Sea, and suggested that finds would be limited to natural gas. Certainly, this was the conventional wisdom among politicians throughout the 1960s and the issue of 'natural gas/oil' played no part in the Hamilton by-election of 1967, nor in the subsequent 1970 General Election.

In the early 1970s, the significance of North Sea oil dawned on the Scottish public, albeit gradually. In the October 1973 North Edinburgh by-election campaign, either Billy Wolfe,

Chairman of the SNP and his party's candidate, or his supporters, when pressed to say how they would pay for their proposals, stumbled on the slogan, 'It's oor oil!' The SNP immediately sensed that they had struck oil in more senses than one. The slogan was transmitted to Glasgow, where the by-election at Govan was also taking place, and where it had a greater impact than in Conservative North Edinburgh — to such an extent that, as we shall see, the SNP captured the seat from Labour. At the two General Elections of 1974, the question of who would benefit most from the North Sea oil reserves moved to the centre of the political stage. The Scots exclusively? The Scots for the most part? The Scots in part? Or the British people as a whole?

Partly because daily press headlines told the Scots about the North Sea bonanza, and partly because Shell, Esso and BP are imagined to be the Croesuses of the modern world, the argument soon deteriorated to the level of unreal slogans. What few people realised was that winning oil from the inhospitable waters of the North Sea was a far greater technological feat than had at first been supposed — and one that would cost five times as much as originally estimated. As Monty Pennell, Technical Director of BP, has pointed out, the difficulty of the transition between land drilling in Texas and sea drilling in the Gulf of Mexico was significantly less than the transition between sea drilling in the Gulf and work in the cold, storm-ridden North Sea. The costs of extracting the oil continue to soar in relation to expectations, even though the deposits are even greater than anticipated. However, such hard facts have done little to erode the myth of the 'crock of gold' due to every Scottish family from the North Sea, if only Scotland can keep her birthright. Even if the myth of Scottish oil did not launch the SNP's success, at least it sustains the credibility of an independent Scottish state, which would have evaporated long ago without it.

Understandably, it is tempting for Scots to look abroad and ask themselves what exactly the Westminster Government has done and can do in relation to North Sea oil that a Scottish Government in Edinburgh could not achieve. If other small countries with smaller populations and fewer other resources than Scotland can harvest huge sums of money from the oil reserves off their shores, why cannot the Scots do the same?

This looks a plausible argument at first sight. However, the Scottish situation is not quite so simple. Huge payments have been made to oil-rig and platform companies involved in the North Sea operations and these have come from the pockets of United Kingdom taxpayers, and not exclusively from those of Scottish taxpayers. They have taken the form of Regional Employment Premium payments and a variety of other grants and tax remissions. Furthermore, there have been considerable infrastructure payments to local authorities in Scotland — again from the pocket of the British taxpayer. The involvement of the British National Oil Corporation is on a United Kingdom, and not an exclusively Scottish, basis. To unscramble all the payments of this nature which have been made over the past five years would be an administratively impossible task, even if it were desirable to do so. Were the Scots somehow to 'hog' the North Sea oil revenues, it is inconceivable that resentment in the rest of the country would not force Westminster into demanding its money back.

Nor would it be possible for a Scottish Government simply to license fields and blocks in the North Sea to giant international oil companies purely as an accounting operation. The ramifications are far deeper than that. How would the English feel if, with the prospect of their taking the lion's share of North Sea oil revenues, the Scots suddenly decided to hive-off from the United Kingdom, after thirty years of Regional Development Policy operating greatly in their favour? Relations between the Governments in Edinburgh and in London would be sour, to put it mildly. A separate Scottish state would have enough problems as it is: one that was faced with a commercially hostile English Government, and deep resentment throughout English industry, hardly bears thinking about. Just imagine how the Scots would have felt if oil had been discovered in the English Channel rather than in the North Sea in commercial quantities. How outraged they would have been if the English had suggested that the Scots should not have a full share of the benefits of Channel oil.

One of the great attractions for the SNP in using North Sea oil as a political weapon is the superficial simplicity of the issue. It is a God-given panacea, manna from heaven for those who are pressed to explain where the cash is to come from to pay for various and wonderful schemes for the public good. One of the most telling political advertisements ever produced in Britain is a poster used by the SNP over the last three years, and doubtless to be used for the next three years. A needy pensioner is shown in a large photograph; and underneath is the caption, 'It's his oil'. An elderly widow, equally in need, appears opposite the old man; underneath is the caption, 'It's her oil'. Below is a large-scale photograph of an average children's school playground, with pupils scampering about, carrying the caption, 'It's their oil'.

These are very seductive slogans to an electorate which, as we have seen, is discontented with the management of the British economy, and wants to make its protest felt.

The Scandinavian Example

If the grass tends to look greener on the other side of the fence, it is none the less true that Norway may well look more attractive from the Scottish side of the North Sea than from the Norwegian side. The suggestion that Scotland should be like Norway has helped to sustain a belief in the credibility of independence.

The comparison appears to be validated by history, in that the Norwegians seceded from Sweden in 1905, with apparent success. (In fact there are Norwegians and Swedes, working for example, for Scandinavian Airlines, who would question the wisdom of Norway's secession.) What is less often taken into account is that in the case of Norway and Sweden the comparative distances were huge, natural geographical features formed a frontier, the peoples spoke different languages and, above all, in 1905 both Norway and Sweden were then predominantly agricultural states. A far cry from an interdependent industrial community, like that formed by England and Scotland, in which the surgery of partition would undoubtedly result in industrial and commercial chaos.

North Sea oil in particular has encouraged comparisons with Norway. In the early 1970s it was widely believed that the Norwegians had handled their share of oil in the North Sea, particularly in the Ekofisk field, more advantageously to themselves than the United Kingdom had handled the Forties Field.

Further, the Norwegian government seemed to have been wise in the help they gave to platform-construction companies, and in the concrete designs which they had chosen, at a time when our structures were facing all sorts of difficulties and delays. British politicians and journalists, if not professional oilmen, were always going on pilgrimages to view the construction yard wonders at Stavanger. All those apparent Norwegian advantages look more tarnished now than they did five years ago. But the myth of Norwegian wisdom and excellence has been created — though it was often denied by Norwegians themselves, who are in no mood to boast.

Moreover, whatever the rights and wrongs of the arguments over the speed at which North Sea oil has been extracted, the economic reality is that 2 million Norwegians did not need the oil anything like as urgently as the financially embarrassed British economy. Fifty million people in an intensively industrialised society create far more pressure for rapid expansion; rapid expansion led to difficulties, particularly in relation to diving risks, which the Norwegians did not share. (Much-publicised British diving accidents also contributed to the belief in Norwegian superiority.)

'Small Country Attraction'

Entry into the Common Market has also promoted a new sense of Scottish identity. It was Mr Tony Benn who perceptively warned the pro-Marketeers among the Scots at the time of the Common Market referendum that for Britain to remain in Europe would provide an added impetus to Scottish nationalism. Although I do not regret for one moment the United Kingdom's membership of the European Economic Community, it is probably true that had Britain rejected EEC membership, there would have been a stronger desire in Scotland to cling to the United Kingdom raft, and less confidence that Scotland could 'go it alone'. Be that as it may, the fact that, for example, Mr Max van der Stoel, the Dutch Foreign Minister, was at one stage President of the Council of Ministers, while the Belgian Prime Minister, Leo Tindemanns, was responsible for a key report to the heads of government on the future of Europe, and a Dane occupied the key post of Agricultural Commissioner of the EEC, all contributed to a feeling that Scotland too should have an independent voice in Europe.

On the face of it, this seems a natural enough question for the Scots to ask: if Ireland and Luxemburg can have their own representatives in Brussels and in the higher echelons of policy-making, should not the same privileges be extended to the Scots?

The way in which this question would be answered in Scotland would partly depend on whether the person asked thinks of Scotland as a separate nation or not. In fact it is open to doubt whether separate representation of Scotland in the Council and in the Commission — were it acceptable to our European partners — would be a privilege, however flattering it might be to national self-esteem. Certainly there might be a kind of glamour in having a Scot representing Scotland on the Commission; George Thomson, the ex-Regional Commissioner and former MP for Dundee East, sat on the Commission by virtue of his appointment by a British Government. Having a Scot on the Council of Ministers would certainly provide the trappings of power. Yet two years' membership of the European Parliament, examining the work of both Council and Commission at close quarters on a day-to-day basis, has convinced me that the large members of the European Community carry the political clout when it comes to crunch decisions. For example, at the peak of their difficulties over fishing limits, the Scottish trawlermen recognised the advantages of negotiating in the Community from the vantage point of a large member, and merged with the British Trawler Federation. Danish and Irish colleagues in the European Parliament tell me that they often wish that their interests were looked after in Brussels by a bigger unit. Even the Dutch and the Belgians recognise the short-comings of 'small country' status, while the Luxemburgers cheerfully accept any decision (or, at any rate, any decision which does not involve the removal of certain cherished Community institutions from Luxemburg City!).

Even if it were to Scotland's advantage, there is another reason why separate Scottish representation is a pipe-dream. Our European partners would not agree to it. The Scottish National Party, and Mr James Sillars's Scottish Labour Party, may issue clarion calls for Scotland to take her place as the

Tenth Member in a Europe of the Ten. Yet for the existing members of the Community it is one thing to welcome old nation states such as Greece, Portugal and Spain; it would be quite another matter to welcome part of an existing member-country which had hived off in inevitable rancour and bitterness from the mother country. The answer was tersely put to me by a highly placed German:

> Do you think that in order to solve your Scottish problems, affecting 5 million people, we are going to risk the break-up of government from Bonn? If Scotland were to have an equal place in the Council and European Commission, what do we say to 17,000,000 Bavarians and Franz Josef Strauss? Think again!

Nor would the Government of France be any more sympathetic. Grant membership to the Scots, and Basques, Bretons and Auvergnards would be descending on Paris asking for equal treatment. In Rome, the government would be reminded that there was a Kingdom of Piedmont, and a King of the Two Sicilies, two and a half centuries after the Union of the Crowns, and one and a half centuries after the Union of the Parliaments between Scotland and England.

The Myth of the Poor Scot

Another factor which has contributed strongly to the demand for separation is the belief that Scotland does not receive its fair share of the cake — that Scotland is poorer, more neglected and suffers higher unemployment than the rest of the United Kingdom. This feeling has probably been enhanced by Scots' wonder, tinged perhaps with envy, at the apparent wealth of countries like Austria and Holland. It is very easy to suggest that, were it not for London and the English, Glasgow would have been rebuilt like Rotterdam and problems of deprivation and poverty overcome. And people tend to believe what they want to believe, especially when their own woes and shortcomings can be blamed on others.

Whatever the ills of Scotland, they cannot reasonably be attributed to the fact that the Scots have been unable to obtain their fair share of the cake. If anything, the reverse is true. The

TABLE I   *Unemployment and earnings in Scotland and the UK*

	Unemployment rate per cent (a)		Average weekly earnings of full-time male manual workers in manufacturing at October each year (in £)	
	Scotland	*UK*	*Scotland*	*UK*
1949	3·0	1·6	—	—
1950	3·1	1·6	—	—
1951	2·5	1·3	—	—
1952	3·3	2·2	—	—
1953	3·0	1·8	—	—
1954	2·8	1·5	—	—
1955	2·4	1·2	—	—
1956	2·4	1·3	—	—
1957	2·6	1·6	—	—
1958	3·8	2·2	—	—
1959	4·4	2·3	—	—
1960	3·6	1·7	13·50 (b)	14·82 (b)
1961	3·1	1·6	14·79	15·76
1962	3·8	2·1	15·00	16·34
1963	4·8	2·6	15·92	17·29
1964	3·6	1·7	17·41	18·67
1965	2·9	1·5	19·02	20·16
1966	2·7	1·5	20·18	20·78
1967	3·7	2·3	21·24	21·88
1968	3·7	2·5	22·95	23·62
1969	3·7	2·5	24·84	25·54
1970	4·2	2·6	28·09	28·91
1971	5·8	3·5	30·30	31·37
1972	6·4	3·8	35·45	36·20
1973	4·5	2·7	41·14	41·52
1974	4·0	2·6	48·92	49·12
1975	5·2	4·1	60·38	59·74

(a) The denominators up to 1970 are the mid-year counts of National Insurance cards and, for 1971 and later, are the mid-year Census of Employment plus the numbers unemployed at the June counts.   (b) April.

SOURCE: Compiled by the Library of the House of Commons from *British Labour Statistics Historical Abstract*, Tables 57, 168; *British Labour Statistics Yearbook*, Table 117; *Regional Statistics* (1974), Table 82, and *Regional Statistics* (1976), Tables 8.4 and 13.7.

alleged bias against Scotland has lent itself to flights of grand oratory; yet, as Table 1 shows, the position has greatly improved over the past decade, and was never as marked as the orators would have us believe. Moreover, the Scots were never significantly worse off at any time by comparison with areas other than London, the East and West Midlands and the Home Counties. The myth that the Scots were being 'done down' by the English originated in the 1960s, partly because of the publicity given to wages in the motor industry, which were higher than in any other. Not until the British Motor Corporation brought part of their truck and tractor division to Bathgate did Scotland have a share in the magical motor industry. By the time devolution was first mooted, the differences in wages between Scotland and England had narrowed — but myths die hard.

Alien Industry

Again, much resentment has been stirred up against the alien ownership of industry. Ownership and control of the private sector of the economy are out of Scottish hands as such. Mr John Firn of Glasgow University has estimated that about 41 per cent of the employees in manufacturing industry work in Scottish-owned or Scottish-controlled companies, very slightly more than those employed by companies from other parts of the United Kingdom. Nearly 15 per cent of all manufacturing employees work in North American-controlled plants, such as Honeywell, Hewlett Packard, and Cameron Ironworks, the world's largest forge company. In certain vital sectors of industry, outside control was even more marked. The Scottish share of employment in chemicals was only 11·8 per cent; even in the traditional industry of metal manufacturing, only 18·3 per cent; in electrical engineering, 7·8 per cent. Only in shipbuilding, textiles, leather, furniture, paper and printing were more than half the employees working for Scottish companies. Most dramatically of all, of the eight platform- or rig-building yards in Scotland, two are US-owned, one is partly US-owned, two are partly Dutch and one is partly French. Of the remaining two, one is English-owned and the other owned by the British Steel Corporation.

Against this background, it is easy to see that when anything goes wrong, there is a temptation to blame others.

The Appeal of the SNP

For all these reasons, the Scottish National Party has emerged as a seemingly credible political party over the last few years. We shall trace its electoral success in the next chapter; but it might be helpful at this stage to examine what the party stands for, and what its political aims are.

The image of itself which the SNP would wish to convey, and has been extraordinarily successful in conveying, is that it alone is the 'Party of Scotland'. Whatever the level of election — District election, Regional election, Parliamentary by-election or General Election — the same cry comes over the mobile loudspeakers: 'A vote for the SNP is a vote for Scotland! Vote for Scotland today! This is your chance to cast a vote for Scotland, today!' The SNP appeal is based on a conscious attempt to tap the wells of national feeling, which are somewhere inside most of us, and to claim that it alone has the interests of the Scots people at heart.

Allied to this is the widespread and none-too-subtle use at the hustings of 'scapegoat politics'. Now, it ill behoves me to be unduly prim about this matter — at elections since time immemorial the Labour Party has laid all sorts of shortcomings at the door of the Conservatives, and the Conservatives have not been an inch behind in laying blame for all sorts of things, that politicians in power could do little or nothing about, at the door of Labour Governments. What is different about the SNP campaigns is the intensity of the assault on their opponents, and in particular the fact that it is usually 'the English' rather than 'the Tory Government' or 'the Labour Government' who are the object of attack. 'Go home, English' is the slogan of the graffiti makers. 'Rich Scots, poor British?' in relation to oil, was the more official slogan of the SNP. For everything that is less than perfect in Scotland, the English can be and are made out to be conveniently responsible — even though, as we shall see, most of the bitterly resented decisions, such as the proposed merger and closure of certain teacher-training colleges in 1977, are made by Scots Ministers and Scottish officials, operating from Edinburgh. Similarly, failure to reform the marriage laws in Scotland until the mid-1970s, which has caused so much bitterness over the last half century, has entirely been the responsibility of Scots operating from Scotland, and has nothing to do with the English. The fact remains, however, that when complaints are made, it is all too easy to explain matters in terms of blame the 'English' Government.

Here we come to another clue to the success of the SNP's appeal — its sheer simplicity. Establish a Scottish Government and all will be better, is a clear, simple political message. A supporter of Mr Callaghan's Government, who has to justify a phase of the pay policy or make an argument about prices and incomes, cannot deliver his message in black-and-white terms — and is less effective as a result.

Sometimes the degree of anti-Englishness borders on the racial. Few who watched it on their television screens will forget the venom exuded during the course of the SNP Annual Conference at Motherwell in 1976, or the tone in which Douglas Henderson, MP for East Aberdeenshire, then SNP Whip, denounced the 'rag tag and bobtail down there in England — Callaghan and Thatcher!' It was extremely unpleasant for those who live in a basically tolerant society.

Nor is it entirely fortuitous that each year the major annual rally of the SNP is on the Field of Bannockburn, where history has it that Robert the Bruce won a great battle against the army of the Earl of Surrey in the reign of Edward II of England, in 1314. If the objective is not to promote anti-English sentiment, why choose the less than adequate facilities at Bannockburn for the site of an annual rally?

In attempting to appeal to the electors, like every political party, the SNP tries to exploit grievance. What is new about the SNP in this respect is that they tend to harness grievances that have nothing whatsoever to do with government, and by some alchemy turn non-political grievances into 'the politics of insult'. For example, following a headline in the *Scotsman*, 'English Clubs snub Willie Ormond' (the then Scottish football team manager) the SNP 'went their duster' in the spring of 1976 about English football clubs putting their own needs in the League before those of Scotland in relation to Under-23 international matches. Doubtless a lot of Scots were, like the SNP, very angry; yet apart from the fact that the Scots who were refused permission to play for the Scotland Under-23 team went to England in the first place in order to get more money than they would have done with Scottish clubs, no British Government can tell the Football League what to do.

The SNP have been most adept in exploiting local and regional grievances. In particular, they alight on issues where a British Government is constrained by international obligations or difficulties, or responsibilities to other Members of the European Economic Community. For example, they pose as the champions of the Scottish fishermen in disputes with French, Belgian and fishermen from other countries with whom we have reciprocal relations, and who have recently helped the United Kingdom during financial and other difficulties. The SNP can make an effective appeal precisely because they are unencumbered by the obligations of Government, either at home or abroad. Conservative and Labour spokesmen are more careful, in time of Opposition, since they know that they might well be called upon to face the same problems as the Government of the day, should they themselves become Ministers of the Crown.

Political Aims of the SNP

However single-minded leading members of the SNP may be on the subject of attaining a separate self-governing Scottish nation state, they are united in precious little else in terms of traditional left–right political argument; they draw support right across the political spectrum, from extreme right to extreme left, and quite what would happen to the party if the SNP ever achieved a Government in Scotland is very much an open question.

To be fair, the SNP response to those who ask whether they are a left-wing or a right-wing party is in terms often voiced by Ian McCormick, MP for Argyll, namely that Scottish politics has been too long bedevilled by considerations of social class, and left-wing versus right-wing confrontation. To many people this sounds an attractive posture; the reality none the less remains that a political party actually in Government has to make up its mind on a whole range of policies where there are, like it or not, distinctive left or right points of view — rents and council house building, comprehensive schooling, health charges, to name but a few. The fact is that the SNP have been extremely shy on thorny issues of this kind, preferring to leave the answers to individual Parliamentary and local government candidates, who can tailor their statements to suit the areas in which they happen to be seeking the support of the electors. The line they take in former Conservative strongholds such as Perth, East Perthshire and South Angus, on the delicate issues of bread and butter politics such as council house rents, is very different from that taken in predominantly working-class constituencies in Glasgow and industrial Lanarkshire. Indeed, this dilemma is personified in Mrs Winifred Ewing, MP: when she sat for Hamilton, we were told that she was a better socialist than most Labour Members of Parliament, yet now that she is a Member for rural Moray and Nairn, she does not flaunt left wing views.

As the opening sentence of the leading article in the *Scotsman* of 10 February 1977 shows, much of the appeal of the SNP is negative:

> Whatever the members of a Scottish Assembly, its Executive and their entourage may get up to, if devolution goes ahead, could it be more disconcerting than the tales and counter-tales released by extracts from Mr Joe Haines' book* in the 'Daily Mirror' and 'Daily Record'? These two newspapers are the Labour Party's closest supporters among the daily Press in Britain, and in 1974 they did their blatant best to gather in the Labour vote. What will their readers think of this week's unusually large dollops of the history of the Wilson era, as seen by the Press Secretary? Even the dullest readers, anxious to look up to the great men and women at the centre of British politics during the Wilson years, must have some serious qualms when they read the Haines version, and the torrent of denials, supporting stories and counter-accusations provoked by it from senior and sundry characters in the cast. Even those who believe Sir Harold's and Lady Falkender's current assessment of Mr Haines' credibility must wonder why he was allowed to last so long on the job.

The vague impression that, somehow or another, Labour

* *The Politics of Power* (London: Cape, 1977).

politicians are unfit to govern the country which such revela-
tions help to foster, does far more damage to the Labour Party
than any number of policy decisions on straight political issues.
Not surprisingly, the Haines affair helped the SNP enormously,
even though it had nothing whatsoever to do with the merits or
demerits of setting up a separate Scottish state. Many of the
incidents and controversies recounted by Mr Haines and his
former colleagues are in themselves trivial; yet the general
picture which emerged was that of the Wilson Government and
its political staff, their energies sapped and diverted by personal
rivalries, concentrating their minds on matters which had
nothing to do with the problems of Britain. Such scandals only
serve to discredit Westminster politicians up and down the
country; and, in Scotland, to encourage a belief that the sooner
the Scots can dissociate themselves from such goings-on, the
better.

Certain policies, at home and abroad, can be identified,
although SNP domestic policy is remarkable for its muzziness.
This may stem partly from lack of experience of government,
and of running a government machine; it may also be that a
certain vagueness is thought to be expedient, in that as soon as
its policy becomes sharply defined, a party can become involved in disputes about practical matters. And it is precisely
that kind of dispute that the SNP wish to avoid, preferring to
refer all problems to the vague yet total panacea of a Scottish
Government. To be fair, however, they are far from being the
only group of politicians for whom an unaware ignorance has
its attractions.

When pressed, the SNP make frequent reference to a Scottish
industrial revival brought about by extensive state support and
intervention financed from oil revenues. The instruments of
such a revival would be a Ministry of Development and Industry, undertaking work now done by different departments
and boards, such as the Highland Board, the National Enterprise Board, the Scottish Development Agency and a chain of
fairly independent area development officers. These officers,
whom the sympathetic Mr Neal Ascherson of the *Scotsman*
describes as 'almost a race of economic prefects', would draw up
local developments plans, distribute grants and loans from the
budget allocated to them by the Ministry, and manage in-

dustrial estates and advanced factories. Special attention would be paid to encouraging small enterprises by grants, and small firms would be deliberately favoured by government purchasing agencies. Part of the SNP's traditional emphasis on small firms stems from the hope that their products would be able to replace many imports from England and elsewhere. They also favour the development of co-operatives and worker participation. The SNP promise to introduce participation — a vague term which covers a multitude of meanings — for any enterprise employing more than 200 workers, if the work force so desired, has a certain appeal. The SNP propose that firms should have a policy board, composed of employees, investors, and representatives of the public interest, and a day-to-day management board. They claim that state support would diminish when a 'more self-confident industrial structure' had emerged under the impact of Scottish economic, fiscal and industrial policies. Initially, there would be a degree of protection. The SNP also propose anti-dumping tariffs and compensatory duties on some imports. State agencies and nationalised industries would have to justify purchases made outside Scotland. 'Suitable' foreign investment would be welcomed, but foreign-owned firms would be encouraged to give autonomy to their Scottish units, to operate in partnership with Scottish firms, and to put past profits into reserve funds within Scotland. 'State holding companies', too, are proposed by the SNP, with investments in public and private firms with large financial requirements.

At this stage only one point needs to be made. With an economic policy along the lines outlined above, the frequent claims by nationalist spokesmen that no passports would be needed within the United Kingdom, that there would be no customs posts between England and Scotland, and that there would be no interference in the free movement of workers throughout the United Kingdom become increasingly hard to believe. There could be no open border.

The SNP and Local Government

Whether they should take part in local government elections, or decline to do so on the understandable grounds that their main aim — independence for Scotland — cannot be achieved through the medium of local government representation, has been a matter of some debate within the Scottish National Party. Except in the case of a city like Dundee, where the difficulties into which local government has fallen have persuaded the SNP not to get their hands dirty by seeking election, the faction in favour of participating in local government has won. This is partly on account of the wholly honourable reason that members of a political party want to participate in decision-making in their own locality, and partly for the more strategic reason that a political party must keep its membership interested, and involvement in local government is one way in which to achieve this end.

The point at which the Scottish National Party really were able to make political hay was in the wake of reorganisation. As we have seen, the Royal Commission on Local Government, under the chairmanship of Lord Wheatley, made recommendations which were partially implemented; it might have been better if the whole Wheatley proposal, a carefully balanced package, had been accepted. The Conservative Government then implemented a reorganisation which involved abolishing the old County and City Councils, and putting Regional Councils, such as Strathclyde, Lothian, and Grampian, in their stead. The truth is that any reorganisation has its teething troubles. It happened with the reorganisation in England, following the Maud Committee; it happened in London, following the creation of the GLC. It happened in Scotland.

In particular, a number of officials who had been in rather important posts were found jobs which were virtually little more than sinecures, or given fairly generous golden handshakes, often after long years of good and faithful service to the community. Others were promoted to significantly better-paid jobs in larger units, and a few, amid a great deal of unwelcome publicity, kept their former jobs, with a new title and a larger salary for performing just about the same tasks as those they had performed before reorganisation.

However, in local elections it is always easy to pinpoint grievances, especially if the object of the grievance is well known personally in the community. When grievances about waste and inordinate salary rises could actually be pinned down to individuals, either by name, or by the local post held, this has the ingredients of a political orgy. The SNP have absolutely wallowed in the jealousies created by stories of rises in salary for particular individuals — often exaggerated in the telling and invariably bearing little or no relation to take-home pay, taxed at source — and therefore unavoidable.

In fact, though one might expect them to say it, given the positions they hold, separately James Anderson, Convener of the Central Region, Sir George Sharp, Convener of the Fife Region, Peter Wilson, Convener of the Lothian Region, and Dr Lawrence Boyle, Chief Executive of Strathclyde, have all made out good cases to suggest that, given the level of service provided, the District and Regions are a good deal *more* efficient, and not less efficient, than the Councils which they replaced, and that costs for the same level of service would have been significantly higher had the former Councils remained in being.

Defence and Foreign Policy

Since SNP suggestions that there should be a Scottish air force and a Scottish navy and Scottish army are usually greeted with incredulity, let the SNP speak for themselves. Mrs Ewing is not only a Member of the Westminster Parliament, but the SNP representative in the European Parliament. Below is the letter she wrote to her constituents during the 1974 General Election, from which it will become apparent that a Scottish Royal Air Force is indeed SNP policy:

Dear Elector,
R.A.F. and S.N.P.

I am often asked 'What happens to the Royal Air Force when Scotland becomes Independent?'

The answer is simple: it continues as the Scottish Royal Air Force and doubtless as English and Welsh Royal Air Forces too. The RAF is in fact the simplest of the Services to apportion as the proportion of RAF stations in Scotland is much the same as Scotland's share of the population of Britain. The air stations at Kinloss and Lossiemouth among others would continue in operation (the SNP is the only party committed to this) along with their aircraft and equipment.

We need these airfields. We need them to fulfil our commitment to NATO of which we would be a member. Near home we need them because they are a very important factor in the economy of Moray.

And what of the Serviceman who is not Scottish but who wants to go on serving in the R.A.F. in Scotland? He has two choices: He can opt for Scottish citizenship to which he will be entitled by his domicile in Scotland at the time of Independence or we hope that he will be able to serve in the Scottish Royal Air Force in the same way as men from Commonwealth countries such as Canada and Australia do now and will so continue to do. Of course, this depends on agreements being reached with England and Wales and the other Commonwealth nations which would be to the benefit of all.

With Scottish Independence becoming nearer, some non-Scottish servicemen who have bought, or are planning to buy, houses here are asking if they can own houses in Independent Scotland. The answer is a clear yes to owner occupiers of whatever nationality, and servicemen will be entitled to let their houses while on tours of duty abroad.

I know that a great number of you, many not Scottish born, voted for me in February. I thank you most sincerely for your support then. I think you will agree that I have not disappointed you as your M.P.

Yours sincerely,
Winnie Ewing

Foreign Policy

The SNP have plans for Scotland to become a Member of the United Nations and the Nordic Council of Scandinavian Countries and to join in 'a special relationship with England' under the Queen within the Commonwealth. Trade links with Scandinavia would be increased and a Scottish Government would try to start talks with the Nordic Council, NATO, the US and the Soviet Union for an 'arms control zone in the North Sea'. The SNP are opposed to political or monetary union in Europe, and promise a referendum on Scottish membership of the EEC. Even with a referendum, they are pledged to renegotiate a more advantageous position for Scotland in relation to fishing, oil and industrial development and are against any extension of the powers of the European Parliament. In a later chapter, I shall deal with the unreality of Scotland being accepted as a Member of the EEC on these or any other terms.

5

Vacillation in Scotland

The Scots are no different from the other peoples of Britain and the world in that they have a natural pride of region. Talk to a Sicilian, a Sardinian, a Bavarian or an Auvergnard and he will speak with pride of the characteristics of his region, and its virtues. In a world in which governmental units have tended to become larger, and the nation state more intrusive into peoples' lives, that pride of a local or regional nature is being fostered is a healthy development. And a sense of local identity is precious in an increasingly uniform world.

However, Scotland currently differs from many other areas of Western Europe in that there now exists an institutionalised political party which is in business to capitalise upon any feelings of national and cultural identity for political ends, to exploit them and to use them for the purpose of creating a separate state. And once a lot of people find themselves caught up in the cameraderie of a movement, storming the citadel of political power takes on a momentum of its own.

It was not until the late 1960s and the crucial breakthrough at Hamilton that the process of transition began in earnest, whereby the SNP ceased to be something of a 'joke party' and crossed the Rubicon to become a serious political force. To understand what had happened over the last decade, it is necessary to take a brief look at the antecedents of the modern SNP.

The Cradle of the SNP

Ever since the Union of the Parliaments in 1707, a minority — small in some periods, larger in others — have continued to believe that Scotland should be a separate nation and not simply just another part of the United Kingdom. Such people have been labelled as romantics, idealists, patriots, dreamers or weirdies, according to the prejudices of those who have described them. For the century after the fiasco of Bonnie Prince Charlie and the '45, this tradition was muted even in the Highlands; it fell almost silent in the central belt of Scotland, one of the centres of the Industrial Revolution.

There is some evidence, albeit flimsy, that a sense of Scottishness was rekindled in the 1840s and 1850s, after the immigration into Scotland of Irish peasants as a result of the potato famine, many of whom found employment in the coal mines there. However, it is perhaps no coincidence that any impetus to translate a sense of Scottishness into political institutional change did not manifest itself until the late 1870s, which marked the beginning of Scotland's relative decline from industrial pre-eminence. In 1885, the position of Secretary for Scotland was created: not from a demand for better government but — as is always the case when concessions are made — from a conscious or subconscious desire for increased nation-status. By present-day standards, little power accrued to the Secretary, though comparisons are a little unreal since the state itself did not play the same pervasive role in the life of the country. In 1926 the post was upgraded to that of Secretary of State for Scotland: but 1939 was a watershed year. That spring most of the Scottish Office work was transferred from London to Edinburgh, into the newly finished St Andrew's House block of offices; in the autumn, the second World War broke out. The responsibilities of the state in general increased by leaps and bounds — and, in particular, the Secretary of State for Scotland took on all the responsibilities of a Home Secretary during the war years. And the occupants of the post, Tom Johnston and Lord Rosebery, were figures of influence and ability, who gave authority to it.

Far from diminishing a sense of national separation, the establishment of the Scottish Office in Edinburgh actually served to increase it. As government has become even larger and more pervasive, it may well be that people in Scotland have become more conscious than they were of their individual identities. Yet, even these administrative changes had more to do with political pressures than with good government. (This was certainly the opinion of Lord Rosebery, by then a very old man, when he talked to me at Dalmeny, shortly after I had been first elected as Member of Parliament for West Lothian. On balance, he thought that the creation of a Scottish Office had been an error, in terms of governmental and administrative efficiency. And as the son of a Liberal Prime Minister, and himself a Member of the 1906–10 Parliament, Rosebery was no crusted Anglo-Scottish aristocrat, but a man of shrewd political awareness and a successful Minister.)

It is true that by 1939 there was an amorphous feeling that Scotland was a separate entity and not just another region of the United Kingdom. The conscious or subconscious desire for nation-status thrived chiefly on lack of economic success. On the other hand, a number of those who were politically active at the time have told me that those who were 'Home Rulers' forty years ago emphatically did not think in terms of a separate Scottish state in the way that the SNP do today; and however woolly and vague their ideas may have been, they never contemplated the break up of the United Kingdom or the dismantling of the Act of Union. Many of those who waved the Home Rule banners probably thought that Scotland could somehow be a nation without becoming a separate political entity. They may have sought the best of two mutually incompatible worlds, but this was what they believed in. They were never called on to hammer out the confusion inherent in their position on the anvil of argument.

The Home Rulers

Between the world wars, the pressure for Home Rule came most vocally from some — though not all — Scottish socialists. The name of Keir Hardie is often invoked in this connection. Whatever he may have said on the subject at various moments of his life, Keir Hardie left Scotland for Wales, and found a Parliamentary seat in East London. His son-in-law, the late Emrys Hughes — MP for South Ayrshire and a Welshman sitting for a Scottish constituency, who was not unfriendly to the SNP — told me that Keir Hardie never seriously envisaged a separate Scottish state, and to imagine that he had was, to use one of his favourite phrases, mumbo-jumbo. Emanuel Shinwell was active in the National Union of Seamen and in Glasgow politics just before the First World War and the MP for West Lothian from 1922–4 and 1928–31. He has made it clear to me that some of his colleagues, notably the Reverend James Barr, Jimmy Maxton and Campbell Stephen, declared that they were in favour of Scottish Home Rule. In Shinwell's opinion, however, they were only posturing, since they knew in their hearts that Home Rule would never come about, and they would have been horrified if it had. It happened to be convenient at the time to make stirring speeches to the effect that since it would be impossible to achieve a 'real socialist Government' in Britain as a whole, there might be a greater chance of creating a socialist society in Scotland, alone. John Wheatley, the hardest-headed of the Clydesiders, and the only one with senior Ministerial experience, would have no truck with Home Rule.

This is not the appropriate place to recount all the ups and downs of the various shifting Home Rule factions in the 1920s and 1930s, all of which contributed to the ancestry of the Scottish National Party of today. It is sufficient to say that at no time did any combination of these factions look like returning a Member of Parliament. The late Douglas Young, Lecturer in Greek at St Andrews University and a central figure in the various nationalist factions of the 1930s, told me in 1966 that he doubted whether many of his associates of thirty years before had really wanted political power: they were more interested in middle-class romantic ideas about Scotland's culture and past history.

There were, of course, pockets of genuine Home Rule feeling, depending very much on the existence of enthusiastic individuals or cells. One of these was Motherwell which, in a freak by-election towards the end of the Second World War, returned Dr Robert McIntyre to the House of Commons, where he remained until he was swept away in the Labour landslide of 1945 a few months later. Partly as a result of the Motherwell result, the election addresses of most Labour candidates in Scotland at the 1945 election included a reference of some kind to the notion of Home Rule. In that sense, the Motherwell result provoked a similar commitment from the Labour Party as the Hamilton by-election result did two decades later, at which Mrs Winifred Ewing was returned for the SNP. Yet any commitments were soon forgotten: the issue of Home Rule went temporarily to sleep and hardly featured at all in the 1950, 1951 or 1955 General Elections.

This can be attributed to a combination of three separate factors. First of all, these were elections in which the differences between the Labour and Conservative Parties were clear and apparent. In 1950 and 1951 in particular, vigorous party machines fervently contested for the favours of the electorate, each strongly believing in its own cause; the Attlee Government had been a great, reforming administration, and it was easy to make up one's mind whether one was for, or was against, the Labour Party. In no election since has it been quite so obvious that a vote for a smaller party is a wasted vote.

Second, in 1948 and 1949, the Home Rulers had put forward the Scottish Covenant, which was a petition demanding Home Rule. It was claimed that the Covenant had attracted 2 million signatures. It soon transpired, however, that many of the signatures were those of people who simply did not exist, while others had been obtained without the knowledge of the people involved. (One of my vivid childhood memories was the consternation of my parents at church one Sunday, when they discovered that the Covenant had been signed on their behalf by a friend, who supposed that they would sign it!) One of the chief instigators of the Covenant was Dr John McCormick, who stood as Liberal candidate against me in 1959, in Roxburgh, Selkirk and Peebles. He ruefully told me that the whole Home Rule movement had been set back by the disrepute into which the Scottish Covenant had been brought by zealots and by the jovial pranking involved in concocting signatures.

Third, the Home Rule cause was greatly damaged by various escapades, for which sincere Scottish nationalists were hardly responsible. There were the bizarre activities of Miss Wendy Wood and her group of Scottish patriots. More damaging still was the dramatic theft of the Stone of Scone from Westminster Abbey and the blowing up of pillar-boxes. These episodes were sensibly and gently handled by successive Secretaries of State — Arthur Woodburn, Hector McNeill and James Stuart — with the result that the perpetrators were regarded as cranks and not as martyrs.

Despite the claim made at the Scottish Labour Party Conference in Perth in 1977 by William Ross, Scotland's longest-serving Secretary of State, that devolution had been part of Labour Party policy since 1945, the truth of the matter is that by the early 1950s the concept of Home Rule in any form had receded into the political background. As Hugo Young of the *Sunday Times* put it, Mr Ross's speech on that occasion 'rewrote autobiography with a passion that would make even a member of the politburo blush'.

Serious Home Rule sentiments were resurrected for the first time since the war at the Scottish Labour Party Conferences of 1957 and 1958. Various factors contributed to this. It was the period of what the late John Strachey called, in an influential book, 'the end of Empire'.* Strachey said that he feared above all else the 'Belgianisation' of Britain — borrowing Trotsky's phrase to describe a people who had entirely divorced themselves from honourable national objectives and surrendered themselves to commercialisation. It was a period of maximum disparity between wages in Scotland and England; and feelings over this were exacerbated by the publicity which surrounded the level of wages being earned at that time by the car workers in the Midlands. Neither the truck and tractors division of the British Motor Corporation nor Rootes's car production factory had yet come to Bathgate or Linwood, nor was there any sign of their doing so.

The case for Scotland having a greater say in its own affairs had a most persuasive advocate in John Mackintosh, then, as now, one of the most gifted orators of his generation. He dazzled the Scottish Conference of the Labour Party with brilliantly delivered and authoritative speeches and influenced a generation of students from his position in the Department of History at Edinburgh University. Had he not departed from the Scottish political scene for a period as Visiting Professor of History at the University of Ibadan in Nigeria, he would certainly have become Member of Parliament for Paisley in 1960; he had to withdraw on account of his academic contract from a by-election short list, in which he had the formidable backing of George Middleton, then General Secretary of the Scottish

* See p. 83.

Trades Union Congress. Had he entered the House of Commons in 1960 rather than in 1966, he could hardly have been denied a place in the Labour Party hierarchy, from which he could have pursued a constructive devolutionary case. With the departure of Mackintosh for Africa, and a number of other pro-devolution academics to posts elsewhere, the positive case for some kind of devolution in the late 1950s and early 1960s went by default in the Labour Party, as it had never had the sympathy of Will Marshall, the powerful Secretary of the Scottish Labour Party during that period.

Instead, an altogether less healthy form of activity was going on inside the Parliamentary Labour Party. In the late 1950s and early 1960s Members of Parliament were paid a paltry sum, with the result that many Members had other jobs in London during the week in order to make ends meet. The digs which most of them could afford were uninviting. The result was that the Scottish Labour members had little better to do than to remain in the House night after night when Parliament was sitting, teasing the Tory Government. At that time there were no time limits on House of Commons business such as have since been introduced. If they were in the House anyway, why not take part in any debate which happened to be going on? So, on Monday, Tuesday and Wednesday nights — though not on Thursdays, when they caught the night sleeper home — the Scottish MPs over-indulged themselves in making speeches on every conceivable subject which came up for debate at night. Moreover, having been out of office since 1951, and feeling perhaps that office would never come their way again, their sense of responsibility was dimmed. It was all too easy to complain that virtually anything the Macmillan Government did was bad for Scotland; and from there it was a small step to blaming the English for all the ills of Scotland. If ever a body of men fashioned a cane with which they themselves would be scourged, it was the loquacious Scottish MPs in the period leading up to the 1964 General Election. Their extravagant propaganda trickling into the Scottish press week in and week out came to be believed. They cannot be surprised if they or their successors reap a political whirlwind.

The first indication of the approaching nationalist storm appeared at the Bridgeton by-election of 1961. In 1959, the

Labour candidate had 21,048 votes and his Conservative opponent 8,909 votes, in a contest in which 68·5 per cent of the electorate took the trouble to vote. Two years later, James Bennett, the Labour candidate, had 10,930 votes, his Conservative opponent 3,935 and the Scottish National Party 3,549. Not only did the SNP come a good third, but only 42 per cent of the electorate bothered to go to the poll. Disenchantment with both the major political parties in Scotland was beginning to show itself. As in any other by-election, there were local factors which contributed to the result. For example, just as the Roman Catholic vote tended to be pretty solidly for Labour at the time, so the Protestant and Orange vote, actively organised in Bridgeton, could never bring itself to vote Labour. Traditionally, Bridgeton had a Tory vote; but the Tories had been brought into disrepute in the West of Scotland as a result of persistent unemployment and other factors and the Orange vote was searching for somewhere else to go. Scottish nationalism seemed to provide a respectable alternative; besides, as a creed, it was not temperamentally uncongenial to the Glasgow Orangemen.

The Bridgeton result can reasonably be compared with the result in the by-election at Kelvingrove, a neighbouring constituency, four years earlier rather than with the 1959 General Election result, since country-wide polls and by-elections are rather a different species. At this election — which followed the death of the ex-Cabinet Minister Colonel Walter Elliot, MP, and was contested by his widow, now Lady Elliot of Harwood — I detected no real sign of Scottish National Party sentiment during the campaign. If it existed, it was dormant.

At the West Lothian by-election of June 1962, the storm signals appeared loud and clear for the first time. Although I more or less held the Labour vote, which I inherited from John Taylor, who had died unexpectedly, the Conservative vote plummeted from some 18,000 two and a half years earlier to a meagre 4,000, with the candidate forfeiting his deposit. William Wolfe, a well-known local figure and a Scout Commissioner, polled 9,750 votes on behalf of the Scottish National Party, of which he was later to become Chairman.

There were various reasons for this startling result. The

Macmillan Government was at a low ebb: indeed the late Sir
Knox Cunningham, MP, then Mr Harold Macmillan's
Parliamentary Private Secretary, later revealed that the West
Lothian by-election result was the final straw which prompted
the Prime Minister to sack half his Cabinet — the 'wrong half',
as Harold Wilson used to say — including Charles Hill, the
former Radio Doctor and Housing Minister, David Eccles, the
well-remembered Education Secretary, and Selwyn Lloyd.
Years later, during Selwyn Lloyd's period as Speaker of the
House of Commons, he used to rib me cheerfully as the man
who was responsible for getting him the boot as Chancellor of
the Exchequer. The Conservative candidate — now deservedly
a highly respected judge of the High Court, and at one time
Solicitor-General for Scotland — was a busy lawyer, irritated at
having to become involved in the stramash of a by-election,
which he had no chance of winning. The conservative campaign seemed lackadaisical and little more than a token effort.
This was one of the first by-elections in which television played
a prominent part. Cross-examined by Professor Esmond
Wright, the Scottish political pundit of the day, the Conservative candidate made an unfortunate and unlucky showing,
which greatly damaged his image. The outcome — to which
such minutiae inevitably contribute — was that although little
had appeared to be at stake, the SNP candidate received twice
the vote of the Conservative candidate, placing him firmly in
the position of an alternative to Labour in future contests. For
the SNP it represented the breakthrough to credibility and
seriousness.

In the 1964 General Election, whereas the Labour share of the
vote in West Lothian remained at just over 50 per cent, that of
the Scottish nationalist went up from 23·3 per cent to 30·5 per
cent. Elsewhere, notably in Perthshire and Stirlingshire, the
SNP polled respectably. The Labour Party manifesto and the
policy document *Signposts for Scotland* were chiefly concerned
with the control of the location of new factories and offices,
inducing firms to move to areas in which industry was declining,
establishing new public enterprises and checking the drift to
the south. Labour promised to create Regional Planning
Boards, which would work closely with the representatives of
the local authorities and other interest in the region. A pledge

was made to create the post of Secretary of State for Wales 'to facilitate the new unified administration we need'. There was no suggestion of recognising a Scottish or Welsh identity as such! The main issue of the election was economic efficiency: those were the brave, optimistic days when Mr Wilson's 'white heat of the technological revolution' was going to mend the damage inflicted on the economy by 'thirteen wasted years' of Tory rule.

Although the Scottish nationalists did significantly better in some constituencies in the 1966 General Election, there was still no breakthrough to Parliamentary representation. Neither the Labour Party manifesto nor indeed Ministerial speeches of the time indicated that members of the Labour Government were at all serious about 'devolution' or a greater degree of Home Rule for Scotland. However, there was a demand for greater scrutiny of governmental actions — including a demand that there should be a Select Committee of the House of Commons on Scottish affairs, which could take evidence from senior civil servants at the Scottish Office and from Scottish universities in particular in order to produce a report. This, it was supposed, would open up the options, force officials to defend their proposals and make Ministerial thinking more explicit: when a final decision was taken, all those concerned would at least feel that they had had their say, and had understood and been able to answer the case put by others. The Select Committee was indeed established, but is currently in abeyance. It was argued that in modern government this process was essential if decisions were to be accepted as legitimate. It was thought to be not only politically disastrous, but an undermining of the whole system, if large and important sections of the community were to feel that bad decisions had been taken for incomprehensible reasons by unknown officials, hiding behind unbending Ministers. Possibly it was too late by this time for the establishment of a Select Committee on Scottish affairs to head off the drive for more say by Scots.

Those of us with vivid memories of the period could but chuckle when we heard Mrs Judith Hart, who was to play a critical role in Labour Party policy formation in 1974, assure the House of Commons:

I have been a positive devolutionist for more than twenty

years. I became a positive devolutionist when I was living
and working in Scotland, when I came to the belief that an
Assembly or Parliament in Scotland was necessary because
of the remoteness of democracy for the Scottish people,
and because of the difficulty in expressing in legislation and
administration affecting Scotland, the very different
economic and social circumstances of Scotland [Hansard,
14 December 1976].

Mrs Hart was Under-Secretary of State for Scotland from 1964
until 1966; she was being groomed as one of the leading ladies
of the Labour Party, and had the ear of the Prime Minister,
Harold Wilson, at the time. Yet she said little about an
Assembly — and appeared to do still less about it — when
she had the power to do so.

As we have already remarked, some of the recent public
pronouncements of William Ross, the former and distinguished
Secretary of State for Scotland and a figure of weight and importance in two Wilson Governments, are even more breath-
taking in their audacity. For years he was the major bulwark
against giving in to nationalist demands towards an independent
Scotland and setting out on the slippery slope. For a quarter of a
century he was the 'hammer of the Nats' — though in retrospect
it is clear that some of the epithets which flowed from his
biting tongue, such as 'Tartan Tories' were counter-productive
in terms of Scottish support for the Labour Party. As we shall
see, his position was crumbling and he was under some pressure
from the Prime Minister not to revolt both on the Common
Market and on devolution. For reasons which are given later in
some detail, a certain charity should be extended to those like
Mr Ross (and myself) who displayed weakness in the autumn of
1974, when proposals for an Assembly seemed to involve freez-
ing the Wheatley recommendations for implementing Regionalisation in Scotland and the creation of an Assembly which would
be a super local government unit rather than a subordinate
Parliament. After holding a position strenuously over a period
of years, it is difficult to return to former beliefs when one has
changed one's mind: as Churchill put it 'It is difficult enough to
rat — it is infinitely harder to re-rat!' What does scar Mr Ross's
scutcheon — and is highly relevant at this point in the narrative

— is his incredible suggestion that he had been in favour of an Assembly or something similar to it ever since 1945, and was just waiting for the Kilbrandon recommendations on the Constitution before taking action.

The fact is that Mr Ross, along with a large and distinguished company of almost all his Ministerial colleagues and most Members of Parliament, believed that SNP electoral advance was nothing more than a flash in the pan and was best dealt with in dismissive and scornful terms. Not even a token gesture was made in the direction of the SNP by any Minister who was in a position to make one, in the immediate aftermath of the 1966 General Election.

One non-Scottish colleague, however, displayed a sustained curiosity in the size of the SNP vote and, until her last and tragic illness, used to ask me at regular intervals how I was faring with the Scottish nationalists: that marvellous lady, Megan Lloyd George. She believed that as soon as the Labour Party succeeded in becoming the party of Government, the natural ruling party, the Establishment, then the natural anti-Establishment minorities and the young in Wales and Scotland would take to nationalism: radicalism must find a political home, and it might be a little difficult for the radical young to identify with the Labour Government of Mr Wilson, as she would call him.

Ironically enough, Harold Wilson's own human kindness in intervening in order to allow Megan Lloyd George to stand in the 1966 General Election, although he knew that she had terminal cancer, gave the nationalists in Wales their chance. She died within weeks of winning Carmarthen at the General Election and her seat became vacant. At the by-election which followed, the Chairman of the Welsh National Party, Gwynfor Evans, was returned to the House of Commons.

If Harold Wilson had not been over-decent to Megan, a new Labour candidate would have contested Carmarthen at the 1966 General Election, and would have won. The Welsh nationalists would not have won the seat; and in the absence of a Welsh example, it is doubtful whether Mrs Winifred Ewing could have convinced people that as a nationalist she had much chance in Hamilton the following year. The party's advance might have at least been delayed, and Scotland's recent political history would have been rather different. Leaving aside speculation about the 'ifs' of history, it is ironic that it should have been Megan Lloyd George's own fiefdom in Carmarthen which heralded a series of nationalist electoral successes. Although the formal links between the Scottish and Welsh nationalist parties are somewhat tenuous, and there is a certain edginess on the subject of North Sea oil revenues, it cannot be denied that SNP successes in Scotland encouraged Plaid Cymru and vice versa. Visiting fraternal delegates from the other Celtic land are made welcome, and their meetings tend to be so well reported that people imagine that there is a stronger link than is actually the case.

The by-election in Hamilton in 1967 was the next major watershed in Scotland. Only then did many people in the Labour Party — apart from myself and a few others who had actually experienced SNP campaigning — take the nationalist threat seriously. I do not say this to prove my own perspicacity and prescience to be greater than that of my Parliamentary colleagues; but I realised that what happened at the Hamilton by-election could very easily have happened in West Lothian in 1966, as many of the SNP members expected that it would. The election of Mrs Ewing went off like an electoral atom bomb in the Labour Establishment. To say that party leaders in Scotland were shell-shocked for weeks is an understatement. After all, Hamilton was not just any old Labour seat: a Scottish Ebbw Vale, with close links to Keir Hardie, Bob Smellie and other pioneers and folk-heroes of the movement, it embodied the socialist heartland. For a quarter of a century, its MP had been the Rt Hon. Tom Fraser, a Cabinet Minister in the Wilson Government.

Sensing danger on our first visit to the constituency three and a half weeks before polling day, my wife and I returned frequently and took a very active part in the campaign, canvassing many a doorstep in Hamilton and the neighbouring towns of Larkhall, Lesmahagow and Blantyre. Ten days before the result, I told an incredulous Harold Wilson and an unbelieving Willie Ross that Labour would lose. To his credit, the only Labour Party leader who listened to my forebodings was the present Prime Minister, James Callaghan, then in rather a depressed mood.

I offer no apology for burdening the reader with some of the down to earth details of the contest in Hamilton, since it is a story which has been repeated, in one form or another, on various occasions. The first thing to be said is that I am quite convinced that very few of the thousands of electors who voted for Winifred Ewing did so because they hoped to see a Scottish Parliament or Assembly established in Edinburgh. Of course it is true that in any election people's motives for voting for a particular candidate or party are mixed. The Labour Party in 1977 could hardly claim that all those who voted for the 1974 Government had a burning desire to see the Dockwork Regulation Bill put on to the Statute Book. People vote for a particular party for all sorts of dubious reasons, which may have next to nothing to do with that party's politics. It is equally true that if a majority of electors decide to plump for a particular party, then the party is entitled to claim their support for its policies: to deny this is to get bogged down in Rousseau-like concepts of the General Will. I must content myself with the simple claim that, as a first-hand witness to what occurred in 1967 in the Hamilton constituency, the idea that thousands of electors voted for a separate Scottish state is absurd.

A very live talking point in those weeks before polling day in Hamilton was the behaviour of Tom Fraser. He was local. He had been a miner. He became an MP in a wartime by-election. He was well-liked and immensely hardworking, and had been a successful Junior Minister at the Scottish Office during the Attlee Government. During the thirteen years of Conservative Government, he had risen steadily in the Parliamentary Labour Party hierarchy and had done well in the annual Shadow Cabinet elections. However, more recently it was being said — perhaps unfairly — that he had not kept up his previous constituency service, at which he had been so good. He had grown up with many of his constituents and was very much a part of the closed community of the Lanarkshire towns, and people were beginning to ask whether he had forgotten about them. To many people in Lesmahagow, it was less important that he should do his duty as a Cabinet Minister, responsible for a vital sector of the British economy, than that he should be there frequently to listen to complaints about a Council that would not get round to repairing Mrs McGinty's door which was causing an awful draught in the house.

Tom Fraser was an admirable representative of the real
interests of the Scottish working class; yet, by 1967, under the
extra strain of sickness at home and working as a Cabinet
Minister in an unfamiliar Department with many problems,
the man whom I knew in the House of Commons as a good
colleague was in bad odour among his 'ain folk'. Damagingly, if
unfairly, it was put about that Tom had become too important
for them.

That year, the Prime Minister offered Tom Fraser a different
job, outside the Cabinet, but still highly placed in the Government; this he refused, partly because he did not want a post
outside the Cabinet while remaining an MP, and partly because
he wanted to spend more time at home in Scotland, for understandable reasons. So he accepted the post that Wilson and Ross
offered him of Chairman of the North of Scotland Hydro-
Electric Board. It was, in fact, by no means an unreasonable
appointment. As well as being an ex-miner, Fraser had studied
power industry problems for years as a Shadow Minister; it had
been his great misfortune that, in the game of Ministerial
musical chairs, he had landed up at Transport, about which he
knew very little compared with his expertise in power problems
and the working of the Ministry of Power.

But, of course, his new and apparently well-paid appointment
at the Hydro-Electric Board was seen by thousands in Hamilton
as a case of 'Tom getting a cushy job for himself' and deserting
them just when things were getting rough for the Government.

Worse still, the Hamilton Constituency Labour Party — or
what remained of it, since electoral victories had been taken for
granted for years — were furious with him. Not only had he not
consulted them about his decision to leave the Government and
the House of Commons; they felt that he had not even said
'thank you and goodbye' to them properly. I vividly remember
calling at the house of a Labour Party stalwart, the Secretary
of one of the large Hamilton old age pensioners' associations,
for a cup of tea before the final effort on polling night. 'Tom
Fraser,' she exploded, 'after all these years together, treated us
like that cloot', pointing to a washing-up cloth lying on her sink.
She was deeply hurt and angry. The fact that such behaviour
was not at all characteristic of Tom Fraser did not count. Having been given a non-political post, he felt — through an excess

of political purity and proper convention — that he must on no account be seen to have further relations with the Labour Party!

Again, some members of the Labour Party, following an unsatisfactory selection conference to choose that party's candidate, were in a sourer mood. They were angry with the candidate's election agent, the Provost of Hamilton, as a result of matters which had absolutely nothing to do with the latest policies being pursued by the Wilson Government. The result was that such work as was done in the Labour cause was mostly done by outsiders, coming to work in the Hamilton constituency.

No less important than the unsatisfactory state of the Labour Party machine were a whole series of niggles, some of which I made a note of at the time. It is worth listing them here since it is from such apparent trivia that by-election results are often made. What politicians see as the great issues of the day often take second place to considerations which, seen from the centre of politics, look like sheer triviality.

First, there was more than usual dissatisfaction with the local housing authority, Labour-controlled since the proverbial year dot, or at any rate within living memory. Repairs reported months previously had failed to get attention. The Council needed 'someone who would get them off their backside'. Since the Labour candidate, Alex Wilson, later MP for Hamilton, was closely identified with the Council, through his agent, the powerful local Provost of Hamilton, it was thought that he was not the person for this task — not that carrying the can for a Council is really an MP's job at all, since Parliament leaves responsibility for such matters to the local authority. But these fine distinctions were not present in the collective mind of the angry housewives of the Hamilton constituency.

Second, there was much ill-feeling in the influential teaching profession. One of the causes of this was that primary school teachers were up in arms at discovering that they were paid somewhat less than their equivalents in England — which was true, if a little exaggerated. It was no less true that, on average, Scottish teachers were no less well off than English teachers, since Scottish Honours graduates, by virtue of the separate Scottish salary negotiations, earned substantially more than equally well-qualified English counterparts.

Third, there were troubles in the steel industry, centred on nearby Ravenscraig and Motherwell. It was widely believed that certain categories of steelworkers were paid less than workers at Corby and Shotton for doing exactly the same work — supposedly indicative of bias by the nationalised British Steel Corporation against the Scots!

Fourth, there had been a spate of accidents on the road skirting Lesmahagow and the rest of the constituency, carrying the main traffic between Glasgow and the West of Scotland to the south. Why did England get all the motorways and Scotland get so few? And what was the point of having the local MP as Minister of Transport if you could not even get a motorway for your own constituency? Adding insult to injury, was the permanent grievance in the Scottish press at the time that we Scots had to pay tolls on the Forth Bridge, while the English did not pay tolls on their more costly motorways.

Fifth, the election took place during one of those perennial rows involving English league football clubs which refused to allow the Scottish team manager of the day to have their players for practice and 'friendly' internationals. This was the English doing the Scots down in the way they always had — methods by which they had won the World Cup some months before, in the summer of 1966. (Some years later, the cause of Scottish nationalism was to be greatly helped in the summer of 1974 when Don Revie, then manager of Leeds United, forbade six of his Scottish players — Harvey, Bremner, McQueen, Jordan, Lorimer and Gray — to play in a friendly match against the West Germans in Frankfurt, some weeks before the World Cup of that year.) It is not the business of governments to tell football clubs how to conduct their affairs; but it is no less true that such pin-pricks influence public attitudes, as soon as nationalism becomes an option.

This sort of thing tied in very well with a political campaign to suggest that Scots were being insulted by the English. Besides which, the SNP candidate not only appeared to be a 'bonnie lass'; she claimed to be an authentic socialist, and indeed a better socialist than the Labour candidate. Authentic socialism is not a drum that Mrs Ewing has beaten since 1974, when she won the seat in the rolling agricultural acres of Moray and Nairn, but she had indeed been a socialist as a Glasgow

University student. Time and again on polling day I met people who said, 'Och well, we voted to give the lass a chance.' Of course, they added, it would be different at a General Election. It was, in the event. Hamilton returned to the Labour fold. But the damage was done. From the sea of trivia which resulted in Mrs Winifred Ewing's triumphal entry into the House of Commons, there emerged a momentous decision — though it hardly appeared like that at the time. Mr James Callaghan, then Home Secretary, took it upon himself, with Mr Wilson's consent, but certainly without a Cabinet decision, or consultation with the Secretary of State for Scotland, Mr William Ross, to set up a Commission on the Constitution under the chairmanship of Lord Crowther. By doing so, he clothed the Scottish Nationalists' case with the mantle of respectability. We shall be examining the reactions of politicians in Westminster to the rise of the SNP, and the implications of the Royal Commission, in the next chapter.

6

Puzzlement in England

When I arrived at Westminster in June 1962, in the wake of the West Lothian by-election, many MPs were mildly curious to learn why the Scottish National Party candidate had fared so well, coming a decisive second, pushing not only Liberals and Communists, but the Conservatives, too, into the ranks of those who lost their £150 deposit. Leading figures in the Scottish Labour Group of MPs, such as Miss Margaret Herbison and the late Lord Hoy, attributed the result chiefly to the level of unemployment in Scotland, compared with that in the South and Midlands of England.

Only two Scottish MPs were clearly not entirely satisfied with this explanation. One was George Lawson, the Scottish Labour Whip; he had succeeded to the Motherwell seat on the sudden death of Alex Anderson who had ousted Dr Robert McIntyre, the first SNP MP, in 1945. Lawson, a severe Scot through and through, and one of the half-dozen best Burns orators of our time, displayed a profound interest in the SNP achievement, though like other Scottish MPs he was inclined to write it off as a flash in the pan, the kind of temporary seizure which electorates sometimes permit themselves in by-elections. Lawson, having retired voluntarily at sixty-five from the House, is now the vigorous Secretary of the 'Scotland is British' campaign.

The other Scottish MP — in a geographical sense at least — was John Strachey, who represented Dundee West. He had recently completed two seminal books, *Contemporary Capitalism**

* London: Gollancz, 1956.

and *The End of Empire*.* I recollect Strachey's words to this day.
'I know', he drawled engagingly, 'everyone says I am the
worst, least Scottish, Scots MP in the House of Commons, and
they may be right. Because, however, writing my books, I have
had to reflect deeply on what happens to countries when they
divest themselves of colonies and dominions, I am most concerned at your result. Now that the Empire is vanishing, we
must prevent the "Balkanisation of Britain" at all costs.' Like
so many other striking phrases in common political parlance,
the concept of the 'Balkanisation of Britain' originated with
Strachey, whose untimely death in 1964 was a great loss to the
Labour Party, and to intellectual socialist thought.

Most other Scottish Labour MPs — like Scottish Tory MPs
— regarded nationalism as a purely temporary phenomenon,
and smugly imagined that it would simply fade away in due
course. Incidentally, neither William Ross nor Judith Hart —
senior Ministers, both of whom now lay claim to a pedigree of
favouring devolution for a couple of decades or more — suggested at this time that any kind of moves in the direction of
Home Rule for Scotland were desirable. Nor, in 1964, when
Mr Ross became Secretary of State for Scotland, and Mrs Hart
was a Junior Minister at the Scottish Office, did either make a
move, when they had the power to do so. Among major Labour
Party figures, those who displayed a rather more profound
interest than most were Hugh Gaitskell, Herbert Morrison — by
then Lord Morrison of Lambeth, but still a frequenter of the
Members' Dining Room in the House of Commons — and the
present Prime Minister, James Callaghan.

At the end of July 1962, shortly before the summer recess,
Hugh Gaitskell asked me to go to his room in the House. He
launched into a formidable post-mortem interrogation on the
by-election. I replied in terms of unemployment in certain parts
of Scotland, though not in West Lothian, being higher than in
certain parts of England, particularly the London area and the
Midlands. Blanket assertions about unemployment in Scotland
were misleading, since the variations within Scotland were
statistically sharper than loose comparisons with English unemployment figures. I added that a special feature of the by-election

* London: Gollancz, 1959.

had been the latent pools of anti-English resentment in the recently established British Motor Corporation Truck and Factory at Bathgate, which had been Macmillan's 'gift to the Scots' against the wishes of Sir George Harriman and other motor industry leaders in Birmingham at a time when the conventional wisdom had it that the motor industry was a cure-all panacea for unemployment. The trouble was not only that wages were lower than those in the Midlands car industry, which were receiving great publicity at the time: it would have been contrary to human nature to accept that Scottish know-how and productivity in the motor industry, then in its infant stages, was substantially below that of areas in which they had had motor industry in their blood for three generations. It would have been contrary to the nature of the Scottish press, to make a clear distinction between the amounts paid to car workers in the Midlands, and to those, like the workers at Bathgate, making trucks and tractors, who were receiving less bonanza-like wages at the time.

Worse still, I told Hugh Gaitskell, was the fact that parts had to arrive from Wilmot Breeden, Rubery Owen, Fisher & Ludlow, Lucas's, and other component makers, and the words 'SCAB LABOUR' were often chalked on the boxes destined for Bathgate, since the Midlands motor workers, even more than management, resented the dispersal of 'their' industry to Bathgate, Linwood, and Halewood, Liverpool. Such epithets were dynamite at the time of the by-election, for many Scots with their own different tradition of high-class engineering felt insulted. Since the factory employed over 4,000 men at the time, mostly from the West Lothian constituency, it is not surprising that the SNP vote was astonishingly high. It is hard to exaggerate the role that the politics of insult, real or alleged, have played in the rise of Scottish and Scottish nationalist feeling. It is true that London has often been pretty gauche in smallish matters, and equally true that the Scots are a prickly and touchy people, who, moreover, often take a sneaking enjoyment in professing outrage at some 'insult' which has been perpetrated against them. We Scots are unsurpassed when it comes to making a mountain of invective out of some mole-hill of a slight, or an unintentional slight, upon us.

Gaitskell observed that, with his own Cumberland background, he could see these problems only too well. He said he would talk to Bill Carron and John Boyd — Amalgamated Union of Engineering Workers' leaders — to see if there was any way in which the differentials between Bathgate and the Midlands could be evened out over fewer years than had originally been intended. He kept his word. John Boyd, a Scot himself, was always helpful and sympathetic. Lord Carron was salty to me: 'If you think Hugh Gaitskell, Prime Minister or not, can persuade any of my members in the Midlands to see the Scots getting as much as they do, until they do roughly the same work, you and he had better think again.'

But Gaitskell was not to get the chance; he died in January 1963. And I was to learn quickly that anti-London feeling in West Lothian in some sectors of the electorate had quite as much to do with anger at union chiefs like Bill Carron, and was as much anti-Peckham Road (Headquarters of the Amalgamated Union of Engineering Workers) as anti-Westminster.

Contrary to widespread belief, Herbert Morrison had a considerable interest in politics outside London. (Indeed, it is a slander on London MPs to imply that they are not interested in Scotland and the Regions — Douglas Jay, the architect of the Industrial Development Certificate Policy, Peter Shore, Reginald Maudling, to name but a few, are some who have shown by their Ministerial actions that they were prepared to antagonise their own people to disperse industry.) What is even less generally known is that Morrison came to Scotland almost every year at the end of January; he was in great demand as a Burns Supper guest, at which ordeal he was astonishingly adept.

In 1962, Morrison thought that too many academic and even public school candidates were being chosen for winnable Labour seats — which may have prompted his opening remark to me: 'Laddie,' he said, 'you may think, and your Scottish colleagues may think, that you have done a good job in getting Macmillan's candidate to lose his deposit. I think you may have great problems!' Some weeks later, I had the opportunity to talk to him alone at length, and despite his initial disapproval, no man could have been more friendly and forthcoming subsequently. Herbert Morrison challenged the view that the SNP result was either a flash in the pan, or that it was simply concerned with economics — wage differentials and unemployment. 'That's what Hugh Gaitskell will tell you,' he quipped acidly. For Morrison, the central issue resolved itself into two questions of fact: 'First, is there a real demand for a different form of governmental organisation in Scotland? [The ugly word 'Devolution' had not then been invented.] And if there is a demand for a different governmental organisation in Scotland, will reform of local government satisfy it?' Herbert Morrison saw the answer in terms of local government reform. As one of the most wily business managers the Commons has ever seen, he knocked down my naive view that the Scottish Grand Committee, discussing Scottish Bills, should meet in Edinburgh so many times a year, and pointed out that, unless such meetings were confined to the Westminster Parliamentary recess, it would make the Scottish Members into second-class MPs, since they would be in Edinburgh during important party meetings and the regular parliamentary business of Departments, such as the Treasury and the Board of Trade, which were no less vital to the people of Scotland than the Scottish Office.

'Besides,' reflected Herbert Morrison, 'what Government is going to allow its MPs, if they are in the majority, to be in Edinburgh, when the fate of the British Government could easily depend on their presence at Westminster?' That was the clinching argument against having the Scottish Grand Committee, which meets on Tuesday and Thursday mornings, meeting in Edinburgh — an idea which has been espoused by some 'minimalists' for Devolution among Scottish Conservatives, fifteen years later.

The third really interested leader to make more than a cursory polite enquiry was James Callaghan, at that time immersed in the work of learning the job of Chancellor of the Exchequer, from the berth of Shadow Chancellor. He wanted to know in some detail what had happened and why the Tories had lost their deposit. He was naturally worried about the 'danegeld' that the Scots would want to extract from a Labour Government in order to put things right, and saw the problem mainly in terms of regional policy.

The 1964 General Election saw Labour returned to power with a wafer-thin majority. At Westminster, if not in West Lothian, the Scottish nationalists were far from the minds of Labour politicians who had come to office after thirteen years. However, in the spring 1966 General Election, there was a landslide victory, consolidating the position of the Wilson Government. Shortly afterwards, as we have seen, the Commons were jolted out of complacency, first by the arrival of Gwynfor Evans, as a result of the by-election at Carmarthen, and subsequently by Mrs Ewing's spectacular victory for the SNP at Hamilton in November 1967.

The Setting Up of the Royal Commission: 1969

Cynics who claim that it makes very little difference who occupies a particular Ministry at any one time are very much mistaken. It matters a great deal — and has continued to matter throughout the whole Devolution saga. For example, it mattered a great deal that the Home Secretary at the time of Winifred Ewing's success in the Hamilton by-election was James Callaghan, who was, as we have just seen, one of the few Labour MPs to have shown a concerned interest in Welsh and Scottish nationalism. In these early days at the Home Office, he was no longer an overworked, over-burdened Chancellor of the Exchequer: Dick Crossman rightly described him as liberated, almost carefree. It was in this mood of relative yet mature abandon that he decided to set up the Crowther — later the Kilbrandon — Committee on the Constitution, under the chairmanship of Lord Crowther, the ex-Editor of the *Economist*.

The setting-up of the Commission in April 1969 was, of course, a direct result of the Hamilton by-election. As we have seen, the SNP fared badly in the 1964 and 1966 elections; and as far as Westminster is concerned, out of sight all too often means out of mind. Mrs Ewing's arrival there startled MPs from both sides of the house into the realisation that Scottish nationalism could perhaps be a force to be reckoned with.

The Government itself was divided over how Mrs Ewing's victory should be interpreted. Some Ministers — including the Secretary of State for Scotland, William Ross — took the view that SNP successes at Hamilton and in local elections were a passing phenomenon, and unrepresentative of the real views of the people of Scotland. Others believed that deeper feelings were at work in both Scotland and Wales, and that — if only for cosmetic and purely political reasons — the Government should try to find out what these feelings were, and how they could most reasonably be satisfied. Among those who felt this way was the late Richard Crossman. In his diary entry for Friday, 24 November 1967, he records:*

> At my press lunch at the Garrick I had among others George Clark, the number two at *The Times*, and found myself discussing devolution; the possibility, for example, of a Stormont-type Parliament in Cardiff and in Scotland. Since I had been wanting to launch a trial balloon on this subject, I aired my views at length and won't be surprised if Clark's story gets on to the Front Page.

Crossman records that it did, provoking questions next morning from all the Sunday papers.

Three days later, Crossman recorded:

> I dined with John Mackintosh, David Marquand, and David Owen to discuss devolution. I've mentioned already that on the previous Friday I'd had a long talk to George Clark of *The Times* and that the story I'd given him appeared unattributed on the front page. But it caused very great interest and the *Glasgow Herald* man [Jack Warden], and a good many others, wanted me to talk a lot more about it. Since most of the Scottish M.P.s, with the Secretary of State [Willie Ross] at their head, detest the idea of devolution, John Mackintosh had been terribly pleased by the article, and arranged the dinner. All this suited me because for a year now (ever since I found Welsh local government being reorganized in such an insane way) I have thought there is a lot to be said for devolution to Welsh and Scottish Parliaments. The whole thing has got to be looked at as a problem not merely of appeasing the Scottish Nationalists and the Welsh Nationalists but as sensible regional devolution and I've been popping off minutes to the Prime Minister for the past six weeks. He's very cautious and holding his options open.

* *Diaries of a Cabinet Minister*, Vol. 2 (London: Cape, 1976).

In the end, it was decided to set up a Royal Commission —
always a convenient way of postponing an awkward decision
(leaving its implementation or rejection, if possible, to one's
Ministerial successor!) while making those whose grievances
are being investigated feel that something was being done on
their behalf. The exact circumstances in which the Kilbrandon
Commission was established are shrouded in a good deal of
mystery. Some of those who must have been in a position to
know the truth now produce significantly contradictory versions
of events.

There is agreement on a few basic facts. In the first place,
neither the Scottish Labour Party, Scottish Labour MPs nor —
astonishingly enough — the Secretary of State for Scotland,
were consulted before the decision to set up the Commission
was made.

Second, the idea of setting up a Commission was the handiwork of the Prime Minister, Harold Wilson, and his Home
Secretary.

Third, the Prime Minister and the Home Secretary hoped to
be able to kill two birds with one stone by setting up the Commission. They hoped to be able to placate Mrs Ewing in the
Commons by pointing to the establishment of the Commission;
and they hoped that its findings would give them a far clearer
idea of the nature and strength of Scottish and Welsh nationalism. To dismiss the setting-up of the Commission as a crude
exercise in buying time and political expediency is to fail to
take into account the extenuating circumstances of the time.
Nationalism was something new on the political scene: politicians had to ascertain whether it was a flash in the pan or a
long-term issue, and how the grievances which gave rise to it
could best be met. Setting up a Commission did, of course, have
the additional benefit of putting the problem on ice: but to have
acted precipitately without trying to find out what should be
done for Scotland and Wales would have been extremely
foolish.

On the other hand, one cannot help feeling that neither the
Prime Minister nor the Home Secretary showed as much
interest in their brain-child once it had been established.

As an Englishman of Irish extraction sitting for a Welsh seat,
James Callaghan had a shrewd idea that the Crowther (as

opposed to the Kilbrandon) Commission would come up with
the answer he wanted. Despite his own awareness of nationalist
sentiments, neither he nor the Prime Minister were interested
in meddling with the Constitution, finding it boring and irrelevant to the real problems facing the Government. They felt
that they could count on Lord Crowther — a firm advocate of
regional planning — to come up with a sensible and unconten-
tious solution, which would satisfy any Scottish and Welsh
sense of grievance and defuse the nationalist challenge in local
and national elections. The Commission could be expected to
come up with various appetising yet sensible schemes for the
economic development of the two countries: as far as constitutional changes were concerned, Mr Callaghan's advisers at the
Home Office felt sure that they would not recommend anything
that went beyond the negative findings of the Speaker's Conference of 1920, which was mainly concerned with Ireland, and
recommended no change in the Scottish relationships.

Powerful evidence in support of the view that neither Mr
Wilson nor Mr Callaghan took the Royal Commission that
seriously when they set it up is provided by the fact that Lord
Wheatley and Lord Redcliffe-Maud both offered to cease work
on their own Royal Commissions on Local Government Reform
— in Scotland, and England and Wales respectively — when
they learnt that a Royal Commission on the Constitution was
being set up. Both were asked to carry on. Any Government
that was that serious about constitutional reform — let alone
the establishment of Assemblies in Edinburgh and Cardiff —
would surely have asked Lord Wheatley and his colleagues on
the Royal Commission in Scotland to put their work on ice for
an interim period of time at least, or at any rate to stop work
until the Government had considered the views of the Crowther
Committee.

The Home Secretary's assumptions seemed reasonable
enough at the time — but then occurred one of those odd
quirks of fate which make politics such an unpredictable business, and confident forecasts of the future so unreliable. Lord
Crowther suddenly and tragically died of a heart attack at
London Airport on 8 February 1972. He was succeeded on
13 March by Lord Kilbrandon, a Scottish judge.

No one becomes famous by recommending that things should

remain as they are — and members of a Commission which fails to come up with new and exciting proposals tend to feel embarrassed about the time and money spent on their activities. As it turned out, the Commission's recommendations went far beyond the expectations of most politicians — though not of those who had remarked the resignation of two of its most able and experienced members, Douglas Houghton, a former Cabinet Minister and Chairman of the Parliamentary Labour Party, and David Basnett, General Secretary of the National Union of General and Municipal Workers — and provided an invaluable impetus to the SNP.

The Kilbrandon Committee Reports

In October 1973, the Kilbrandon Committee's recommendations were finally published. We shall be examining its main proposals shortly: in the meantime, it is worth noting two consequences of the 1970 General Election, following which a Conservative Government under Mr Heath was returned to power — a Government far more concerned with entry into the EEC and industrial relations than with devolution, which slid down the ladder of its priorities.

In the first place, the SNP had done unexpectedly badly at the polls. Mrs Ewing was defeated in Hamilton by Alex Wilson, the Labour candidate, whom she had vanquished in the by-election three years before: in my own constituency of West Lothian, a saddened William Wolfe did significantly less well than in 1966. Had it not been for the Provost of Stornoway, Donald Stewart, who captured the Western Isles from Malcolm Macmillan — their Labour MP since 1935 — the SNP would have lost its frail toe-hold at Westminster, and the course of recent history might have been very different. Whatever the reasons for the SNP's poor showing — and many of its sympathisers put part of the blame on Mrs Ewing — its effect on the Labour Party was to push the problem to one side like a bad dream: from which the party did not wake again until November 1973, when Margo MacDonald won the unlikely seat of Glasgow Govan for the SNP.

Second, the new Conservative Government began its term of office by pursuing more abrasive, right-wing policies than had

been anticipated. As a result of the Government's short-lived
determination to take a hard line with so-called 'lame-duck'
industries, industrial Glasgow soon found itself in direct confrontation with them, and the Labour Party — rather than the
SNP — became once more the natural focus of opposition to the
Government's policies. Throughout 1971 and 1972, the issue of
nationalism appeared to have been submerged by industrial
controversy over such matters as shipbuilding on the Clyde.

Not surprisingly, then, the publication of the Kilbrandon
Committee's findings created little more than a ripple in stormy
political seas. Voluminous government reports seldom capture
the public imagination to the same extent as a surprise by-election result; and although the Kilbrandon Report was a godsend
to the SNP and those politicians who were beginning to toy with
the idea of devolution, Scottish nationalism remained a side-
issue until the Govan by-election.

Before discussing the Kilbrandon Commission's proposals, it
is worth mentioning two points. First, although the political
developments which led up to the setting up of the Commission
pre-dated the Ulster crisis, its actual deliberations were conducted in full awareness of developments in Northern Ireland.
Yet the Committee was forbidden to include Ulster in the scope
of its investigations — which led to the absurd situation of a
Commission debating devolution without being able to draw on
the experiences of the one part of the United Kingdom which
had actual experience of it, however unfortunate.

Second, the Report emphasises (in paragraphs 770 and 771)
that its proposals must be accompanied by a measure of good
will and agreement on all sides — qualities which are, alas, all
too seldom in evidence at the time of writing: 'If it is not
accepted that both central and regional authorities could be
relied upon to strive to administer a scheme of legislative
devolution in this spirit of co-operation, legislative devolution is
not to be contemplated.' The bickerings since 1974, and the all
too clear absence of any co-operation of the kind the Kilbrandon
Committee postulated prompted Mrs Nancy Trenaman,
Principal of St Anne's College, Oxford, a Member of the Commission, to write in *The Times* that whereas she had voted —
just — for the majority recommendations, with hindsight of
what has transpired since, she would not now do so.

The main recommendations of the Kilbrandon Commission can be summarised as follows: that the essential political and economic unity of the United Kingdom should be preserved, though unity does not necessarily imply uniformity; that separatism would neither serve the purposes of good government in Scotland and Wales nor enhance the prosperity of those countries — quite the reverse; that there was very little demand for federalism in Scotland or Wales. On finance, Kilbrandon contended that a block grant system would help to foster regional independence and responsibility, and that an independent exchequer board would be necessary, to apportion resources between England and Scotland. Powers, said Kilbrandon, should be transferred to a regional Assembly to determine policy on a selected range of subjects, to enact legislation to give effect to that policy, and to provide administrative machinery for its execution. By devolving responsibility for prescribed matters only, leaving the Westminster Parliament with the sole right to legislate on matters not so prescribed, Kilbrandon thought that maximum precision would be given to the devolved powers. The United Kingdom Government would also have a power, exercisable only perhaps with the approval of Parliament, to veto regional legislation considered to be unacceptable. Voting for the Assembly was to be by the transferable vote system of proportional representation, so that the proper interests of minorities could be best secured. Each region was to have its own Civil Service and though it would be 'difficult to justify the separate offices of Secretary of State for Scotland and for Wales, it would be to the advantage of the Scottish and Welsh people to have continued representation in the Cabinet'.

Govan: 1973

Like Hamilton, six years earlier, the by-election at Glasgow Govan at the beginning of November 1973 was a landmark, even a watershed. Mrs Margo MacDonald, later to become policy-maker-in-chief of the SNP, and their senior Vice-Chairman, wiped out a Labour majority of 16,000, winning by 571 votes. The attitude of the Labour Party in Scotland before Govan was clear enough, and there is no basis for supposing that

that of the leaders of the Labour Party at Westminster was any different. But timing can mean a lot in politics. Govan occurred at a critical moment. A week before the by-election, the Kilbrandon Commission had reported. Without question the shattering by-election result helped to determine Wilson's response to the Kilbrandon proposals, and marked the beginning of the Prime Minister's conversion to Devolution.

If ever there was a case in recent British political history of chickens coming home to roost, the Kilbrandon Committee was it. What had started half a decade earlier in the minds of James Callaghan and Harold Wilson as a temporising and expedient device to counter the SNP and Plaid Cymru had now matured into a controversial set of proposals which their incoming Government was going to have to do something about. The mere fact that a Royal Commission on the Constitution had been set up at all had itself become a factor in the situation; its very existence contributed to the need for action.

The extent of Wilson's conversion and that of many Labour people in Scotland can be judged from a cursory glance at the policy document *Scotland and the UK*, a specially published pamphlet by the Labour Party Scottish Council which was circulated in October 1973 during the weeks before polling day at Govan. It started with a reference to the basis on which the Labour Party had fought the previous General Election, in 1970, namely the evidence submitted by the Scottish Council of the Labour Party to the Kilbrandon Commission. The 1973 document endorsed the 1970 evidence to Kilbrandon, that the best interests of Scotland would be served by radical changes in the local government structure, 'such that local democracy as it now exists can be strengthened and extended over greater areas', and by changes in Scottish Office and other government procedures, so that decisions made by existing authorities could become more open and comprehensible.

As in 1970, the Labour Party in the autumn of 1973 considered and specifically rejected the possibility of a separate Parliament, Assembly, Scottish Council, or some other elected authority, with executive and legislative powers covering the whole of Scotland. In 1973, the Labour Party reiterated the final paragraph of their evidence to Kilbrandon that they 'would welcome any further developments in self-government which would bring *real* benefits to the Scottish people, provided that all proposals are consistent with our right to remain in the UK Parliament, and continue full representation in that body'.

In the internal party discussions at that time, the phrase 'We cannot have our cake and eat it' cropped up again and again. It was foreseeable and actually foreseen, predictable and actually predicted, that the right of the Scots to remain in full strength in the Westminster Parliament would be jeopardised by the existence of any legislative Assembly in Edinburgh. In contemplating the reasons why the Scottish Council later shifted position, it ought to be remembered that the composition of its members was also a shifting element, and that some of the wisest of those on the Scottish Council either did not seek re-election in later years, or lost their places for reasons unconnected with the devolution issue.

The 1973 Scottish Council of the Labour Party agreed that consideration would have to be given to devolution of further central government functions to the new Regions in the future, but preferred that this shift of power should be allowed to evolve until they had seen how the performance of the new Regional and District authorities worked out in practice. 'Meanwhile,' said the Labour Party officially in a policy document published in October 1973, 'it would be preferred by new Councillors and Officials alike, that they deal with the Scottish Office, rather than any new-fangled Assembly or other administrative or executive machine they do not know.'

The Scottish Council made the tentative suggestion that the Scottish Grand Committee, for example, could meet for a week or so in Scotland in January and in September, with occasional one- or two-day sittings in other months. But this 'must not affect the question of Scottish Members in the House. Time must be set aside for Questions in the House to Scottish Ministers, and for Second Readings of Bills.'

It might be asked, said the Scottish Council, why they should use this route for further devolution. Referring to their many objections to all the other alternatives that had been put forward over the decade, their reply was:

We are still of the opinion that an assembly, other than a committee of the UK Parliament, would be a mere talking shop and would not attract the right calibre of member.

Previous experience of assemblies which have no executive powers is that they are highly unstable in the sense that they do not endure, become merely symbolic, or in fact secure some executive power.

We reiterate our distaste for solutions which would involve the withdrawal of Scottish and Welsh Members, and thereby leave the UK Parliament as basically an English Parliament ...

We are convinced that the Scottish people do not wish total separation. Britain's democracy has been well served by a gradual evolutionary development of its constitutional processes. The alternatives are ineffective change with a window dressing assembly or constitutional upheaval with its attendant political and economic chaos.

We are convinced that the gradual but continual extension of administrative and legislative devolution within the UK Parliament is in the best interests of the Scottish people.

This then was the official position of the Labour Party on the night when her ecstatic supporters acclaimed Mrs Margo MacDonald at Govan Town Hall. Whether the alarum bells were not a bit too loud was open to question, since on the same night, in the Edinburgh North constituency, the Chairman of the SNP was slumping to a disappointing defeat, along with the Labour candidate, in a decisive Conservative victory for Alex Fletcher.

For our purposes, however, the Govan result was overtaken by events, in that the Christmas season followed, and then suddenly, before any kind of alternative strategy on devolution could be devised, Mr Heath unexpectedly went to the country in February 1974. The miners' strike and the three-day week dominated the campaign, and though Mrs MacDonald just lost the Govan seat, the SNP results confirmed the incoming Prime Minister's shift of opinion to the belief that something had to be done about the 'Nats' (the electoral progress of the SNP over the years can be seen by glancing at the figures in Table 2).

The Scottish nationalists gained six seats, four from the Conservatives and two from Labour — both of which could be

TABLE 2 *SNP Votes and MPs*

Year	Total vote	Vote as % of Scottish electorate	MPs
1945	30,595	1·2	—
1950	9,708	0·4	—
1951	7,299	0·3	—
1955	12,112	0·5	—
1959	21,738	0·8	—
1964	64,044	2·4	—
1966	129,112	5·1	—
1970	306,796	11·4	1
1974 Feb.	632,032	21·9	7
1974 Oct.	839,628	30·4	11

SOURCE: The Library of the House of Commons.

interpreted to some extent in terms of local factors. As in so many situations, the facts are incontrovertible; the interpretation is not. What can never be proved or disproved is the extent to which this increase between elections in the SNP vote was determined by pledges on devolution, in general, and the machinery of government in particular, or by matters such as housing and prices. The point is that statistics of this nature weighed even more heavily with Harold Wilson than they would have done with most politicians.

For the Prime Minister, the results also seemed to confirm a series of private polls taken by Market and Opinion Research International in January and February, under their Director, Bob Worcester, which purported to reveal a 17–21 per cent vote for the Scottish National Party. In general terms, MORI looked correct. In particular terms, MORI confidently predicted the loss of certain seats, such as my own — where in fact there was a 6,422 Labour majority in February. More significantly in terms of Prime Ministerial thinking, MORI indicated that whereas only 19 per cent wanted complete independence, 78 per cent wanted some kind of Scottish Parliament; and among Labour voters, this rose to no less than 83 per cent. Mr Worcester then concluded: 'Scottish Nationalism is a unifying force for a wide variety of Scottish people ... North Sea

Oil and Devolution are the two most important issues the new Government should tackle for Scotland.'

As so often in British politics, the Government's policy was, in effect, decided by the Prime Minister's choice of people to carry it out. By choosing two Ministers who were themselves committed to devolution to prepare a White Paper, Harold Wilson in effect decided what Labour's policy was to be. Certainly, there was no discussion at Cabinet as to whether or not the Party should opt for devolution. As various Cabinet Ministers were to lament later, 'We were told by our elders and betters that the *status quo* was not an option.'

Not that many Members of the Cabinet were in any mood to dispute the Prime Minister's will at that time. First the men chosen for this task were the Deputy Leader of the Parliamentary Labour Party and Deputy Prime Minister, Ted Short, and Lord Norman Crowther Hunt, whom few Cabinet Ministers knew, but who had been a member of the Kilbrandon Committee and had produced a minority report, which had enjoyed a decent press. When a Prime Minister assigns a task to his Deputy, it is a little difficult to challenge the decision, at the best of times.

Second, by no stretch of the imagination could the spring of 1974 be said to be the 'best of times' in this context. Labour had won by a whisker and it was only too evident that there would be yet another election soon. The political arithmetic of the House of Commons suggested that this would be within the year — which is exactly what happened.

It is impossible to exaggerate the long-term significance that the fluke chance of a near-tie in the House of Commons can have on the attitudes of the major parties to a delicate constitutional problem. In any electorally normal period, a party which has either won or lost at the poll has time in which to settle down and formulate its policies, after a lot of argument at conferences, and a reasonable amount of mature reflection among the leaders of the party. But times were not normal in 1974, and there was little time to spare. The closeness of the February and October polls meant that many decisions which would normally have been taken in a deliberative manner were hasty and rushed.

The Queen's Speech, delivered on 12 March 1974, merely

stated, 'My Ministers and I will initiate discussions in Scotland
... and bring forward proposals for consideration'. Harmless
enough.

Lo and behold, that very same afternoon of 12 March, the
Prime Minister, making his formal speech in which he explained
the Government's measures to the House of Commons, referred
to 'our intended discussions'. Interrupted by a somewhat can-
tankerous Mrs Ewing, demanding 'proposals instead of discussion', Mr Wilson replied: 'We on this side believe in full consultation and discussions. We are not an authoritarian party. Of
course, we shall publish a White Paper and a Bill.'

This was news indeed. Since the General Election result,
there had been no formal discussion within the Labour Party as
to the right course to adopt in view of SNP success. This was
scarcely surprising, since the Government's main preoccupa-
tion was getting Britain back to work after the miners' strike
and the three-day week.

The damage was done. The Prime Minister had given an
off-the-cuff assurance that his newly elected Labour Government would not only publish a White Paper but also an actual
Bill based on the proposals of the Kilbrandon Commission on
the Constitution; yet the Queen's Speech a few hours earlier
had mentioned little more than 'discussions' on the report and
'proposals for consideration'. Thus it was that a Labour Government, on the day of the opening of the new Parliament, and in
response to a Parliamentary interjection that could easily not
have taken place, either had to become committed to legislation
on the Kilbrandon proposals, or somehow or other disown a
statement made by its Prime Minister.

I do not believe that Mr Wilson had reached some Machia-
vellian decision at all. If he had determined to promise a Bill, he
would have done it in a different style, either through a Prime
Ministerial Statement, or in answer to a staged Private Notice
Question, but certainly not in such a way that would enable
Mrs Ewing and the SNP to claim that they had 'extracted the
promise of a Bill from the Prime Minister'.

From that moment, however, the pressures were on to bring
the Labour Party, and particularly the Labour Party in
Scotland, into line. But the party was to prove recalcitrant. The
majority of its members were unwilling to run directly counter

to what were, until very recently, the settled and passionately held belief of most of them, and certainly of most members of the Government.

A White Paper in name — but actually a Green Paper for discussion — was published on 3 June 1974 under the title *Devolution Within the UK — Some Alternatives for Discussion*. This was a hurried effort — how could it be otherwise? — suggesting an Assembly, but bearing all the marks of being ill thought out and designed simply for the purposes of an imminent General Election.

On Saturday, 22 June 1974, two major events occurred which affected people in Scotland. First, and infinitely more important at the time not only for the public, but for most members of the Scottish Executive of the Labour Party as well, was the fact that Scotland was playing Yugoslavia in Frankfurt in the final rounds of the World Cup.

This meant that the second event — the meeting of the Scottish Executive of the Labour Party at Keir Hardie House in Glasgow — was somewhat overshadowed. The Secretary of State, Willie Ross, was very properly in Frankfurt for the soccer match. Out of twenty-nine members of the Scottish Executive of the Labour Party, only eleven turned up.

I joined the Scottish Executive of the Labour Party only the following month, when I became Chairman of the Scottish Labour Group of MPs in the House of Commons, but I heard colourful and authentic descriptions of this celebrated meeting.

On the instigation of the Prime Minister and the promptings of Ted Short, Ron Hayward, the General Secretary of the Labour Party, had written to the Scottish Executive urging them to accept Devolution; furthermore, with the acquiescence of the National Executive — a decision which was squeezed through among a mass of administrative trivia — John Forrester, Clydebank-born and an AUEW Tass Member of the National Executive, had been despatched to Glasgow to help the vote go 'the right way' from Transport House's point of view.

During the meeting it became clear that five of those members of the Scottish Executive who were present were against an Assembly, and five were in favour. The blandishments of Mr Forrester were more than matched by the tough eloquence of the Chairman of the Scottish Labour Party, Allan Campbell

McLean from Inverness, who was steadfastly opposed to an Assembly. When the vote was taken, all eyes turned to the one member of the Scottish Executive not to have spoken, the petite and comely Mrs Sadie Hutton of Glasgow, who had drifted in after doing her morning's shopping. Loyal to her Chairman, and resentful of the pressure that was being put on him from Transport House, she raised her hand. Thus are momentous decisions actually made!

So, by six votes to five, the Scottish Executive of the Labour Party reaffirmed their policy that an Assembly was 'irrelevant to the real needs of the people of Scotland'.

In restrospect it has been claimed that had there been a fuller turn-out of members, and had the Scottish Football side not been encountering Yugoslavia at Frankfurt, a very different, pro-Assembly, result would have occurred. I doubt this. On joining the Scottish Executive the following month, I made enquiries among my colleagues as to which way they would have voted, had they been present. Even allowing for the influential presence of Old Basso Profondo himself, as Harold Wilson affectionately called Willie Ross, my reckoning was that the 6:5 vote reflected the majority feeling of the Executive at that time; the vote would have been 18:11, or even 19:10, in favour of McLean's anti-Assembly view.

This was not the way the result was portrayed by the Scottish press, who accused the absent members of the Scottish Executive of succumbing to the lure of a soccer match. (To my certain knowledge, at least two of the press scribes who castigated the absent members of the Executive were glued to their own television sets on the Saturday, however they expressed themselves in Monday morning's papers.) 'Six silly men' screeched the *Daily Record*, apparently forgetting that Mrs Hutton was among the six.

The following Wednesday, 26 June 1974, the National Executive Committee of the Labour Party met at Transport House. Towards the fag-end of the meeting, and certainly after several important Cabinet Ministers had left for luncheon engagements, the Scottish Executive's decision was lambasted by Alex Kitson of the Transport and General Workers' Union, and Mrs Judith Hart, MP for South Lanark, and essentially a national figure rather than a Scottish figure, at any rate since she had left the Scottish Office as Under-Secretary in 1966. Their colleagues on the NEC assumed that, as the only Scots on the Executive, they must know about the situation, and agreed to their proposal for a recall conference of the Scottish Labour Party. The truth was that neither had very much day-to-day contact with the Labour Party in Scotland, but this did not prevent them from being regarded as authorities within the NEC as far as Scottish Affairs were concerned.

On 6 July 1974, I attended my first meeting as a member of the Scottish Executive Committee of the Labour Party. Confronted with a demand for a recall conference of the party, the executive, now in full attendance, felt in no position to refuse. My impression is that had there been a larger attendance and a more decisive vote at the 22 June meeting, my colleagues would have summoned up the muscle to refuse. But defying Transport House was a major step, rendered more difficult by the unfavourable press reaction concerning the lack of attendance at the previous meeting. Trivial considerations, it may seem in retrospect — but then minutiae do loom large when decisions are being made, however trivial they may look afterwards. Nor should the sheer embarrassment factor over the poor attendance be underrated.

However, I must also confess that Allan McLean, other anti-Assembly Members and I reckoned that we could persuade a recall conference of the Scottish Labour Party to our way of thinking — against an Assembly.

We were wrong. We had failed to foresee the power and energy that Alex Kitson was to bring to his task. At the meeting of the National Executive Committee of the Labour Party in London, he was instrumental in pushing through a resolution recognising the 'desire of the people of Scotland for an elected Assembly', and calling for party support and Government legislation. All this momentous handiwork was accomplished towards the end of the meeting, when once again members were leaving. The slap-dash way in which decisions seem to have been made may appal many readers; in reality, however, there are extenuating circumstances in that trades union leaders and politicians are under such pressure these days that they tend to act hastily in matters which are not going to have immediate consequences, and which seem to have little bearing on their own activities. A Scottish Assembly was by no means the most pressing matter occupying the minds of the members of the National Executive of the Labour Party.

More importantly, Mr Kitson undertook some neat lobbying to line up the major unions in Scotland behind the idea of an Assembly. Most trades union leaders were taking their well-earned holidays – and even if they were not, many of their members were. Consultation with full-time trades union officers, let alone lay members such as chairmen of local committees, was negligible. For example, men of standing in the Labour movement, such as Ronald O'Byrne, Chairman of the West Lothian Labour Party and a convener of ICI shop-stewards, negotiating pension rights for the entire United Kingdom with his company, heard not a word from his union (the Amalgamated Union of Engineering Workers) before their vote was cast on the undiscussed issue of an Assembly; nor was an important National Union of General and Municipal Workers official, Archie Fairlie, West Lothian constituency agent, even consulted.

Mr Kitson had done his work well. The Scottish Executive, until then resolute and determined, met its Waterloo on Saturday 17 August 1974. The freshest description is a comment I wrote the following day on what was obviously a crucial event to those of us involved: how crucial to the future of the country was only – and gradually – to become clear later.

On Sunday 18 August, I made an unusually long entry in my diary, and I reproduce it in full, as its immediacy gives something of the flavour of this very critical event, not only for the Labour Party in Scotland, but for all concerned with British politics for the foreseeable future:

Yesterday, it was a bad, bad, day. I picked up Ronnie in Winchburgh [Councillor Ronald O'Byrne, Chairman of West Lothian Constituency Labour Party], and he told me that he had had bad news on the AEU grapevine, that Alex Kitson had fixed Gavin Laird. When I arrived at the car-park, Ronnie and I bumped into Janey and Norman [Buchan]. Janey said bluntly that we [the anti-Assembly group] had had it; Alec Donnett of the NUGMW had been squared! I could hardly believe it. I had a quick word with Frank [Gormill of National Association of Colliery

Overmen, Deputies and Shotfirers] who was to chair the Conference, and he said he would do his best, but he had his doubts about being able to carry the Conference.

Frank did well as always. He started by saying bluntly that the Executive would have greatly appreciated it if the NEC at Transport House had held back from making any statement on Scottish Devolution until after this Conference had been held. I clapped hard from my place on the platform, but noticed Alex [Kitson] looking embarrassed and sour; Judith [Hart] did not look too pleased either. Frank went on to tell Conference that the timing of the decision was 'most unfortunate' — I thought some pit language would have been more appropriate, but Frank has exquisite manners and is no Will Lawther. Frank said rightly that the reason given by the NEC that it would have been helpful to this specially convened conference to know the views of the NEC was 'strange'.

I take this from the handout: 'One of the duties of the Scottish Council is to advise the National Executive on Scottish opinion in the party on a wide variety of subjects and this we do, but on this most crucial issue the National Executive decided to make their own pronouncements in advance of any advice that they might have received from the Party in Scotland.' Frank said that we were in a better position to assess Scottish opinion, and surely it would have served the interests of the Labour Movement better if the NEC had awaited the outcome of the special conference.

Then Allan McLean spoke. I thought he did well. He moved that Conference oppose the setting up of a Scottish Assembly as being irrelevant to the needs and aspirations of the Scottish people. He thought it would be an Oliver Twist situation. It would be a wonderful sounding-board for our political opponents. All the ills of the Scottish people, inflation, employment, inadequate housing, environment, juvenile delinquency or overcrowded schools would be attributed to and blamed on the lack of power vested in an Edinburgh Assembly and their subservience to Westminster. Allan and I have talked a lot together about scapegoat politics; he hammered it home. Perhaps he should not have got on to the Crofters of Drumbuie which slightly confused the argument.

Jim Sillars was first to the rostrum. He's tremendously eloquent, and has a beautiful rich voice and a handsome youthful presence — but I do get irritated the way he supposes that only he, and not the rest of us, can interpret the aspirations of the Scottish People. How does Jim know that they have a deep desire for the devolution of powers from Westminster? I hardly think that people in Mauchline are queueing up, asking Jim for Devolution of Powers; more likely, they want to know why the Council has got them or their offspring so far down the housing waiting list. Then Jim went on about decentralisation. I recollect that during the South Ayrshire by-election Jim gave me a mouthful on how Education in Ayrshire should never be run from Edinburgh, but from Ayr. He used to be very certain of his opinions even when he was Alex Eadie's agent, when we were working together in 1963. But yesterday he made a speech that mattered. He obviously does not like Westminster very much, and I thought many delegates were in the mood to believe the worst of most MPs. John Mackintosh, too, was effective, arguing that many decisions affecting Scotland were not taken politically by any public body. He had an odd passage about how directors of education, the inspectorate, or colleges of education were taking policy decisions. Clearly, John's Assembly is going to meddle both with the local authorities, and with the professional representation on *ad hoc* bodies. Ronnie [O'Byrne] went next and spoke excellently, putting the case for sorting out local government finance, which was the source of so much of the original discontent. If the local authorities had enough money for 'folk's housing repairs' to be done promptly, 'we would not be here to-day'!

Oh, Heavens, and then came Gavin Laird. He said he did not have time to prepare a speech since he had just interrupted his holiday to come to the Conference. He stumbled out that the AEU would not support Devolution simply for reasons of expediency. Gavin, who normally speaks well, produced a number of platitudes about improving the democratic process. He seems to think all the

work of the House of Commons concerning Scotland is
done in the two hours after midnight. This is really a load
of rubbish. George Lawson followed and as an ex Scottish
Whip in the House told Gavin that we Scots had more than
our share of time. George wanted to know where the demand for an Assembly was to be found. He pointed out
that seventy SNP candidates had got 21·9 per cent of the
vote, but this did not mean that there was an overwhelming
demand for a separate Scottish set-up. Brian Wilson, our
Ross and Cromarty candidate, who runs that extraordinarily successful and radical West Highland Free
Press, just thought the party should square up to the
challenge of the SNP and not run away, instead of shelter-
ing under the umbrella of a Scottish Assembly. He thought
it would lead to the destruction of the Labour Movement.

Then came the dagger. How Alex Donnett, believing
what he does about the Assembly, will be able to look at
himself in his shaving mirror, I know not. Anyhow, he
trundled to that rostrum and solemnly told us that there
had been a considerable amount of administrative and
executive devolution in the last few years, and that he
considered the time had come for making a systematic
approach for a Scottish Assembly. Though Andy Forman
of USDAW followed him, opposing the Assembly, I
realised the game was up, and so did the whole Conference.
In vain did Andy say defiantly that if a political party of
the stature of the Labour Party resorted to political expediency, then we were on a very slippery slope. Andy
Forman warned us that any further disillusionment could
lead to Separation, if the Assembly did not produce the
goods expected of it. Alex Kitson coolly told us that the
NEC at Transport House were expected to give a lead, and
this they had done in declaring their support for an Assembly. All too obviously it *had* been 'fixed' — and as Allan
McLean whispered to me, we never had a chance. There
was no earthly point in prolonging the agony into a Second
Day, and we would be well advised to throw in the towel
after lunch. Two other speeches stuck in my mind. A
competent effort from John Smith saying that delegates
who were pressing for devolution to a Scottish Government

could not have their cake and eat it, by insisting that they
keep the office of Secretary of State for Scotland, and all
seventy-one MPs. The other was by Willie Mack, the
delegate from Maryhill. Willie said that he would vote for
the Assembly, without fully understanding what it was all
about. 'But if you fail to make it work, you will have
destroyed the Scottish Labour Party, and the national
Labour Party will be in perpetual Opposition and eventual
decline.' Willie added, 'If a Scottish assembly is to be the
answer to the problems confronting us, please don't put it
up as a vote catcher, and then run away from it. This is one
of the reasons why political democracy is treated with contempt by the man in the street. He doesn't believe you. You
make promises and don't keep them, and the sort of devolution I would like to see is that which brings for ordinary
people policies which eliminate fear of want, bad housing,
and fear of minority oppression. But I am very much
afraid that unless we deal with these problems on a national
level, no Scottish Assembly will save the Labour Party.'

I was itching to speak but as a member of the Executive
had to sit silent on the platform; I told Allan towards the
end that it was a basic error to conclude that if one only
adopts Nationalist-type policies, all will be well. Things
don't follow like that at all. The tartan curtain was falling
all around us. There was no point in calling for a card vote,
(though thinking about it later I believe we made a bad
mistake not to) for we would have been beaten. Nor did I
realise until last night that the AUEW delegation had
divided 8:6 for the Assembly, with several anti-Assembly
absences. Oh, Lord, how are decisions made in the Labour
Party? Ironically, I bet the SNP chances have been greatly
helped by the Labour Party in Scotland having to dance to
the SNP tune. Devolution is little more than a political life
jacket — and a life jacket, what's more, that will not inflate
at the right time, as John Burns of West Lothian Constituency Labour Party acidly retorted to me.

After the Conference, I took Norman Crowther Hunt
home for the night. We talked in the car and later, and he is
very charming. But I am far from convinced that he has his
feet on the ground. I am conscious that for all his soothing

words that all will be well, and that we should not worry, he neither knows us Scots, nor our history of faction; in fact, I sense that he regards us as interesting guinea-pigs on which to practise his constitutional experiments. He is obviously very close to Harold Wilson, and will play a vital part in the coming months and years, in shaping these ideas. The real trouble is that he thinks that the SNP exists because people want a different constitutional set-up; Ronnie and I know the SNP flourishes on account of the greed of the people for North Sea oil revenues, disgust at local council corruption scandals, stirring up Rangers supporters' clubs by Orangemen because there are too many Catholics in the Labour Party, and a host of other matters, which are well known to those of us who struggle along in the gutter of political life, but which are somewhat novel, if known at all, in Oxford University Common Rooms frequented by Norman. But as Ronnie said, 'He's a rare talker!'

Archie [Fairlie — West Lothian agent at elections, and full-time officer of the National Union of General and Municipal Workers] told me he was disgusted, but that the trouble was that the unions did not know the SNP as well as we do in West Lothian, and that nothing would appease them. He thinks Alex's attitude is a lot to do with the union leadership.

As Mr Willie Mack of Maryhill had had the foresight to point out, he and many other delegates did not know what devolution really meant. Extravagant pledges, however, had been given, and there was a commitment for a Scottish Assembly, so he supposed he ought to go along with it.

On Wednesday, 21 August, a sub-committee of the National Executive Committee of the Labour Party met, and decided on a paper to be drawn up. The wording was largely left to Mr Geoff Bish, Research Secretary at Transport House, and Mr Philip Wyatt, Secretary of a working party of the NEC. Their report was published with the imprimatur of the Home Policy Committee of the NEC on 5 September 1974. The document contained much that was unexceptionable in the light of what had happened:

We propose the creation of directly elected Assemblies for Scotland and Wales. We have of course an equal commitment to democratic accountability of government and of equality of political rights in the English regions ... An essential element of our policy for both Scotland and Wales is the retention of their existing number of MPs at Westminster, and the maintenance of both the posts of Secretary of State for Scotland and for Wales in the Cabinet.

There would be a block financial allocation, and regional imbalance of areas of industrial decline had to be redressed.

There was, however, one sentence in the document of 5 September which was squint, mistyped, and from which there was obviously an erasure, unusual in documents of this nature which are put out for the benefit of the press. Yet this sentence was of thunderous significance. It read:

It was the Labour Party in Scotland, the party of Keir Hardie, which in 1958 reaffirmed its support for the principle of maximum self-government for Scotland consistent with remaining within the United Kingdom; it was [erasure and miss a double-spaced line of typescript] the Scottish Council of Labour which, in 1974, after an open, honest debate, overwhelmingly called for an elected Scottish Assembly with legislative powers.

The press reports on Sunday, 18 August 1974 and Monday, 19 August 1974 make it clear that the delegates did not realise that on Saturday they had called for a legislative Assembly; most of them were under the impression that they had called for a super-local authority. The crucial word 'legislative' had been deftly inserted into the press hand-out and was repeated in the White Paper on devolution published on 17 September 1974. On 18 September, Harold Wilson announced as Prime Minister that he was calling for a General Election.

On the Monday following the General Election, the Scottish Group of Labour MPs held a press conference in Keir Hardie House in Glasgow. As Chairman of the Group, I assented to the proposition by a journalist that Labour would not go back on the campaign promise for a Scottish Assembly, and was duly reported as having done so, and pictured, shoulder to shoulder with my friend and colleague Harry Ewing, MP, an ardent devolutionist, who was Secretary of the Group. Moreover, I was correctly reported as having said that the Secretary of State should make haste and produce the Assembly, as soon as possible. I mention this press conference in some detail, as for three years and more I have not been allowed to forget it, either by Mr William Ross, or by other pro-devolution colleagues.

My side of the story is, however, rather simple. I was most disappointed by the 17 August conference result. The press statement of 5 September occurred when I was snatching my only three days' holiday of 1974, and did not moreover highlight the point about the legislative nature of the Assembly. Possibly I ought to have read the White Paper carefully, but since it was not physically in our possession when the election balloon went up, I did not. Nor, because one has a million other things to do in the course of a hectic election campaign, did I read it or the Party manifesto, which repeated the White Paper pledge, before polling day. In the forty-eight hours after the result of the poll, I caught up on lost sleep, and had not read the White Paper by the time I faced the press on the Monday. I really imagined I was endorsing the super local authority, which we understood had been agreed on 17 August. So did most of my colleagues.

For suggesting that the Assembly should be produced quickly, I make not the slightest apology. If one was going to have an Assembly which was essentially a super local authority and in no way a legislative body, obviously it should have been introduced quickly, and indeed could have been done quickly, since Regionalisation could at that stage have been frozen in its tracks: what would just have been possible in November 1974, was no longer so the following year. A super local authority for Scotland could have been on the Statute Book by now, since there would have been none of the problems attendant on a subordinate Parliament. The truth was that those who wanted a Scottish Parliament had inserted the word legislative, and had subtly used a one-way ratchet to achieve their wishes or at least a significant move in the direction of their wishes.

In 1974, the promise of a Scottish Assembly appeared harmless enough in London's eyes. It did not seem to cost too much. It seemed a neat enough solution to a worrying problem; if there was the widespread impression in Scotland that what had been promised was in effect a form of super local government, that impression was almost universal south of the Border. The confusion was easily explained. In Scotland, as elsewhere, the whole argument had been conducted up to that time in terms of over-easy slogans, trundled out as the needs of each politician's speech required. Tragically little thought had even then been devoted to thinking the problem through, in any serious manner. Phrases and catchwords were devised, with the following morning's headlines in an excitable Scottish press as the major consideration.

The results of the October 1974 General Election were highly — if unevenly — favourable to the SNP and confirmed Scottish nationalism as a central issue in British politics. The SNP retained all their existing seats, and gained an additional four seats (see Table 2). The Government had actually got to do something, unlike Mr Heath in 1970, who was confronted by only one Scottish National MP who had strayed in from the Western Isles; and the case for the *status quo* against separation had to be robustly made, and could not longer go by default.

1975

On Monday, 6 January 1975, Gerry Fowler, MP, then Minister of State at the Privy Council Office, and Harry Ewing, Scottish Office Minister, came to a meeting of the housing sub-committee of the Scottish Council of the Labour Party at Keir Hardie House in Glasgow. It was a filthy winter's night and only nine souls were present in all. Out of the blue, Mr Fowler started making references to what a Scottish Prime Minister and a Scottish Cabinet would be likely to do in relation to housing policy. At that moment, it dawned on me for the first time — and on others, such as Allan McLean, Party Chairman in Scotland — that Ministers were thinking in terms of a Prime Minister of Scotland and the whole paraphernalia of a Cabinet system.

After the Christmas recess, when I returned to the House of Commons, and conveyed these tidings about a Scottish Prime Minister to my Parliamentary colleagues, I was met by an incredulous, 'You're bloody joking!' 'That'll be the day, a

Prime Minister of Scotland — Bermondsey will be wanting me to be Prime Minister of bleeding London!' laughed the Government Chief Whip, Bob Mellish. I record this ribaldry as evidence that the Labour Party Commons managers had not the slightest notion of what their own Lord President of the Council and his colleagues were up to.

I will spare the reader the details of the cascade of speeches I was to make on the subject in and out of the House of Commons. But it is worth mentioning one of them, less for its content than for the reaction that it provoked after Ted Short had read a full account of it in *The Times*, on 3 February 1975. I was correctly reported as saying that I had been acutely unhappy the year before about the possibility of there being an Assembly, but that I had accepted that it was as far as we could go without breaking up the United Kingdom. 'It now seems that the Government is prepared to go much farther than the original contract with our electors.' *The Times* quoted me as pointing out that the trades unions had insisted that trade and industry should be excluded from the power of a Scottish Assembly, and that these responsibilities had now been given to the Secretary of State for Scotland. However, the more such powers were given to an Assembly, the more swiftly would it lead to the break-up of the United Kingdom. I was quoted as having pointed out that the Scottish Executive of the Labour Party had last voted by 2:1 against the Assembly having powers to raise revenue:

> Nor was it my understanding that there should be a Scottish Cabinet Government, with the probability of a Scottish Prime Minister, backed by a ministerial team. Once you have this you have a situation where every ill, real or imagined, will be blamed on the assembly not having enough power. The same would happen if Westminster had the power of veto and dared to use it.

If the Scots had their own Assembly with strong powers, we could hardly claim the right to keep seventy-one MPs at Westminster, and a Secretary of State in the Cabinet.

I quote this not to boast of my own prescience, for in truth, I was merely stating what was obvious to anyone who cared to think about the topic in any depth, but because my remarks provoked anger of thermo-nuclear intensity on the part of Ted

Short. And since even then it should have been obvious that my points were of considerable substance, and were indeed precisely some of the very rocks on which the Scotland and Wales Bill was to perish exactly two years later, it could hardly have been the irritation that senior Ministers feel when their time is being needlessly wasted. What was obvious, both in interviews in his room as Leader of the House, and from the debate of 3 February 1975 in the Commons Chamber, was that he had shut his mind to anything that he did not want to hear. He could not be talked to. And it is no good saying that Ted Short was never talkable to. As Chief Whip, as Postmaster-General, and as Secretary of State for Education, it was certainly possible to have a dialogue with him. On devolution, it was quite impossible. What had changed? To answer this question, before resuming the narrative, it is necessary to digress, as so much that follows depends on understanding the state of mind of Edward Short, and his successor Michael Foot.

The temptations facing Ministers given responsibility for items in their party's programme are extremely seductive. Honourably, they want to do a job well. As human beings, they rejoice at the opportunity of leaving their mark on history — again, not a dishonourable motive in itself. They have a vested interest of the mind in implementing legislation for change.

Though perhaps his Parliamentary colleagues ought to have known better, few people guessed in October 1974, when Harold Wilson handed the key role of devolution supremo to Edward Short, that he would be other than a critical senior Minister, objective in his approach, ready to listen to argument and displaying all the caution which was to be expected from a Tyneside MP on this issue. Yet, within weeks of his getting the job, it was clear that Mr Short's mind was no longer open on the merits of the issue, even though little discussion on it had taken place in the Labour Party as a whole. Gone was the caution which he had displayed on the subject during the General Election when he visited Scotland. Mr Short had seen his chance to perform a political task of historical significance, to give his name to History, as any of us might, and had suddenly become an ardent devolutionist, positively messianic in the cause of an Assembly in Edinburgh. Anyone who pointed out those very difficulties on which the Scotland and Wales Bill was eventually to founder got short shrift, and was firmly informed: 'the *status quo* is not an option'! Yet eighteen months later, soon after he had ceased to be Lord President of the Council, and a Government Minister, and had become Lord Glenomara, he was telling the North-East of England Development Council, of which he had become Chairman, that their duty was to watch devolution like a hawk.

My purpose in referring to these events is not to make a criticism of an old friend of nearly twenty years, but to point out that it is in the nature of Ministers, in the British system of Government, to take action, and to neglect the possible merits of inaction, for no better reason than that they find themselves in the driving seat. For example, exactly the same phenomenom can be diagnosed from the case of Mrs Barbara Castle, given the job of Secretary of State for Employment, foisting *In Place of Strife* on a doubtful Cabinet, reluctant Government colleagues, a basically hostile Parliamentary Labour Party, and a sullenly furious Trades Union Congress. It was her child, and she was going to fight for it. For her, the validity of the case against, as with Mr Short on devolution, was obscured during the time that she held the Office.

Exactly the same happened when Michael Foot inherited Ted Short's job in April 1976. Close political friends of Michael Foot had little idea that he was an enthusiastic supporter of devolution. As Aneurin Bevan's sympathetic biographer, it was assumed that he shared Bevan's distaste for anything to do with Welsh nationalism, or giving in to demands on an ethnic basis. Both Aneurin Bevan's widow, and his loyal PPS, Donald Bruce, now Lord Bruce of Donnington, have been dismayed by Michael Foot's espousal of the devolution cause. My impression is that this considerable writer and polemicist, who has a real sense of the past, also wants to leave his mark on history, and sees the successful pilotage of a Scotland and Wales Bill through Parliament as a triumphant note on which to terminate a remarkable career.

How else can one explain how a man who ended up his oration on the European Communities Bill in 1972 with the following majestic passage would himself have imposed a Guillotine in such a case as Devolution?

There is a further reason why it is improper for this Government in particular to introduce a guillotine. There is a further limitation on the manner and method which are open to the Government for securing the consent of Parliament to the Bill. No one can say that he has the full-hearted consent of Parliament and at the same time introduce a guillotine. No one can say that unless he emasculates the English language, just as the Government propose to emasculate the British Constitution.

Nobody can say that he has full-hearted consent for a Measure, that he has the full-hearted consent of a majority in Parliament, if he has to impose a guillotine. Nobody says that the Government have the full-hearted consent of Parliament for the Housing Finance Bill, to which they have applied the guillotine. The guillotine is the last resort of a Government who know that they cannot get the full-hearted consent of Parliament but are determined to have their way in any case.

When the Prime Minister originally used that phrase, it was designed to comfort the people of this country into assuming that there would be some special measure of tolerance, that some special measure of acceptance and a wider unity had to be obtained for a Measure of this constitutional importance. No such claim can be made once the Government have forced through a guillotine Motion.

What the Government and the Prime Minister, in particular, are doing is to show full-hearted contempt for the democratic processes of this country; full-hearted contempt for the normal legislative processes of this House of Commons. The stain will remain indelible on the right hon. Gentleman for ever. It is a pity that he did not have the courage to come to the House today to defend his Bill [Hansard, 2 May 1972].

The central point is that it is an illusion to imagine that once even senior Ministers have been given a task to perform, they will step back to take a reflective and critical look at the situation. Given the pressures of high office, and the knowledge that the time in which to achieve anything lasting at all in a certain Ministerial position may be short, and stopped dead at any time, the instinct is simply to put one's head down and charge, doing what one conceives of as one's best.

There should, however, be a counter-balancing and restraining force — the collective will of one's Cabinet colleagues. In relation to devolution, this safety mechanism failed to operate properly for two separate sets of reasons. First, the Secretary of State in charge of devolution was also Deputy Prime Minister and Lord President of the Council, normally a non-Departmental job. However, the Lord President, as Leader of the House of Commons and Chairman of the Legislation Committee of the Cabinet, is also the man who allocates Parliamentary time to his colleagues and their Departments. Most Cabinet Ministers want to get their own measures on to the Statute Book. This means an allocation of Parliamentary time. Whereas it is hazardous and unpleasant to make enemies in Cabinet by criticising too severely the measures of any Cabinet colleague, it is doubly hazardous, even an act of folly, to antagonise the Lord President — especially if the occupant of the post commands the ear of the Prime Minister to the extent that Edward Short had Harold Wilson's ear, and Michael Foot has the ear of James Callaghan.

Even so, Cabinet might still have put the brake on devolution, so unhappy were they about it. But then came the second reason for the failure of the safety mechanism — Harold Wilson's resignation in March 1976 and the leadership contest this forced upon the Labour Party. In order to attract the votes, so they supposed, of the majority of Scottish Members, some candidates for the leadership made more pro-devolution noises than they might otherwise have done, and subjected to direct enquiries on their attitude to a Scottish Assembly by certain Scottish Labour MPs, made public attestations of faith in an Assembly which might not otherwise have been forthcoming.

And just as it is natural that a senior Minister should apply himself to his Departmental task at the expense, sometimes, of the overall picture, so it would be unreasonable to expect Junior Ministers to do other than to forge ahead with the task that has been allotted to them by the Prime Minister. In the first place, they have been appointed for one of two reasons — either, like Lord Norman Crowther Hunt (appointed Minister of State at the Privy Council Office with special responsibility for devolution), because they are enthusiasts for, and knowledge-able on the issue, or because they are thought to be competent men, capable of doing a good job with the Civil Service, and in the House of Commons, or both. Those falling into the first category are unlikely to renege on their beliefs: those in the second will be naturally concerned with impressing the Prime Minister, the fount of patronage and preferment, accruing good will among other Ministers, and in the party in the House and in the country, and demonstrating that they are among those who can handle the House of Commons. After being handed a job such as steering the Scotland and Wales Bill through the House of Commons, they are hardly likely to paddle along to Downing Street three months later, and opine to the Prime Minister that they think the task is impossible, and that their Ministerial errand is simply ridiculous. They would rightly suppose that any youngish politician who treated James Callaghan or Edward Heath in such a fashion could expect a set-back to his career.

So it was that from the autumn of 1974 onwards, the devolution juggernaut developed a momentum of its own, fuelled not only by loud external pressures, but by an absence of any braking mechanism inside the government machine itself. The exercise was a flawed one from the moment in September 1974, when — as we have seen — the vague super-local-authority-type Scottish Assembly assumed the role of a subordinate Parliament or legislative Assembly.

Now any Government may have a bad plan in their programme; what was almost unique about the devolution scheme was that more than half the Ministers in the Cabinet, three-quarters of the Ministers outside the Cabinet, and a majority of the Parliamentary Labour Party knew very well that it was a bad plan, and yet they let it go on.

The original impulse for an Assembly, in both the Labour and Conservative Parties, had little to do with improving the government of Scotland or Wales, or bringing decisions nearer to the people, and a lot to do with saving Labour and Conservative seats at Westminster. As we have seen, in Labour's case, the notion of an Edinburgh Assembly was hardened into a party commitment during the short Parliament of 1974, when there was no time to assess it properly, and consider the implications in any depth. Senior Cabinet Ministers continued to deplore it in private, but they suppressed their scepticism, even at Chequers meetings, when they saw that Harold Wilson was giving his full backing to Edward Short, for between them the two men controlled the Minister's legislative time and, possibly, their futures. Some of these Ministers became supporters of an Assembly when they canvassed the votes of Scottish MPs in March 1976 during the Labour Party leadership election.

Disingenuous in conception, the scheme could not fail to be dishonest in execution. The Scotland and Wales Bill — published in November 1976 — represented a surrender to the politician's most pressing temptation, which is to say different things to different people at the same time. In Edinburgh, and to the political correspondents of the *Scotsman*, *Daily Record*, and other fervent newspapers, it was suggested that cataclysmic changes were to take place in the government of Scotland — for the better. In London, the impression that Ministers too often wanted to give representatives of the heavyweight press was that it was simply a matter of altering matters pertaining to Scotland and Wales, and that the rest of the United Kingdom was not greatly affected.

Out of this fork-tongued approach came the central absurdity of the Scotland and Wales Bill, the rock on which it was to founder in the House of Commons; in the debates on the Bill which followed its publication, the pretence that there can be substantial differences in social or industrial or economic policy within a unitary state, if that state is to remain a United Kingdom, was fully exposed.

I hope that the previous section has provided some insight into the human reactions of senior Ministers which allowed a predictably and preposterously unworkable scheme to get as far as the stage of a Parliamentary Bill. On 6 March 1975, in response to a reasoned outline of the problems he was likely to face, Ted Short wrote me a curt letter saying he was ready to consider publishing another White Paper — i.e. discussion document — in advance of the introduction of the Bill — 'provided that this does not hold up work on the Bill'. The very idea that the Lord President ever imagined for one moment that he could by-pass the White Paper stage of so complicated a proposal indicates in itself the messianic unreality of his thinking. It was not until the Labour Party meeting on the first Wednesday in April 1975, devoted to devolution, that Short was brought down to earth, and told that he must bring in another White Paper. Tom Urwin, Chairman of the Trade Union Group, and a former Minister of State in the Department of Economic Affairs, with responsibility for the North of England, led off the discussion by giving his view that we were embarked on a calamitous course, and that a much more coherent White Paper was needed than that of the previous September.

A new Member, Bruce Grocott, made a powerful speech, deploying the overwhelming case for having more administrative devolution, but treating every citizen in the United Kingdom in the same way in matters of his or her relation to the state. John Parker, for forty years MP for Dagenham, quoted the example of Yugoslavia, where states within a state duplicated resources. Neil Kinnock, the Member for Bedwellty, attacked the concept of ethnic differentiation in politics, of dividing Welsh, Scots and English on a racial basis. By the end of the morning, when Big Ben struck 12.45 p.m., it was obvious to all in Room 14 on the Committee Floor at Westminster, including the Prime Minister, that it would simply not be acceptable to the Parliamentary Party to leap-frog the White Paper stage.

Once it had been established that a further White Paper would be produced in the autumn of 1976, a 'wait-and-see' shroud fell over the political scene. Oddly enough, such dissension as took place on devolution tended to relate to the demand for devolving to the Assembly those functions of the Department of Trade and Industry regarding the development of existing industry in Scotland and the attraction of new, and the demand, also embodied in a successful Transport and General Workers' resolution, at the Aberdeen Conference of the Scottish Labour Party on 21–3 March 1975, to make the Scottish Development Agency answerable to the Assembly. For most non-professional politicians, these were recondite issues. And the professional politicians, or at least those given to strong views on devolution or other topics, were involved on one side or another in a different passage of arms — the referendum on entry into the EEC in June 1975.

Two events following the EEC referendum ought to be recorded. The first was the declaration on Monday, 9 June 1975, by James Sillars, MP for South Ayrshire, that a Scottish nation state within the European Community should be set up. In characteristically simplistic terms, Sillars declared: 'This Referendum does not close the question of Scotland's role in the EEC. It opens up another forum. The Scottish people must make the choice between playing in the First Division or the Second.' In September 1975, he and John Robertson — MP for Paisley — broke away from the Labour Party to form the Scottish Labour Party.

Since it looks as if Jim Sillars and his Scottish Labour Party may not endure as a lasting political force, comment ought to be telescoped. First, the Scottish Labour Party's genesis owed a great deal to Sillars's own personal sense of anger at Westminster, and all its works: 'It's this place that gets me; it can't do much for the people I represent.' Second, he has a brand of *Volkspolitik* which leads him to assume that the Scottish people's views at any given time, on any given subject, happen to coincide with his own. Third, as often happens to exceptionally good speakers, this extremely gifted orator gets easily carried away by his own rhetoric, giving him an often weird interpretation of what Scots people really want. Fourth, Sillars perceived the same truth which I perceived from the opposite end of the devolutionary spectrum, but which none of our fellow-members on the Scottish Council of the Labour Party could bring themselves to believe — that there was not a cat in hell's chance of a devolution Bill, along the lines they were talking about, getting through all its stages in the House of Commons, as composed after the 1974 General Election. Finally, what James Sillars had done is in a good old Scottish tradition — he had created a Schism; we Scots are prone to schisms, and indeed revel in them. In the seventeenth century we had religious schisms of varying ascetic brands; in the eighteenth century there were the Jacobite schisms; in the nineteenth century there was the Disruption, when two-fifths of the ministers of the Church of Scotland walked out to form the Free Church of Scotland, under the pastoral guidance of that commanding figure, the Reverend Dr Thomas Chalmers; earlier in our own twentieth century, there was the Independent

Labour Party, with outstanding figures like Jimmy Maxton; Sillars and the Scottish Labour Party are in this interesting and honourable Scots tradition.

The second event of the summer went almost unnoticed. This was the brief visit to Edinburgh on 2 July of Leo Tindemanns, Prime Minister of Belgium, which was to have reverberations for years to come. Tindemanns had been charged by the EEC heads of government to report by December 1975 'on opinions about progress towards political union and direct elections to the European Parliament'. The Labour delegation, led by Tom Fulton, Chairman of the Scottish Council of the Labour Party, suggested that Scottish representation might be useful in limited fields: law, education, and research in agriculture and fisheries. Populations living far from Europe's 'Golden Triangle' require protection if closer economic and monetary union came about. The Conservatives, led by Ian MacArthur, until 1974 MP for Perth and East Perthshire, spoke of the need to preserve Scottish influence and identity within the overall British representation in the EEC. The Scottish Liberals asked for direct Scottish representation within a federal Europe 'of the regions', with maximum Scottish control of resources and revenue. The Scottish National Party told Tindemanns that they could not be expected to show enthusiasm for direct elections to the European Parliament, when they had no part in the decision-making and no effective sanctions existed for Scotland over Community policy. They expressed their suspicion of common energy and fishing policies, stressed their party's interest in decentralisation, and asked for direct Scottish representation in the Council of Ministers of the European Community, and on the European Commission.

Having heard all this, Leo Tindemanns could not conceal his astonishment, either to the Scottish press at the time, or to me in Brussels later. In Edinburgh, he commented: 'One of the big questions for the parties was the representation of Scotland at Brussels. For me that was new. They were all afraid of centralisation. They said like a slogan: "Westminster is far from Scotland, and Brussels is even farther".' Later Tindemanns indicated to me in Brussels that his visit to Scotland had been unique in his peregrinations round Europe on behalf of the Council of Ministers: nowhere else had he found the demand, on the part of a region on the periphery of the EEC, for separate representation in Community institutions. Certainly, he had found enormous pressures for a regionally biased economic policy, and many discontents in France, Italy, and Denmark; but no one other than the Scots had even suggested that part of one of the nation states of the Community should now demand direct representation. Though less caustic than my highly placed German (see p. 51) on the subject of Scottish representation, Tindemanns was no less firm.

The Scots were doubtless entitled to set up a separate Scottish state if they so wished. Equally, the European Economic Community were no less entitled to reject any application a separate Scottish state might care to make for membership of the Community. For Tindemanns, as for many other European statesmen, it was one thing for old nation states like Portugal and Greece to apply for membership; it was quite another matter altogether to welcome a part of one of the existing large nation states as a new entity in the Community. Tindemanns simply said to me:

> You heard my speech the other night in Brussels to a largely Belgian and Community audience — you heard that I had to start in Flemish, and half-way through the speech change into French. Every major Belgian politician has to switch languages in big speeches. If Scotland achieved separate representation, do you think that within days I would not have delegations at my door, from both the representatives of the Walloons, and the representatives of the Flemings, demanding a separate voice. If I acceded to the request made in Edinburgh for separate Scottish representation, by inference I would also be acceding to the splitting of Belgium into half — and this I'm not prepared to do, as it would be a disaster in Flanders.

In common with Willy Brandt, the ex-Chancellor of the Federal German Republic, and several other European heads of government, past and present, Tindemanns holds the view that a federal Europe of the Regions would be bad for Europe. They dismiss the notion of some kind of United States of Europe. With Bretons, Basques, Catalans, Corsicans, Bavarians, Flemings, Scots, and sixty other peoples, including Londoners,

Parisians and Romans, it would not work as it does in the different conditions of North America.

It is an extraordinary fact that, considering the very future of the country was involved, there was little debate on devolution at the Conservative Party Conference, and none at all at the Trades Union Congress Conference or the Labour Party Conference in the autumn of 1975. But waiting for a White Paper or waiting for a Royal Commission Report is a good excuse for postponing discussion of thorny issues.

The new White Paper on devolution, *Our Changing Democracy — Devolution to Scotland and Wales* (Cmnd 6348), was presented to Parliament in November 1975. Since its proposals are substantially those embodied in the Scotland and Wales Bill, described in Chapter 3, it would be superfluous to repeat them here. The White Paper, however, gave the overall impression that not only was there to be a subordinate Scottish Parliament, but in fact the proposed Assembly was to be another tier of local government superimposed on the Regions, which by that time were in the process of coming into existence following the recommendations of the Wheatley Commission. Those of us who a year earlier were arguing that if an Assembly had to be established, it should be as a super local government unit were not being inconsistent; in November 1974, the Regionalisation proposals could have been frozen (though in my opinion it would have been wrong to do so); by November 1975, it was too late.

This ambivalence in the White Paper which gave rise to the impression that the Assembly would deal with local authority matters was recognised by John Smith, MP, Minister of State at the Privy Council Office, when he spoke to the Convention of Local Authorities at their annual meeting in Elgin in April 1977:

In our Bill, we invented no new methods by which a Scottish Administration would impose new curbs on local authorities. With hindsight our White Paper of November 1975 may have overstressed the national role of the new administration, and implied that it would take over decisions on local expenditure priorities which properly belong to the local authorities themselves.

The only material differences between the White Paper and the Scotland and Wales Bill were contained in a Government Statement of 25 May 1976 in the House of Commons, and the White Paper of August 1976, *Devolution to Scotland and Wales: Supplementary Statement*, brought some further decisions on points so far untouched and some changes of view. The principal features were as follows:

1 For all elections in both Scotland and Wales each Parliamentary constituency would have at least 2 Assembly seats and each constituency with an electorate more than a quarter above the average for the country would have 3 seats on present figures. This would result in a Scottish Assembly of about 150 seats and a Welsh Assembly of about 80.

2 For Scotland the appointment, pay, numbers and so on of the Executive would be a matter for the Assembly alone to determine. Only law officers could be appointed from outside the Assembly. Proposals for Wales were anyway different as Wales would have no separate Executive.

3 Consideration of *vires* of Scottish Assembly Bills would be by the Judicial Committee of the Privy Council and not the Secretary of State. The envisaged power to reject Bills on grounds of policy (subject to affirmation resolution of Parliament) would be restricted to occasions when Parliament considered that an Assembly Bill had unacceptable repercussions on matters for which it remained responsible. Westminster's reserve powers to control executive actions of the Scottish or Welsh Assemblies would be similarly retrenched.

4 It had been decided not to pursue the idea of devolving any revenue-raising powers, for instance through a surcharge on the rates. The Government still considered this the most effective possibility but had decided for the moment to restrict finance to the provision of central government block grants to Scotland and to Wales.

5 The earlier decision not to devolve powers in regard to the Scottish and Welsh universities was confirmed.

6 Responsibility for the operation of the Scottish and Welsh Development Agencies would not after all be divided between Assemblies and Secretaries of State; it would instead be transferred to the Scottish and Welsh administrations.

7 The Scottish Assembly would be given legislative powers in the whole field of Scottish private law, subject to Westminster's general reserve powers.

8 The administration of the Scottish courts would be fully devolved, together with responsibility for the law of evidence, diligence and contempt of court and for the District Courts. Matters affecting Supreme Court judges, sheriffs, appeals to the House of Lords would not be devolved and Parliament would keep sole responsibility for legislation on any jurisdictional matters essential to safeguard the structure of the court system.

9 Both Assemblies would be given closer control than originally envisaged over their respective tourist boards. The Welsh Assembly would be given more say in its assumption of the functions of nominated bodies operating in the devolved field.

10 The regulation of the distinctively Scottish professions — teaching and the two branches of the legal profession — would be devolved to the Scottish Assembly.

The other remarkable fact is that between May 1976 and the publication of the Scotland and Wales Bill in November, the party political conferences took place. One might have supposed that a subject such as devolution, which involved the future of the kingdom, might have commanded a good deal of the time of the parties assembled at the seaside: not so. The Liberals, interested in their new leader, and his performance, had a meandering debate on devolution. The Conservative debate was cursory and confused. At Blackpool, the Conference Arrangements Committee of the Labour Party contrived to spatchcock the only debate on devolution into fifty-two minutes between the Prime Minister's first ever Parliamentary Report, his big speech to the Party, and a debate on the future of rail and road: the Chairman, Tom Bradley, MP, was President of the Transport Salaried Staffs Association and could hardly be expected in his year in the chair of the Labour Party Conference to cut that particular debate to a truncated ten minutes! Worse still, half of those fifty-two minutes were consumed by Michael Foot, speaking from the platform: he amused the Party with a graphic description of his difficulties as Leader of the House of Commons, and a statement about the need for the Government to continue in office, but with scarcely a mention of the whys and wherefores of devolution itself. Surprisingly, a number of major trades union leaders, such as Frank Chapple of the Electrical Trades Union, and Clive Jenkins of the Association of Scientific, Technical and Managerial Staffs, whose unions had supported the devolution resolution at the Trades Union Congress, a month before, changed their minds and voted against the principle of devolution; like many others they were beginning to learn a little more about what precisely was involved. With marked lack of enthusiasm, and out of a vague loyalty to the Government, Conference carried a pro-devolution resolution, partly because they thought there were enough sources of dispute with their Government in the economic field, and partly because the Bill had not been published — and why have a row about something, when you have not seen the actual proposals?

The Demise of the Scotland and Wales Bill

Within living memory, there are only three Parliamentary Bills whose passage can be sensibly compared with that of the Scotland and Wales Bill: that of the Government of India Act, 1935; the Parliament No. 2 Bill, Lords' Reform, 1968; and the European Communities Bill, 1971. Of the three, the last two are such inexact parallels as to require scant reference here.

Unlike devolution, Lords' reform was far from being the Government's central legislative plank for the Parliamentary session: voting was virtually optional even for members of the Cabinet, and his colleagues displayed not the least compunction about deserting Richard Crossman, Leader of the House and the Minister responsible for the Bill, as soon as they realised how unpopular the proposals were proving to be. This was very different from the frenetic anxiety which surrounded the Guillotine motion of 22 February 1977 on the Scotland and Wales Bill, which prompted the Government Chief Whip to go along to Westminster Hospital to find out whether a desperately ill MP — Ray Fletcher — could come by ambulance to sustain the Government in the lobby. His not unexpected answer — that if he came by ambulance, it would be to vote against the motion for the Guillotine, and not for the Government — simply underlines how desperate the Government's business managers were to keep alive their measure, and semi-cooperation with the nationalist minorities in the House, alive. Such pressure was generated by anxiety to retain the Government's slender Parliamentary numerical ascendancy, and not by the merits or demerits of devolution.

Like the devolution proposals, Lords' reform came to grief and perished as the result of a surge of Parliamentary opinion to the effect that the proposals were unworkable, unwanted, and friendless outside the Government Front Bench. After all that has been said and written for years about the weakness of the House of Commons, both issues demonstrated its power on a matter of fundamental importance for Britain. The House showed that it could deny the Government the right to push through a piece of constitutional legislation, the consequences of which had increasingly come to be seen as incalculable to those who were asked to enact it. In the case of both Lords' reform and the Scotland and Wales Bill, a substantial number of Members of Parliament were faced with considerations that transcended normal calculations of loyalty and party advantage, with the result that there was an almost chemical reaction on both sides of the House which Government Ministers could do nothing about.

Like the 1971 European Communities Bill, the Bill concerned the powers of the House of Commons. But there were many differences, only two of which should be mentioned here. First, entry to the EEC did not involve setting up another Government, but the altogether different matter of Britain's Treaty obligations. Second, not only the Prime Minister, who saw entry to the EEC as the culmination of his life's work to date, but a great many other Ministers and Shadow Ministers were passionately committed to the proposals, and really believed in them; the critics of entry into Europe were counter-balanced by those who advocated it, and were more than outweighed in the lobbies. By contrast, during the Scotland and Wales Bill, the friends of devolution — with the exception of Norman Buchan, MP, a man with views of his own — found better things to do in the Palace of Westminster, and left the Chamber to be dominated by the anti-devolutionists. And this happened to be one of those occasions when what is actually said in the House of Commons can curiously contribute to changing the climate of political opinion, and altering events in the outside world.

Richard Barlas, the erudite Clerk of the House of Commons, maintains that the most convincing parallel is between the Scotland and Wales Bill and the India Act. In glaring contrast, however, to the devolution proposals, the India Bill had been fully discussed and digested for over half a decade, in and out of the House of Commons. The Report of the Joint Select Committee, which was published in November 1934, was preceded by the White Paper of March 1933, embodying the greatest measure of agreement achieved at a Round Table Conference, the third and last session of which had ended at Christmas 1932.

'This plan is not born of expediency or fashioned in haste, or the result of any political compromise. As we have worked upon it, we have come to know and to believe in our hearts that it is the best,' says R. A. Butler in *The Art of the Possible** quoting his own speech opening the debate on the Second Reading of the India Bill in 1935. As we have seen, hardly a member of Mr Callaghan's administration — men and women of deep and sincere political beliefs on many other topics — could bring themselves to make such a claim for the Scotland and Wales Bill. Even allowing for the change in Parliamentary customs over a period of forty years, the degree of Prime Ministerial and senior Ministerial commitment was of a different order. After he had delivered his opening speech on Second Reading, James Callaghan, by nature and record a good Parliamentary attender and listener, listened politely to the Opposition spokesman, and quitted the Chamber, hardly, if at all, to put in an appearance during the next fifteen days that the Bill was to occupy the Floor of the House: yet Stanley Baldwin, flanked not only by

* London: Hamish Hamilton, 1971, p. 47.

Sir Samuel Hoare, the Secretary of State for India, but by other senior Members of the Government as well, sat, hour after hour, listening to what was said. One could say that nowadays the Red Boxes and responsibilities which Cabinet Ministers take home at night are heavier than half a century ago; but the fact remains that Ministerial and Departmental meetings for most Ministers end at about 6.30 p.m., and the debates go on until midnight; such concern as was displayed by Ministers other than those in charge of the Scotland and Wales Bill during the difficult nights of its passage was limited to popping into the Chamber to ask the whips at what hour they could reasonably expect to retire to a well-earned rest, or perhaps what effect the proceedings were likely to have on the Government's chances of survival. Not much interest in the issues and the substance of the Bill under discussion could be detected, and it became clear to me again and again that many intelligent Ministers were either hazy or downright ignorant about them.

This is not a generalised stricture, designed to discredit Ministers. On many other issues they have been well informed of what was happening outside their own Departments, and have shown themselves more than willing to do without sleep in causes in which they really believe. The fact that Ministers and MPs in the 1930s knew a great deal more about the provisions of the India Bill than their successors knew about the Scotland and Wales Bill really tells us that the hearts of those who were nominal supporters of devolution simply were not in it.

Again, the votes in the House of Commons reflected the different degrees of enthusiasm between implementing the India Act and implementing Devolution. Prior to 1,951 speeches on 473 clauses and 16 schedules filling 4,000 pages of Hansard with $15\frac{1}{2}$ million words, the Second Reading of the India Bill was passed by 404 votes to 133. On 16 December 1976 the Scotland and Wales Bill passed its Second Reading by 292 votes to 247; many of the 292 votes were given on the express understanding that those who voted did so not because they endorsed the proposals, but because they thought that it would be wrong to deny them a hearing. This accounts to some extent for the fact that when, on 22 February, the Government argued that the House should therefore accede to their request for a timetable motion, this was denied by a majority of 29 votes.

The change of opinion in the House had been mainly brought about by MPs becoming aware of many of the problems with which we have been concerned in this book. In general terms, plans for devolution had looked vaguely as though they might be a good thing; but once the House of Commons had to get down to the nitty-gritty of scrutinising the particular effects of what was proposed, the picture looked very different indeed. For example, one of the turning points was when it dawned on the majority of Members that Scots MPs would be able to vote on matters affecting England, which they could not vote upon as far as they affected their own backyards. Like other people, MPs tend to think more clearly and urgently where their own interests are directly affected.

Gradually MPs on both sides began to agree that perhaps we really ought not to embark on profound constitutional changes with, at best, the narrowest of majorities, and precious little inter-party agreement. After all, in other countries there are the most stringent Articles in the laws concerning constitutional change; for example, in the United States, a three-quarters majority in the Senate and two-thirds in the House of Representatives are required, and not just a simple majority. In no other Western country would a slender, and perhaps ephemeral, majority be an acceptable basis on which to introduce such basic constitutional changes.

The instruments of the Government's defeat were the Conservative Party, which did not like the form of the Bill, and during the discussion increasingly came to doubt whether any form of devolution was possible which did not involve embarking upon the slippery slope to Separation; a majority of Liberals, who quickly perceived how ill-digested the measures were and who were annoyed that the Assembly was to have neither tax-raising powers nor proportional representation; and forty-three Labour MPs who realised that the Government's enthusiasm for the Bill had more to do with the natural and not necessarily ignoble desire to remain in office than with the good governance of Scotland and Wales. This assessment was later corroborated by Richard Evans, Lobby Editor of the *Financial Times*, on 22 April 1977: 'Senior Ministers are well advanced with fresh proposals for devolving power to Scotland and Wales which, they believe, will enable Mr Callaghan's minority Government to remain in office for a further Parliamentary session.' For Labour Members of Parliament remaining in power is naturally a desirable objective, but a substantial number of us think that this should not be at the expense of the integrity of the United Kingdom.

The Labour dissidents were fortified in their defiance of the whips by the knowledge that, as far back as the middle of June 1976, I had collected the signatures of seventy Labour Members of Parliament, warning Michael Foot and the Government that in the event of their introducing a Guillotine motion on the Scotland and Wales Bill, they could not count on our support in the lobbies. Ministers had been alerted; but they chose to disregard the alarm bells, which had been rung in very good time. If a rebellion is sprung on a Government out of the blue, without appreciable warning, Parliamentary colleagues have grounds for resentment, and the rebels have to contend with their annoyance. On the other hand, if warning is given months in advance by MPs who are known to have a serious interest in a subject, the odium that attaches itself to disloyalty tends to evaporate. Perhaps the best epitaph on the strangulation of the Scotland and Wales Bill was provided by a Government whip after the Guillotine vote on 22 February 1977. 'The Cabinet jolly well asked for this defeat — and we've got exactly what we bloody well deserved!'

7

The Aftermath

It is not clear, and it may not be clear even for some time, whether the Scotland and Wales Bill proposals have been defeated in the House of Commons for the foreseeable future, or whether they have simply suffered a temporary setback. What is clear, however, is that the effects of the Government's defeat in Scotland were very different from those which pro-devolution-ists had been forecasting. Predictably enough the *Scotsman* and the *Daily Record* screeched with fury, while BBC Scotland was full of gloom. But the average Scot was not greatly concerned either way. There were none of the predicted demonstrations by incensed crowds in favour of devolution. In the week follow-ing the Government's defeat public opinion was muted, apa-thetic and agnostic, and appeared to be far more concerned with the unending problems of British Leyland and Chrysler. The only public demonstrations to be organised in Scotland were protesting over the planned closure and merger of four teacher-training colleges: a rally in Edinburgh, organised by the friends of Craiglockhart Roman Catholic Training College, attracted a capacity crowd of 2,600 people to the Assembly Rooms in Edinburgh. Realising that the turn-out would be paltry, not even the SNP tried to organise a rally over devolution.

This reaction, or lack of reaction, to the fate of the Scotland and Wales Bill simply confirms once again that Scottish public opinion is not interested in plans to change the form of govern-ment or the political institutions of Scotland, however drastic their long-term implications may be. In the same week that the Second Reading of the Scotland and Wales Bill was taking place in December 1976, the SNP were achieving success over an issue which is far removed from the central concerns of the party — the dumping of nuclear waste. The SNP declared all-out war against any government attempts to bury radio-active nuclear waste in Scotland. At Irvine in Ayrshire, 2,000 signatures were collected in a matter of hours to be sent to the Prime Minister 'because of the potential danger we would cause to ourselves and generations yet unborn, whose future we hold in our hands'. George Thompson, SNP Member of Parliament for neighbouring Galloway, one of the areas being considered for possible nuclear storage, declared that the proposals to use Scotland as a nuclear waste bin provided a 'life and death' justification for Scottish independence. The SNP claim — and they may be right — that they have won a lot of support by launching a new policy document, which states that as long as Scotland has control over adequate alternative energy sources, it isn't in the national interest to generate more nuclear power. The significant point here is that they recognise that an issue of this kind, albeit important in itself, is also far more rewarding in electoral terms than beating the simple devolutionary or independence drum.

In my experience the most widespread reaction among people in Scotland to the fate of the Bill was one of relief that at the eleventh hour they thought they were to be spared extra burdens. The devolution bandwagon had rolled so far that many people who did not in the least themselves want an Assembly had reconciled themselves to the inevitable. New hope was given to the silent majority who had come to feel that there was little they could do about it. 'Black Tuesday' — Michael Foot's name for the day that the Guillotine motion was defeated — uncorked a flood of anti-Assembly feeling and this was beginning to filter through to the politicians.

The reaction of the politicians and the media was, predictably, much more excited than that of the Scottish public. Least excited of all were the forty-three Labour Members of Parliament who had brought about the Government's defeat. Since many of us had never in our lives voted against our party, our mood was sad, but unrecalcitrant. Since, in the face of every kind of (civilised) political pressure and political arm-twisting, they were the men and women who halted the Assembly juggernaut, their names should be recorded:

The twenty-two Labour MPs who voted against the Government were: Mr Leo Abse, Mr Ronald Brown, Mr Harry Cowans, Mr George Cunningham, Mr Tam Dalyell, Mr Joe Dean, Mr Bruce Douglas-Mann, Mrs Gwyneth Dunwoody, Mr Fred Evans, Mr Ted Garrett, Mr William Hamilton, Mr James Lamond, Mr Tom Urwin, Mr Ted Leadbitter, Mr Arthur Lewis, Mr Ken Lomas, Mr John Mendelson, Mr Eric Moonman, Mr John Ovenden, Mr John Parker, Dr Colin Phipps and Mr Reg Prentice.

The Tory Reaction

The normal Opposition reaction to Government defeat on a major vote in the House of Commons is to go into ecstasies of juvenile joy, waving order papers and yelling 'Resign!' at the top of one's voice. When the Conservative whips announced the result of the vote on 22 February, no such outburst occurred. Apart from the odd backwoodsman, who had not followed the proceedings, the result was greeted with subdued seriousness — and fury on the Scottish National benches, with Mrs Margaret Bain, M.P., bursting into tears.

The explanation for this is not hard to find. Tory MPs reacted in one of three different ways. First, there were the predictable reactions of the out-and-out opponents of an Assembly, led by Members such as Maurice Macmillan, Julian Amery and Betty Harvie Anderson and ably organised by George Gardiner, MP for Reigate. For this large group, the Union between Scotland and England matters very much, and is the Ark of the Covenant. Should the decisive majority of Scots ever decide that they want to bring the Union to an end, this faction would say Scotland must live with the consequences without expecting undue sympathy or co-operation from the English. They believe that the Scots will soon get very bored with all the talk about devolution and separation and having contemplated the prospect of yet more bureaucracy and additional expenditure, they will decide that they are not really so keen on an Assembly after all. However, this general view could be dismissed as being that of the remote English aristocratic wing of the Tory Party, who know little or nothing about life in Scotland.

Yet support for such views is provided by Mr Teddy Taylor, whom not even his fiercest critics could reasonably call remote, English or an aristocrat. 'Just how angry are the Scottish people?' wrote Mr Taylor in the *Guardian*, the weekend after the vote on the Guillotine motion:

> When I returned to my home in Glasgow after the vital vote, without any special protection from the overworked Strathclyde Police, I might have expected, having read the press, to find the population outraged, incensed, resentful and infuriated, in a state of mind which would lead them to hang Tory MPs from the nearest lamp post. But I found no such reaction. There may have been parts of Scotland where such violent passions were raging, but in Cathcart the increase in the price of coffee and tea were greater causes of concern [*Guardian*, 5 March 1977].

Mr Taylor outlines various communications from constituents, and a public opinion poll favourable to the Conservatives, and concludes:

> So, what messages can we draw from all this? First that Parliament was right to be brave enough to reject a guillotine on a Bill which I think most MPs in their hearts regarded as a load of constitutional rubbish; second, that Scots are not quite so passionate about the whole issue as many believe. And thirdly, that while there is no doubt that the majority of Scots would like more say in their own affairs, that we should take the necessary time to work out a scheme of devolution which won't result in a massive increase in cost and bureaucracy, and include the seeds of non-stop conflict between Edinburgh and Westminster.

The second faction among the Tories includes their leading spokesman, Francis Pym. He has been circumspect about the whole issue, realising the need to avoid a bitter split in his own party and, having offered inter-party talks on devolution with Government Ministers, he has honourably kept to his offer. (There is not the slightest chance of such talks succeeding, given the composition of the 1974 House of Commons. A precondition for the success of inter-party talks is that the party leaders should be able to deliver the votes of their followers. This would not be possible. Even if he wanted to, Mr Pym could not deliver the votes of Messrs Amery and Macmillan, any more than Michael Foot could deliver my vote, and those of forty-two other Labour colleagues).

The reaction of this moderate faction was perhaps most concisely expressed by Timothy Raison, MP for Aylesbury, who took a leading part in the devolution debate. In a leading letter to *The Times* on 25 February 1977 Mr Raison wrote:

Sir, I found your leader, 'The First Home Rule Bill is Dead' so puzzling in some respects that I will not attempt to comment on it directly; but may I set out an alternative way of approaching the present situation?

I certainly accept that there is a need for some form of discussion of the constitutional position, and that that will have to be able to look at the United Kingdom as a whole and may have to go wider than the present issue. My own preference would be to see if a way can be found of allowing Parliament as a whole to do the job — the Committee Stage of the Scotland and Wales Bill has shown that the Chamber is capable of rather more searching analysis than outside bodies have managed on this issue. Perhaps we should go on using the present Bill as the text on which to hang discussion. But if that seems too impractical, then let us have a conference of members selected from Parliament.

But if that is the decision, two things are important. First, such a conference must represent all shades of opinion rather than simply official opinion — after all, it has been clearly established this is an issue where the back benches are going to have their say in the decisions. Secondly, the conference must not start from any position of commitment to devolution or anything else.

That may sound destructive; but in fact it is realistic. For surely the lesson that should have been learned is that it is not enough to say that devolution is a good thing, so let us have it. It matters very much indeed what *form* devolution (or anything else) would take. It is the dawning realisation of that that largely accounts for the difference between the Second Reading and the guillotine votes. The same point applies to your own apparent leaning towards a federal answer. It may sound all very well in theory; but will it survive detailed scrutiny? Significantly, the Liberals have been remarkably reluctant so far to divulge the details of their approach.

So let us have a forum or conference that can look at all the possibilities, including even separatism (strongly though I am opposed to it). Let it consider whether the present scheme is amendable — say through tax raising powers; whether federalism might be both acceptable and work; whether the Assembly-only approach, based on a new Chamber of Parliament, is the solution (remember, it could meet much of the crucially difficult problem of Scottish representation in the Commons); or whether the status quo (perhaps with such variants as Parliament meeting twice a year in Edinburgh, as well as televising Parliament) is not really the best answer after all.

I do not conceal that I lean towards the last approach; but I am certainly not afraid to submit it to the kind of examination that, in one way or another, my colleagues in the House of Commons might bring to bear on it. If they can establish that there is a better answer, so be it.

One of the variants favoured by this moderate group of Tories is that there should be a Scottish Third Chamber. This Chamber would hear the Second Reading, Committee and Report stages of all Scottish Bills, with a final debate in the Westminster Parliament.

Now, the idea that one lot of legislators could give a Third Reading to a Bill which has been produced by a completely different set of people is odd in itself. But if one thinks about the true function of a Third Reading debate, it becomes quite impossible. Erskine May, the Bible of Parliamentary procedure, puts it as follows:

The purpose of the third reading is to review a Bill in its final form, after the shaping it had received in the earlier stages. For this reason, amendment, other than verbal, is no longer permissible on third reading. Hence, debate is confined strictly to the contents of a Bill, and cannot wander afield as on a second reading.

There is often no debate at all on Third Reading, and the Bill
is passed 'on the nod'. Where debate occurs, it is usually a
formal affair, largely consisting of routine party bickering inter-
spersed with sincere congratulations on the statesmanship and
magnanimity shown by the other side. The suggestions of the
moderate wing of the Conservative Party involve something
quite different: they embody the spirit of confrontation between
London and Edinburgh. Just imagine how Members of the
Scottish Assembly would feel after they had spent weary hours
forging a piece of legislation, only to have it possibly mauled to
pieces by the Parliament at Westminster. Still more seriously,
the whole idea is in conflict with the very nature of the legislative process: what it really boils down to is that the House of
Commons and the House of Lords should each have a veto
on Bills put forward by the Scottish Assembly. If this is what is
meant by giving a Third Reading to Westminster, it would be
better to say so. Lack of candour on this point could put the
Union in peril.

The third Conservative faction is small and comprises half a
dozen Scottish Conservative MPs, with a few English sympathisers, such as David Knox, MP for Leek. It is led by Alick
Buchanan Smith, who was deposed as Shadow Secretary of
State for Scotland after a number of Conservative MPs had
refused to vote against the Second Reading of the Scotland and
Wales Bill. Buchanan Smith questions whether the Kilbrandon
Commission and the Government were right to reject federalism. He rejects arguments that the inclusion of the whole of
England in a federal structure would put the federation out of
balance, pointing to similar disproportionate relationships in
Canada and Australia: ' .. even though in population terms,
England dominated a federation, that domination would only
be dangerous if in the federal parliament division took place on
national lines'.

My impression is that Mr Buchanan Smith and his deputy
Shadow Spokesman, who resigned with him, clearly recognise
that the Scotland and Wales Bill is unworkable, but may quite
understandably feel themselves prisoners of their own repeated
pledges in favour of a Scottish Assembly, which were made
before they had fully grasped the implications of what was proposed. Mr Buchanan Smith himself has formed a cross-party

'Alliance for a Scottish Assembly', together with John P. Mackintosh, MP, James Milne, Secretary of the Scottish Trades Union Congress, and Russell Johnston, Liberal spokesman on Scottish Affairs.

The Liberals

The Liberals are in what might appear to be a contradictory position: they have always been the most enthusiastic party as far as the principle of devolution is concerned, yet they were one of the principal agents in blocking the progress of the devolution Bill. In fact, the Liberals deserve some charity. They had never favoured devolution in the form in which it was presented to the House of Commons by the Labour Government, and they had seen one of their main proposals — proportional representation — cavalierly rejected by the Government at a time when the Government had no reason to suspect that they would have to look to Liberals for support. With some justice, David Steel told readers of the *Sunday Times* on 27 March 1977:

> On the Labour side, the exigencies of minority government required them to consult us and other parties from time to time about specific subjects such as devolution. Yet we were getting nowhere in pressing our views. All they were interested in was support in the lobbies. Mr Foot and I were (and remain) in deep and general disagreement on the qualities of the Scotland and Wales Bill. The Liberals therefore opposed the guillotine, and the whole thing stopped dead in its tracks. To put it crudely, it proved necessary to kick them in the teeth before extending the hand of friendship.

Mr Steel has made it clear that his criticisms of the Government's approach to devolution goes far beyond specific questions such as proportional representation, taxation powers for a Scottish Assembly and so forth. The Liberals say that they want to see a new political contract between the various nations and regions which make up the United Kingdom and a new way of deciding which areas of government are best dealt with in a national context and which are better devolved. As David Steel wrote in *The Times* on 7 February:

The Government is fumbling towards a massive break up of the present centralised system of government with no clear idea of what the new system will be, and as its consultative document before Christmas demonstrated, has yet to start thinking about how England, or the various English regions, will fit in. It fails to seize the opportunity to change the House of Lords into an elected body representing the different parts of the United Kingdom and including those elected to the European Parliament. Yet through this Bill, conceived in electoral expediency in 1974, and nurtured by the midwives of Whitehall, who hate the very idea of real devolution, the Government is seeking to dot the i's and cross the t's of the new constitutional structures for Scotland and Wales. It is the worst way to approach the question.

The SNP Reaction

As we have seen, Margaret Bain, MP for East Dunbartonshire, burst into real tears, and some of her colleagues into crocodile tears, when the defeat of the Guillotine motion was announced. However, the significant fact remains that the SNP did not take the opportunity to organise protest demonstrations in the days that followed: they realised that such demonstrations would show how little support there was for the SNP on the devolution/independence issue. And for all their outward indignation, the shrewder SNP leaders realised that the Government's defeat put their party in an extremely difficult position. If an Assembly were denied them, then an essential stepping stone on the path to independence would have been taken from them — and they knew perfectly well that the Scottish people would never cross the stream at one bound at a General Election. The SNP leaders' real frustration lay here.

The Labour Reaction

Few tears were shed by the nominal progenitors of the Bill — the governing Labour Party. Indeed, apart from those Ministers who had been intimately involved in trying to guide the Bill through the House of Commons, members of the Government were remarkably cheerful after their defeat. At least one Cabinet Minister was unable to prevent himself from grunting

'And a bloody good thing too!' Contrary to popular belief, members of the Parliamentary Labour Party genuinely can get upset when some measure in which they really believe gets into trouble. Labour MPs were less worried about the apparent loss of the devolution Bill itself than about the effect it would have on the Government's voting strength in the House of Commons: with the nationalist members voting against the Government on every conceivable occasion out of a sense of grievance, the Government would find itself in a straitjacket. Such criticism as was levelled at the forty-three Labour dissenters — and it was gentle and civilised, in a way that it would not have been had a matter of fiercely held Socialist belief been involved — was more concerned with the fact that we had put the future of the Labour Government in jeopardy than with the merits of the Bill itself. Understandably enough, some of the Ministers who had worked on the Bill were extremely angry: on the other hand it must be recorded that Michael Foot behaved with exemplary generosity. No one in living memory had made better use of back-benchers' power than he had before he joined the Government — indeed his own successes were an inspiration to the dissidents on the Scotland and Wales Bill.

The Parliamentary Labour Party was less shocked by the Bill's defeat — although it was unexpected until at least a few days before — as by the decisive size of the defeat (29 votes). There could be little question of resurrecting a time-table motion on the same Bill. In this mood, thoughts naturally turned once more to the possibility of a referendum. Nicholas Fairbairn, Conservative MP for Kinross and West Perth, wittily debunked the whole idea. 'What possible question could one put in a referendum before [a Bill on] devolution?' he asked in the House of Commons on 14 December 1976:

What will devolution mean to the ordinary person, who is to be asked 'Are you in favour of devolution?' Is it not rather like asking a child aged 6, 'Are you in favour of sex?' The child will have heard of it, and will understand that people think that it is a good idea, but will not have the slightest conception of what it means. Therefore is it not just idiotic to talk of a referendum on that basis? [Hansard, 14 December 1976.]

Yet since the taboo of a referendum had been broken by its use in relation to the EEC: and since by the beginning of February 1977 it looked as though the promise of a referendum was the only hope of getting the Scotland and Wales Bill through the House of Commons, the proposal was taken seriously.

A Referendum

Whereas Anthony Wedgwood Benn, MP, originally suggested that there should be a referendum over whether Britain should remain inside the European Economic Community, Norman Buchan, MP for West Renfrewshire, a former Junior Minister at the Scottish Office and a Minister of State for Agriculture, was responsible for proposals that there should be a referendum on a Scottish Assembly. As early as 4 November 1975, in a major article in *The Times*, he claimed that a referendum would help with the constitutional crisis, and could not be objected to either by nationalists or those opposed to nationalism. 'A nation', wrote Mr Buchan, 'has the right to decide its own future. Let us take the lead in doing so, before events decide in a way wanted by none of us.' Mr Buchan ploughed a lonely furrow in the House of Commons: the Government did not want a referendum to delay their plans, while anti-devolutionists thought that their cause might be damaged beyond repair if the whole issue were to be reduced to a simple Yes or No.

Edward Short, at that time Deputy Prime Minister and Leader of the House of Commons, had declared on 9 November 1975 that a referendum on devolution would be 'inappropriate'; he was hoping to introduce a White Paper the following month, and a Bill shortly after that.

A number of academics, in particular Dr William Wallace of Manchester University, lent support to Mr Buchan. They pointed out with some justice that it was all very well for the Labour Cabinet to reject the idea of a referendum, but that several leading members of the Cabinet in 1975 had stumped the country proclaiming that the issue of British membership of the European Community raised questions of such constitutional importance as to require popular ratification more direct than that provided through Parliament. The Prime Minister himself had accepted their arguments and indeed Mr Callaghan — as Foreign Secretary — had promoted the idea of the European referendum. How could he and his colleagues claim to distinguish between one fundamental constitutional issue and another? The Government could not run away from the fundamental problem of legitimacy. It had already embarked upon the process of constitutional change, by introducing a referendum in the first place: to pretend now that devolution proposals — which are admitted to be as fundamental to our constitutional framework as entry into the EEC — require only the ratification of Parliament, would be to invite a certain public cynicism.

Yet although a devolution referendum could briefly buy time in the House of Commons, would it settle very much in the long run? A great deal would depend on how the question was framed. Even if the Scotland and Wales Bill had achieved a Third Reading in the House of Commons, to ask voters whether they felt that its provisions should be put into effect would have caused great problems of interpretation. Not surprisingly the SNP would almost certainly have campaigned in favour of a 'Yes' vote. But their argument for doing so — that the Assembly was a major step towards independence — would have had a profoundly unsettling effect on Labour and Conservative politicians, even among those who wanted the Assembly. The creation of an elected Assembly and Executive in Edinburgh would be supported by the SNP as providing a sound basis for the transfer of power, ultimately leading to independence. Labour pro-devolutionists would find themselves in the delicate position of claiming that devolution was not so big a change as to upset Scottish Unionists of all parties, and yet a big enough change to justify thousands of SNP voters supporting the Government's package.

A narrow majority in favour of devolution would be unsettling; a comfortable vote for devolution would settle little or nothing about the form of the Assembly. The interpretation of the result would have to be decided by the outcome of Assembly elections following the referendum. If Labour won the election, they would no doubt claim that devolution meant the rejection of independence. If the SNP won they would claim that the referendum justified their demands for an independent Scotland. If no party won more than half the seats the referendum result would be little more than a source of debate as groups jockeyed for power.

To try to forestall confusion about the way in which the results could be interpreted, Mr Buchan and some of his Scottish colleagues desperately want a second question to be added, asking the Scots whether they favour independence. The Government are understandably reluctant to do so. To add such a question to the referendum ballot paper could make matters even more complicated. The SNP would claim that the second question was an implicit recognition by Westminster that the Scots have a unilateral right to vote to secede from Britain.

The right to vote in a referendum of the kind proposed by Mr Buchan would be restricted to those who live in Scotland. Presumably, if 51 per cent voted for independence, independence would be conceded — to which many people in the rest of the country would very reasonably object that the future of the United Kingdom must surely be a matter for all British voters, and not simply for those resident in Scotland.

Again, it is doubtful whether the tactical objective of the referendum — cracking down on the SNP — would be achieved. Such a poll would have to be taken after a devolution Bill was passed; the SNP would be in high fettle, claiming that they had produced the goods so far, and that nothing would have been achieved without their presence in the House of Commons — in which they would be absolutely right.

The SNP would not campaign on independence but on some such slogan as 'Vote for Scotland'. With some justification, they would imply that to vote 'No' would be to ignore all the attention and concessions that have been granted to Scotland since the rise of the SNP. Supposing, say, 35–40 per cent of the electorate voted for the SNP point of view as opposed to the 20–25 per cent who now declare themselves in favour of independence, their position after a referendum would be very different from that of the anti-marketeers after the EEC referendum. On that occasion, the anti-marketeers got 32 per cent of the vote, and to all intents gave up the battle as lost. The critical difference is that there was no anti-marketeers' party to keep the issue alive. If the SNP could point to the fact that there was now a Scottish Assembly — they would call it a Parliament — and that they had received a decent percentage of the vote in the referendum, they would hardly tear up their party cards, and retire to their homesteads. They will point out that in the 1960s they had a small vote, which had grown very much bigger by the 1970s and that in 1976 one in five of the Scottish electorate had voted for independence. Now, they would say, one in three supports the SNP. The referendum would be seen as another step forward in an inevitable progress to an eventual majority of Scottish seats. The referendum process would have added to, rather than diminished, their momentum. Even if the referendum did not go as favourably for the SNP as they imagine — and, in my view, they would be in for a rude shock — it would not be conclusive. A referendum is no more than a quick sampling of public opinion at a particular point in time and is really not much more helpful than that provided by the more careful public opinion polls. To decide Scotland's future on the basis of a test of public opinion would be the height of irresponsibility on the part of those who are elected to deal with just such difficult issues of policy.

Why then, at an early stage in the progress of the Scotland and Wales Bill did the anti-devolution Members of Parliament — many of whom are among the most ardent believers in the authority of Parliament — put down an Early Day Motion in the name of Leo Abse and others (including myself) in the following terms:

This House considers that the proposals of HMG for devolution of some aspects of Government and administration do not appear to enjoy the public support which would justify the introduction of such major and irreversible constitutional change, and consequently believes that before proceeding with a Bill, the Government should make provision for accurately measuring the opinions of the people of Britain on devolution and the alternatives of maintaining the existing structure of government and the granting of independence to nations within Britain by means of a Referendum conducted separately and simultaneously in Wales, Scotland and England.

First of all, we supposed that time was on our side, and that after months of discussion the chances of the anti-devolutionists

winning a referendum was such as to make the attempt worthwhile, particularly if the Government won their Guillotine
motion and Third Reading (as we thought they might).

Second, it seemed to some Labour MPs to be a good Parliamentary device with which to foul up the Government's devolution plans and play for time in the hope that the electorate
would become more and more disenchanted with the whole
idea.

Why did the Government accept the proposal — or fall into
the trap, depending on one's point of view? For a very simple
reason: having strenuously opposed the idea of a referendum
for perfectly good reasons, they realised an important fact in
December of last year when the Second Reading debate was
under way. They might not get the Second Reading of their
Bill unless they could promise a referendum to those who believed in it, and they wanted to provide an excuse for erstwhile
anti-devolutionists in the Labour and Tory parties to change
their minds on the ground that the position had changed somewhat now that a referendum had been promised.

There can be no possible doubt about why a referendum is
still being discussed. It is not being proposed as a constitutional
check whereby the people, in their ultimate wisdom, may
instruct the Government, but to bind together a political party
that is deeply divided on an awkward issue. It enables opponents of devolution to say that in spite of all the fine speeches
they have made against it, they will bow to the will of the people.
Promising a referendum comes in handy when party managers
suspect that, in spite of their best endeavours, they may be
unable to deliver the votes in the House of Commons: on this
occasion, the referendum was also seen as a well-designed shotgun with which to threaten their Lordships in the Upper House,
should they presume to talk at inordinate length on devolution
— a subject on which many members of the House of Lords,
and not only those with Scottish or Welsh connections, are
highly qualified to speak.

The Scottish referendum also differs from that on the EEC in
that there was disagreement over who should be entitled to
vote in it. In our resolution the Labour anti-devolutionists
carefully stipulated that the English should vote: the Government, in their panicky and characteristically ill-thought-out

response to the possibility of losing the Second Reading vote on the devolution Bill, suggested that the vote should be restricted to the Scottish and Welsh residents. As Richard Wainwright, Liberal MP for Colne Valley, put it in a speech in his constituency, the proposed devolution referendum

> may make the soggy English realise at last how vastly they are being conned out of their democratic rights and their money. The outrageous fraud of a referendum limited to the Scots and the Welsh only stretches beyond all reason the concept that it is more blessed to give than to receive. There is much to be said for a nationwide referendum on changes in the constitution. But for a government to propose, that some British people shall have two Parliaments to shout for them, while others are left with only one, to be referred to only by those on the receiving end for the verdict is the last word in political debauchery.

The dilemma of the non-voting English in the referendum was colourfully put by S. Gorley Putt, the Senior Tutor of Christ's College, Cambridge:

> Brooding glumly on the regressive tendency towards tribalism now in evidence all over the globe, it had not occurred to me until I read that in our own Gadarene stampede towards dismemberment we were proposing to disenfranchise the largest constituent part of our present United Kingdom. Will the French abstain from voting when the Bretons seek to lop themselves off from France? Or the Spaniards remain mute when the Basques and the Catalans decide to add two new sovereign states to Iberia? Must I, to keep in step, campaign for a new Heptarchy, so that I may gain the prestige of flying in Air Wessex planes decked out in heaven knows what new mixture of kindergarten national colours? I had not expected when we made our first timid step towards a United Europe that I should so soon become anxious about the shortage of woad wherewith to deck the truncated trunk of Little Tiny England [*The Times*, 3 November 1976].

The Government also skated over the problem of whether Scots living in England should be able to vote — something which clearly worries the Scottish Trades Union Congress. At a meeting in Glasgow on 17 December 1976, with John Smith, the Minister of State at the Privy Council Office, Hugh d'Arcy, Chairman of the STUC General Council, said: 'We want devolution, not separation, and we will seek to influence opinion within the trade union movement for devolution, no matter how the question is framed.' Earlier in the meeting, however, Mr Smith had been pressed on whether Scottish or Welsh 'exiles' would have a chance to take part and undertook at that stage to consider the matter.

Yet when one really starts thinking about possible qualifications for taking part in a referendum, the mind boggles at the complications of extending the vote to those not actually and currently resident in Scotland. Should Scots people living out of Scotland qualify? Should a woman born in England but married to a Scot qualify? Should a woman born in Scotland, but married to an Englishman, an Irishman or an Ethiopian qualify? Should a man or woman born in England but whose parents and all four grandparents were Scottish qualify? And what about English, Welsh and Irish residents in Scotland?

Once one started trying to put together a voter's roll on the basis of the voter's Scottish pedigree the referendum would never take place, since the roll would never be complete. It would be exactly like painting the Forth Bridge. Yet there is no doubt that a great many Scots, living in England, or earning Britain's bread and butter abroad, would be very angry indeed if they were denied any say in the future of Scotland within or without the United Kingdom.

Another ticklish problem — to which the Government, in their unseemly haste, failed to provide an answer — concerned the use of public money to finance referendum campaigns. During the EEC referendum £250,000 was given to pro- and anti-EEC umbrella organisations; in a devolution referendum, it would be hard to know to whom public funds should reasonably be given.

Moreover, there is a related problem. It is just possible to sustain an argument for the expenditure of public money — £3 million or more, plus any aid to the campaigns — for a referendum which is mandatory on Parliament. It is altogether harder to justify expenditure of this order on a referendum

which, as the Government announced, with typical haste, is
only consultative and not mandatory.

Again, if the referendum is to be purely consultative, the
electorate should be consulted about a whole range of related
issues. I suggest the following questions should be asked in any
consultative referendum:

1 In the midst of the gravest economic crisis of our lifetime,
  do you think that priority in Parliamentary time ought to
  be devoted to a matter of at best supreme irrelevance to
  our economic prosperity?

2 Do you want to fork out money to pay salaries large
  enough to keep 150 Assembly members in the style which
  they will certainly expect, as well as those of at least
  another 1,000 civil servants?

3 At a time when no more nursery schools can be started
  for lack of money, where there is overcrowding in many
  primary and secondary schools, and when teacher-training college places have to be cut back for lack of funds to
  improve teacher–pupil ratios in schools, do you want to
  spend public money on an extra tier of government?

4 At a time when there is a shortage of houses, and young
  married couples often have to live with their parents in
  overcrowded conditions for lack of money for council
  house starts, do you as a matter of priority want an
  inevitably costly shake up in the form of government?

5 At a time when there is not enough cash to allow the
  hospitals to continue even existing standards of service,
  let alone make necessary improvements, and when provision for the mentally ill is hopelessly unsatisfactory, do
  you want as a matter of priority to see millions spent on
  an Edinburgh Assembly and all its trappings?

6 At a time when the ratepayers are angrier than ever before,
  do you think that an additional burden in the form of
  taxes and rates, the inevitable result of devolution proposals, should be proceeded with as a matter of urgency?

7 Do you favour still more laws and regulations which
  would be the result of Scottish Assemblymen trying to
  justify their position?

8 Do you agree that public money which could be spent on

what the Prime Minister describes as our top priority — helping competitive manufacturing industry — should be devoted to an Assembly and all its adjuncts, which produce no real wealth for the country?

9 In the next economic blizzard do you want a situation in which Scotland will inevitably be seen as of secondary priority in terms of the overall government of the United Kingdom?

10 Do you think that decisions on education, housing policy, health and other matters are better taken in Edinburgh, or in Aberdeen for those who live in Grampian, in Dumfries for those who live in the south-west, in Inverness for those who live in the Highlands, in Glasgow for those who live in Strathclyde, in St Boswells for those who live in the Borders, in Stirling for those who live in Central Region, in Dundee for those who live in Tayside, in Kirkcaldy for those who live in Fife, in Kirkwall for those who live in Orkney, in Lerwick for those who live in Shetland, in Stornoway for those who live in the Western Isles?

In my view, no consultative or even mandatory referendum would be satisfactory, or indeed complete, if it ducked the question of North Sea oil revenues. The question here should be along the following lines:

Do you want Scotland to have certain necessarily limited revenues from certain North Sea oilfields, not from Brent, Ninian, and other rich fields in the Shetland basin, and not from Forties, most of which belongs to England, in the sure knowledge that once natural resources are earmarked for a Scottish Assembly, the Yorkshire and Nottinghamshire coalfields will cease to subsidise the Scottish coal industry, and that taxation from resources ranging from natural gas to china clay, found in England, will be used for the benefit of England?

This is a much more pertinent question than the simplistic questions posed by public opinion polls, which merely ask whether Scotland ought to have the lion's share of the North Sea oil revenues!

Political scientists with a purely theoretical interest in referenda — and in devolution itself — may feel such questions to be less than neutral or even absurdly unfair. Yet every one of them is a very real question for the people of Scotland, and should be a matter for consultation, if consultation there is to be. I am quite convinced that the answer to each question would be a resounding 'No!'.

If the referendum were to be consultative the electorate might well begin to ask themselves what MPs are there for. I vividly remember during the EEC referendum being confronted with a down-to-earth constituent, a miner in the Kinneil Colliery in Bo'ness, who had one question to ask me: 'Tam, what the hell do we pay you for, other than to make up your mind and come to some conclusion on these tricky questions, which we do not have the time, nor the facts, to make up our minds on?'

If Parliament does not vote as it really thinks on the issue of devolution, the House of Commons could be faced with the ultimate humiliation whereby a majority of the House of Commons passed a devolution Bill, after hours and hours of debate, and then found that most members campaigned against devolution in the run up to the referendum, or more likely kept a discreet silence in the fervent hope that the electorate would make the final decision for them and overturn the judgment of the House of Commons.

8

The Party Alternatives

For the Tories and the Liberals the considerations have been of a different nature. Though this book is an attempt to analyse the problems of a Government in office, the alternatives offered by the Conservative and Liberal Parties to the devolution conundrum must also be examined.

The Tories

If there has been some confusion in the Labour Party over devolution, it is more than matched by that in the Tory Party — to which we must now turn.

In the 1945 General Election, the Conservative Party in England was routed, with a host of well-known names from the 1930s and the Second World War era tumbling at the polls. In Scotland, the Conservative and Unionist Party also suffered a defeat, but on nothing like so decisive a scale. The Unionists, as they liked to be called, did well at the polls, in 1950 and better still in 1951; and by attaining more than half of the popular vote in 1955, they achieved something which has not been matched before or since by a political party in Scotland. So, if by the end of the 1950s, Tory leaders in Scotland were complacent, they had, at least in terms of electoral arithmetic, something to be complacent about.

It is true that the Conservative and Unionist Party in Scotland had a separate structure from the National Union of Conservative Associations, and could not therefore send delegates to the annual conference of the Conservative Party; but considering the relative unimportance of the annual conference in those days to the Conservative hierarchy — compared to that of the Labour conference to Labour leaders — the absence of the Scots was a matter of the utmost inconsequence all round, not least to themselves. What mattered far more was the presence of a host of Scots in the Governments of the 1950s, even though some of the most influential of them — such as Harold Macmillan, Iain Macleod and David Maxwell Fyfe — sat for English seats.

The first Conservative Secretary of State, James Stewart, later Viscount Stewart of Findhorn, was an undemonstrative aristocrat. (Once when he was reading a Departmental brief in the House of Commons, Labour Members yelled at him to speak up and not to mutter. 'Oh', said Stewart casually, 'I'm so sorry, I would have raised my voice if I had thought anyone was interested enough to listen!') But Stewart had been Churchill's wartime Chief Whip, and discreet boozing companion, and for this and other reasons he was — despite outward appearances — relatively the most powerful politician to have occupied the post of Secretary of State for Scotland. A few words in the Cabinet, and he could get more or less what he asked for Scotland — and the Scots knew that they were getting a fair share of anything that was going between 1951 and 1955. English Conservative Ministers left Stewart to run his own satrapy as he thought fit, and hesitated to interfere with a colleague whom they knew had a private line to the 'old man'. Sir Christopher Soames, Churchill's son-in-law, who was in Downing Street a good deal during the early 1950s, has told me about the strength of Stewart's position both in relation to Churchill and to the rest of the Cabinet. Besides, in Sir William Murie, Stewart had a remarkably gifted permanent Secretary at the Scottish Office; together they were a formidable and highly effective combination.

Stewart's successor, Jack Maclay, later Viscount Muirshiel, was an able and hard-working man, who had a rougher ride, as unemployment on the West Coast of Scotland and in Glasgow rose above the national average. Though popular in his party, Maclay did not carry the same political weight with his colleagues as Stewart. His tenure of office — then a record length of service — was terminated after seven years in the July 1962 night of the long knives, when he had to give way to Michael Noble, then a relatively new Member for Argyll.

Bad results for the Conservatives in Scotland in the 1964 and 1966 General Elections created a somewhat edgy relationship with the Conservative leadership at Westminster, which was exacerbated to some extent by resentment on the part of many Tory stalwarts in Scotland, at the manner in which Sir Alec Douglas Home seemed to have been winkled out of the party leadership in 1965. Consequently, the result of the Glasgow Pollok by-election victory in March 1967 came as something of a shock, despite Conservative glee at the Labour Government's discomfiture. The SNP vote was in five figures, however; the alarum bells sounded and in June 1967, the Tory Party set up a Conservative 'Government of Scotland Policy Group' under the chairmanship of Sir William McEwan Younger, at that time Chairman and Managing Director of Scottish and Newcastle Breweries, one of the few major firms to have their headquarters and head office in Scotland.

The Younger Committee was not the first Conservative committee to consider how Scotland should be governed; but it was the first one that really mattered. They held their first meeting on 14 December 1967; five months later, on 18 May 1968, Edward Heath went to the Scottish Conference of the Conservative Party, and delivered what has become known as the Declaration of Perth, in which he came out in favour of a Scottish Assembly. When a major party leader is converted in a mere five months to a major constitutional change, it is not unreasonable to suspect that his mind may have been made up already, and that the main purpose of the Younger Committee was simply to clothe the decision in a certain procedural respectability and decency. The suspicion is natural, but the facts in this instance are more complex. First of all, contrary to the impression of intellectual rigour which he would like to give, Edward Heath is a man who does not think problems through properly; he had a habit of rushing helter-skelter into problems, with no more than a vague hope that he would make a soft landing at the end of the ride.

But, the most convincing evidence that the Younger Committee was not simply a cloak for what Heath wanted to do anyway, which had been packed with people of his choice, is that they did not begin their deliberations by favouring an Assembly. Of the eleven members, three were MPs: Norman

Wylie, now Lord Wylie, who had served for a few months as Solicitor-General for Scotland before being elected to Parliament in 1964, and was later to be Lord Advocate; Anthony Stodart, who had been a Junior Minister at the Scottish Office, and was later to be Minister of State for Agriculture; and Professor Esmond Wright, who had won the Pollok by-election and was an historian and an influential figure among Scottish Conservatives at the time. The Committee was strong on the legal side, regionally well-balanced, and broadly representative of the different sections of the Conservative Party in Scotland — with the exception of what might be termed the hard-core Glasgow Tories. (This was later discovered to be a costly omission: they were an element in the Conservative Party that has never been reconciled to the need for an Edinburgh Assembly, not so much on account of inter-city rivalry, but because they were more aware of the burdens of administration and costs of bureaucracy than many of the well-to-do gentleman farmers from rural areas.)

The Younger Committee was chosen by Michael Noble (later Lord Glenkinglas), the Shadow Secretary of State, George Younger MP, Deputy-Chairman of the Party in Scotland, Sir Gilmour Menzies Anderson, Chairman of the Party, and Robert Kernohan, then Director-General of the Scottish Conservatives. It is important to record that though Mr Heath approved the membership, he did not himself make the selection. The Committee was not designed to produce a particular answer but to examine all the proposals for change with a constructive but realistic eye; but some of those involved in setting it up did not conceal that they were expecting the committee to take a hard-headed look at the idea of an Assembly and then reject it. And this is exactly what might have happened had not the Hamilton by-election taken place in November 1967, between the appointment of the Younger Committee and its first meeting. Once again, timing was all important. And many doubts about the setting up of an Assembly at that time were dispelled by the success of the SNP in local elections in early May 1968, just prior to the Declaration of Perth. Local election results may be a poor indication of a desire to change the constitution; but, however ephemeral they may be, their interpretation by frightened politicians can alter policy.

The Tories were deeply divided over SNP successes. A number of agents and East Coast MPs were apprehensive; others harboured the happy illusion that it would be Labour and not themselves who would suffer. In the late 1960s, it was fashionable for the Tories to say that an SNP candidate took two votes from Labour to one from the Tory. Yet the rise of the SNP was also part of a more general movement at that time in favour of more say for Scotland. Private polls taken by the Conservatives suggested that an overwhelming majority of Scottish Conservatives favoured some kind of devolution, though in a rather vague way. Yet it was abundantly obvious that such polls, the terms of which were necessarily vague, would produce equally vague answers, albeit ones which pointed in the direction of a Scottish Assembly. It was characteristic of the mood of the times that the younger Tories set up a Thistle Group rather than joining the national Bow Group, because they wanted a specifically Scottish organisation of their own. And the Thistle Group had actually published a pamphlet suggesting a Scottish Assembly, before Mr Heath went to Perth in 1968.

Since 1959 — when the Conservatives lost three seats in Scotland — Heath, like other leading Tories, had become exasperated with the Conservative Party in Scotland and their dismal showing. His dissatisfaction stemmed partly from his experience as President of the Board of Trade in 1963 and 1964; he was in charge of regional policy, and found the Scottish Conservative-orientated industrialists unwilling to show many signs of self-help. And they in turn resented his resale price maintenance Bill, as did many of the small traders in the constituency associations. Mutual petulance prevailed.

Then, Mr Heath made an insensitive speech denouncing the SNP as 'flower people with flower power', which was not only a ridiculous assessment of the political situation, but gave offence far beyond nationalist circles. Watching him across the Floor of the House of Commons as the Opposition Leader, he gave me the impression of being a man who realised that anything he did in Scotland was liable to go sour, that he found the Scots uncongenial, and that he would like to do something to wash his hands of the situation. Probably he felt that the only way to respond to the situation was to give the Scots what they appeared to want; he also hoped that by doing so he would recover some Conservative seats in Scotland at the following General Election.

Heath looked to Sir William McEwan Younger's Committee to provide some kind of an answer for him. As the 1968 Scottish Conference loomed closer, so the pressure on the Committee intensified. I am told that the Committee was deeply divided on the substance of the issue of an Assembly, but united in one matter only — that they had to say something on the topic. It appeared to be one of those occasions, all too frequent in political life, when not to say anything is to give one the worst of all worlds; anything appears to be better than nothing. On his part, Mr Heath's one request to the Committee was for a clear decision, one way or the other; which way he would jump was in the balance, but of one thing he was certain — he must be decisive. He had to know whether to come out firmly for, or firmly against, an Assembly by 18 May, 1968, when he made his speech to the faithful. No less than with the Labour Party, the political imperatives of the moment were of more consequence than the question of the good governance of Scotland or of the United Kingdom.

At the beginning of the month, Sir William McEwan Younger and Professor Esmond Wright had a meeting with Mr Heath in London, at which they proposed an Assembly which would merely deal with some stages of Scottish legislation. Since this was such a modest suggestion, they suggested that the Assembly should be only partly directly elected, and partly elected by local authorities and other bodies, with some Westminster representation. Mr Heath retorted that it must be directly elected, though not, I suspect, out of consideration for the interest of Scotland; the overriding factor in his mind was more probably that if the principle of indirect election to a Scottish Assembly was established, it might then seem over-attractive to British Ministers and MPs, on a subject, far dearer to Edward Heath's heart — the European Parliament. Heath knew better than any other British politician that direct election to a European assembly was an integral part of the Treaty of Rome, and the necessary element of democracy to be injected into the Brussels set-up.

The proposal for a Scottish Assembly went before the Conservative Shadow Cabinet on 8 May 1968 at their regular meeting, and by 13 May, at a specially convened meeting, they had before them an interim report from the Younger Committee, and a paper from Michael Noble analysing the report, as well as summarising its conclusions. Two hectic days later, Mr Heath presented a paper to the Shadow Cabinet, giving the substance of what he intended to say at Perth; I am informed that this was approved with a few minor amendments, but that some members of the Shadow Cabinet suppressed their objections, partly because they recognised that their leader had to say something decisive, and partly because any member who crossed Mr Heath was conscious that he might damage his chances of preferment in the next Conservative Government: arguing with the leader once he had made up his mind was not the best way to high Ministerial office.

I refer to these dates in somewhat boring detail in order to underline the fact that all these meetings, which could have such far-reaching consequences for the future of the United Kingdom, were squashed into a mere ten days; any objective observer could be forgiven for finding it hard to believe that politicians could telescope discussion on matters with such weighty implications into so short a time-span. Yet, this was all-too-typical of the way in which the whole devolution situation was allowed to develop; no wonder it gathered a momentum of its own. Time was pressing, and there was no opportunity for the period of reflection that is appropriate before a decision of such importance.

Shadow Cabinet Ministers knew of the existence of the Younger Committee; but the committee itself was having to work against the calendar in order to produce its conclusions in time, and there is no evidence that most Shadow Ministers felt that it was in any way their duty to keep in touch with its thinking before the interim report. No wonder that they drifted casually into the commitment on the strength of three meetings within ten days. Talking to a number of Mr Heath's colleagues at the time — and not just those who have since become antagonistic to him — it is remarkable that either they fail to remember anything about the discussions at all, or say that the discussion made little impact upon them. They took the relaxed view that if the boss wanted it, and the party in Scotland thought it a good idea, then it was presumably all right — a classic example both of the way in which modern British Cabinets and Shadow Cabinets become compartmentalised in their thinking, with members not wanting to tread on their colleagues' toes, and perhaps of the inattention with which English politicians tend to consider Scottish questions. I was told by one of the participants that most members of the 1968 Shadow Cabinet regarded a Scottish Assembly as just another Scottish question, albeit an important one.

This was true not just of the Shadow Cabinet, but of the Conservative Parliamentary Party as a whole. The 1922 Committee was not consulted before the decision, though perhaps this was less than remarkable, in view of Mr Heath's authoritarian style in those days. The only people who bothered to protest to the Opposition whips were a minority of Scottish Conservative MPs, led by Miss Betty Harvie Anderson, who remained adamantly opposed.

The following exchange in the Commons in December 1976 is illuminating:

Mr Bell (Beaconsfield): The Secretary of State for Wales said that this was not a new debate, but it is new to the people of England. It would be hard to exaggerate the suddenness with which this question has come to the English public and to English Members. There was virtually no consultation, I am sure, on either side, outside of the Scottish Members and organisations [An Hon. Member: 'And not much there, either.'] That could well be. I could not know that. However, outside of Scottish Members and organisations, I am sure that on neither side was there any real consultation about the manifesto paragraphs affecting Scotland and Wales.

Mr Edward Heath (Sidcup): In order that this myth should not grow any more than the innumerable myths that we have heard already in the debate, perhaps my hon. and learned Friend will accept from me, as Leader of the Conservative Party throughout the whole period involved, that there was intensive discussion not only in this House and in the Scottish Members' Committee but in the whole party in Scotland. As for the party manifesto, this matter was discussed in the policy committee of the party, which included the Scots and English and members of the whole party and in every arm of the party. There was thorough discussion throughout.

Mr Bell: No doubt there was thorough discussion among Scottish Members and in the policy committee. I am saying that certainly no one asked me, and I did not know when these paragraphs were being prepared. I am prepared to say that nine out of ten English Members knew nothing about it and were never asked.

Mr Heath: This was discussed in the policy committee of the whole party. It was also discussed in the party committees in the House and throughout the party organisation. If my hon. and learned Friend is not a member of these committees and discussed it at no time in any of the committees, that is not my responsibility as party leader at the time.

Mr Bell: If I may respectfully say so, that is just the trouble about my right hon. Friend's attitude. He thinks that if something is discussed in the policy committee of the Conservative Party, which is a very small body, it is somehow percolated and permeated through the whole party, and we all know about it. That is a lot of rubbish, and I dare say — although I do not know this — that it is rubbish on the Government side of the House, too. That is my view. [*Hansard*, 16 December 1976.]

English Conservative MPs acquiesced in the deed at Perth. There were two striking exceptions: both were heavyweight politicians, who had forfeited high office when the 'magic circle' chose Alec Douglas Home as Prime Minister — the late Iain Macleod, and Enoch Powell. Mr Powell was never Heath's confidant; Iain Macleod was working his passage back to the inner sanctum of the Conservative Party, and did not want a row with Heath at the time. However, in July 1968, when I jokingly chided him about how the Tories had been so 'soft-in-the-head' as to go along with this Assembly nonsense, Macleod's crisp remark was, 'Tam, you can rest assured that it was none of my doing!'; and without being disloyal to his colleagues and leader, he gave me to understand that, as a Scot, he disapproved of the entire Assembly proposal; but because being out-of-step on the issue would give the appearance of yet another disagreement with Alec Douglas Home, who was pro-Assembly, he preferred for personal reasons to desist from public comment. Had Macleod delivered one of his withering speeches against an Assembly, along the lines of his own feelings, he might well have swayed the Tory Party into opposition to devolution. But that is one of the 'ifs' of recent political history.

The second striking exception was Enoch Powell, by then estranged from his colleagues in the leadership of the Tory Party. In September 1968, at Prestatyn in Wales, Powell declared that unless Scotland and Wales wished to be separate nations, Great Britain must be governed and administered as one nation. In private, Powell's counsel was neither sought nor given; and the fact that he took a stand on the issue was positively counter-productive to his side of the argument, as far as the Conservative leadership was concerned.

So at Perth, and after Perth, Mr Heath seemed to have his own way. He declared that the Labour Government ought to set up a small Constitutional Committee to examine proposals for the reorganisation of Scottish government. The Conservative Party would then propose to it the creation of an elected Scottish Assembly to sit in Edinburgh as a single chamber, and take part in legislation in conjunction with the Westminster Parliament; he did not specify whether it should be elected directly or indirectly. Whether Mr Heath honestly thought that the Prime Minister would hasten to follow his advice, one cannot know; what is certain is that had Mr Wilson had any intention of setting up a Constitutional Committee in 1968, it would have been delayed by the very fact that the suggestion had come from Ted Heath. In politics, ideas are too often judged by their sources rather than on their intrinsic merits. There was no better way of ensuring that the Government would do nothing, than for Mr Heath to make a constructive suggestion. Mutual dislike between Mr Wilson and Mr Heath transcended actual consideration of what was right for Scotland.

When the Government predictably failed to act on his advice, Mr Heath announced in July 1968 that he himself was setting up a committee of distinguished men and women to consider the question, not all of whom were Conservatives or Scots. To chair it, and give it an undoubted prestige, who better than Sir

Alec Douglas Home, the former Prime Minister? Talking to a number of those concerned, I have found it hard to work out exactly what went on in the Home Committee. To begin with, some members thought that their task was to determine what kind of an Assembly there should be; others were under the distinct impression that they were being asked whether there should be an Assembly at all. Eventually the issue was fudged, producing a formula to the effect that it was open to the committee to reject the idea of an Assembly altogether, but that its primary task was to recommend how an Assembly could work. From the start, the Committee was bedevilled by the same problem which was later to afflict the Scotland and Wales Bill. It had not one but two purposes; it was trying to kill two birds with one stone, only the birds happened to be flying in opposite directions. It was designed both to reform the system of Government in Scotland and make a political impact with proposals for doing so. The methods appropriate for one were counterproductive for the other. To bring about a constitutional change of enormous consequence, it is absolutely essential to prepare the ground in advance, so as to secure the necessary basis of consent. That means moving gradually, with the commitment not merely slavishly following the reports of whatever committees are deemed necessary, but appearing to grow out of those reports as if they were an almost inevitable consequence. That no such process took place suggests that for the Conservatives — as for Labour — the question of party advantage carried more weight than the good government of Scotland.

The draft proposals of the Home Committee appeared for the first time at the celebrated Selsdon Park meeting of the Shadow Cabinet in January 1970. On 16 March, Sir Alec presented his report to the Shadow Cabinet, with a proposal for a directly elected Scottish Convention in Edinburgh which would discuss Second Reading, Committee, and Report stages of Bills referred to it by the House of Commons, which would give the final seal of approval on Third Reading.

There appear to be several reasons why Sir Alec's report was allowed a safe passage through the Shadow Cabinet, several of whose members were — and still are — profoundly sceptical about devolution. First, some of members had the gravest doubts as to whether the Conservative team under Ted Heath could win the 1970 election; in which case, why bother too much about good government? What mattered was the supposed electoral appeal of devolution: if they did not win, nothing would be lost, and the position could be re-thought at a later date, possibly by Conservative leaders other than themselves; if by chance they did win, some way could doubtless be found for constructing a less barmy scheme. Sufficient unto the day was the evil thereof!

Second, if Tories had been reluctant to contradict the party leader in 1968, they were even more reluctant to do so just before an election. Those with some hope of office were unwilling to offend both a possible Prime Minister and his Foreign Secretary. Besides, the mere fact that it had been Sir Alec chairing the Committee, that the Conservative Party felt guilty about the way he had been treated in 1965 when he was ejected from the leadership, and that he had behaved since with commendable honour, all reinforced the instinct of Shadow Ministers, however doubtful they may have been, not to challenge the leadership.

Third, after Selsdon, and Mr Wilson's mocking speeches about Selsdon Man, the Conservative leadership was preoccupied about the handling of the economy, and devolution had become a bit of a side-show.

The Committee's report was published on 19 March 1970, and discussed again in the presence of Sir Gilmour Menzies Anderson on 8 April at the Shadow Cabinet. On 27 April the Shadow Cabinet examined drafts of the manifesto for the election, which was to be held in June. On 6 May, the full manifesto was considered by the Conservative Party Advisory Committee on policy, and later in the month the Scottish Conservative Conference accepted the Douglas-Home Report by a large majority, 'as a basis for implementing the policy of devolution'.

Unexpectedly in Mr Wilson's view, and that of many others, Mr Heath became Prime Minister in June 1970. Why then did the incoming Government fail to implement the proposals on devolution? It was not forgetfulness, once the election had been won. Speaking in the Second Reading of the Scotland and Wales Bill in 1976, Mr Heath told the Commons:

My declaration at Perth was not some mental aberration

after a conference night out in Perth, agreeable as those
occasions always are. It was the result of carefully considered papers — papers before the Shadow Cabinet, and
agreed by the whole Shadow Cabinet — and discussions
with the Party in the House. Therefore, I made my
declaration, which has stood firm ever since 1968 [*Hansard*,
16 December 1976].

Yet after June 1970, the Conservatives had the opportunity
and the power to honour their promise of a Scottish Assembly.
They did nothing about it. Why?

Various reasons or excuses are given; that the Government
were involved in getting Britain into the European Common
Market; that Robert Carr's industrial relations legislation was
more urgent; that they had to wait for the Royal Commission
under the chairmanship of Lord Kilbrandon to report; or that
they were anyhow engaged in a Bill to reform Scottish local
government, which had to come first.

There is some credibility in the first of these excuses. It would
be difficult enough to get one major constitutional measure —
entry into Europe — on to the Statute Book; it would be quite
impossible, it was said, to push two constitutional measures
through at the same time. Since the Prime Minister's life's
mission was to get Britain into the EEC, and since a Bill to set
up an Assembly, running in harness with the EEC Legislation,
would undoubtedly have made the EEC legislation more
difficult to get through Parliament, any thought of a devolution
Bill was out of the question until the EEC Bill was safely signed,
sealed, and delivered in late 1972. By that time, the end period
of the Government's term was in sight — and British Governments only successfully embark on major measures at the beginning of their terms. Impetus runs out, and, as Dick Crossman
showed in his *Diaries*, the Civil Service determination to help
force major measures through the government machine wanes
as the life of the Government goes on. Besides, a simple political
fact weighed heavily with Mr Heath: the House of Commons
had been sensitive enough about surrendering some of its
powers to the EEC: those who supported his Common Market
Legislation might not fancy giving away more power, so soon
after the EEC Bill, to a Scottish Assembly.

The suggestion that the Industrial Relations Bill competed with a possible devolution Bill requires explanation. First, the time, minds and energies of senior Ministers became so focused on the intransigent problems of industrial relations that they could contemplate little else. The Cabinet became obsessed — understandably — with industrial relations, and had no desire to stir up another hornet's nest for themselves, in the form of devolution. Second, was a mundane but extremely important consideration: the number of Parliamentary draughtsmen of the skill and quality to translate proposals on subjects like EEC entry, industrial relations, and devolution is limited; they are hard-working and conscientious lawyers, but their limited numbers do constitute a real restriction on the amount of legislation Governments can pass. There simply were not enough of them available to tackle the devolution on top of all the other legislation which the Government wanted to place on the Statute Book.

While both the EEC legislation and the industrial relations legislation provided on the whole credible reasons for not going ahead with devolution, the explanation given in Scotland was rather different. Two excuses are most frequently made: that the Conservative Government had to wait for the Kilbrandon Commission to report, and that they therefore decided to reform local government in Scotland first. However, before swallowing this particular line, we should glance at the terms of the Conservative Party's 1970 manifesto commitment. This referred to the report of the Home Committee — which, as we have seen, had been published two months earlier — in the following words: 'The contents of that report including the proposal for a Convention sitting in Edinburgh will form the basis of proposals which we will place before Parliament, taking account of the forthcoming re-organisation of local government.'

Now this was extraordinary, in that there was no reference at all to the existence of the Kilbrandon Committee. One or two Conservatives, including Lord Kilmany — who, as Sir William Anstruther Gray, was Chairman of the 1922 Committee when Edward Heath became party leader in 1966 — have told me that Mr Heath took the view that if the manifesto had promised to do something only in the light of the Kilbrandon Committee Report, it would have much reduced its electoral impact in Scotland — which, as we have seen, was really always the main purpose of the entire exercise, anyway.

Another explanation, which is quite compatible with Anstruther Gray's view, is that Heath and his colleagues had little esteem for the membership of the Royal Commission. I myself sensed this from a lively conversation with Quintin Hogg, who, as Lord Hailsham, was Lord Chancellor in the Heath Government. Moreover, even if it had been a Royal Commission of impeccably distinguished membership, it still was one which had been chosen by Harold Wilson. I have often heard that Heath on several occasions referred to the Kilbrandon Commission as 'just another of Harold Wilson's awful gimmicks'. Whether true or not, the fact remains that relations between Mr Heath and Mr Wilson were so poisoned at that time that any body which had been set up by one would be regarded by the other as a monstrosity to be disbanded or ignored. Heath reckoned that Crowther/Kilbrandon had been set up by the Wilson Government in the aftermath of SNP success, chiefly as a delaying device. Various Scottish Conservatives have told me that they thought that in 1970 Heath did intend to proceed to devolution legislation, but was soon diverted for the kind of reason that I have given.

However, over six years later, Mr Heath himself points to the fact that he was asked by successive chairmen of the Royal Commission to wait until they had reported. On 16 December 1976, I heard Mr Heath say in the Second Reading of the debate on the Scotland and Wales Bill:

> We also said that we would hold off the directly elected assembly for Scotland, until local government reorganisation for Scotland was complete. I must say that this was the request first of Lord Crowther, and then Lord Kilbrandon. They asked whether I could not arrange our legislative programme so that they could finish their discussions and then make a complete recommendation about devolution.

The Tories did not say in their manifesto that they would hold off until local government reorganisation had been completed. They said something quite different: that their proposals for an Assembly would take account of the reorganisation of local government. The general lines were already known. As we have seen, the Wheatley Commission had already reported in 1969, and the Conservatives themselves had accepted the two-tier structure of local government. Still less did they say that they would wait for Kilbrandon — which is a bit of a retrospective excuse. Nothing happened on the Scottish or constitutional scene, as such, to prevent the commitment to an Assembly from being redeemed, which could not have been foreseen when it was given. By the time Kilbrandon actually reported in October 1973 the country was lurching under the effects of the world oil crisis, and if Mr Heath's mind was on Scotland at all, his thoughts were focused entirely on Mr Michael McGahey, and what he should say to the National Union of Mineworkers.

Looking back from five years later, one can probably make the following generalisations. Mr Heath himself, as Prime Minister, can be acquitted of cynically wanting a Scottish Assembly simply to get votes in 1970; vaguely, he wanted to do something about devolution. But it was not high on his list of priorities; certainly not in the same league as Europe and the Industrial Relations Act. And both Kilbrandon and local government reform provided respectable excuses, if not actual reasons, for failing to grasp the nettle; the Secretary of State for Scotland, Gordon Campbell, heeding the anti-Assembly advice he was getting from his Permanent Secretary at the Scottish Office, Sir Douglas Haddow, and other senior officials, was tepid about the whole business, and was certainly not prepared to take up the cudgels on behalf of a Scottish Assembly in Cabinet. Above all else, however, the political imperative seemed to evaporate. The crucial fact here was that only one SNP MP was returned in 1970 — Donald Stewart, Provost of Stornoway in Lewis, whose arrival seemed to have more to do with his personal qualities and his popularity in the Western Isles, and with criticism of his predecessor, than with political policy as such. Had the incoming Heath Government been faced with six SNP MPs, as Harold Wilson was after February 1974 — let alone eleven SNP MPs, as he was after October 1974 — he might have put an Assembly higher on his list of priorities.

One of the casualties of the February 1974 General Election

was Gordon Campbell himself, who lost to Mrs Ewing in Moray and Nairn. He was succeeded as Shadow Secretary of State by Alick Buchanan Smith, who with Mr Heath at the Conservative Party Conference at Ayr in May 1974 advocated an Assembly whose members would be drawn from the new Regional and District Councils. The proposal was endorsed by the Party Conference but had a cryogenic reception in the Scottish press. Heath, who had had misgivings about allowing himself to go along with such a proposal, became very testy. He himself had, as we have seen, more or less exercised a veto on a similar suggestion, before reaching his original commitment six years earlier. Change, however, was too late. In October 1974, the Conservative manifesto said: 'Initially the Assembly's membership will be drawn from the elected members of the new local authorities, though direct elections could evolve in the future.' During the campaign, this was realised to be a case of having the worst of all possible worlds, and Mr Buchanan Smith came out in favour of a directly elected assembly at the earliest moment, consistent with decency, after the election. He set up a committee under Malcolm Rifkind, MP for Edinburgh Pentlands, and endorsed their view that there should be a directly elected assembly to take Second Reading and Report stage of specifically Scottish Bills, but without there being any separate Scottish executive.

Then, in the autumn of 1975, the devolution story was to be significantly altered by an event which was quite extraneous to it, as many other events had been. Mr Edward Heath lost the leadership of the Conservative Party.

On the evening that Mrs Margaret Thatcher was elected Leader of the Conservative Party, it happened by chance that I was going to the College Mews Studio opposite the Victoria Tower of the Palace of Westminster to do a TV programme and passed her coming out of the studio. Having warmly congratulated her on her success, I said cheerily, 'Well, if you ever become Prime Minister, don't hive us Scots off!' I sensed that she took the remark seriously and said 'No, I won't do that!' in a friendly manner.

This chance exchange prompted me to ask two of her closest campaign managers precisely what her views on devolution were at that time. I was told that this was one of the issues that she did not fully understand, but that instinctively and temperamentally she had 'little sympathy at all' with the idea of a Scots Assembly, and was passionately hostile to anything that might disrupt the United Kingdom. I have no doubt that my informants were candid and knew what they were saying at the time.

Why then within weeks did she come out with a pronouncement in favour of an Assembly in Edinburgh? Calculations of sheer political advantage and vote getting? Not so, in my opinion.

The truth is fairly simple and instructive, rather than dishonourable. Mrs Thatcher had seldom been to Scotland. Her world had been the Outer London suburbs and her constituency of Finchley, followed by a period in the Conservative Government as Secretary of State for Education, one of the English portfolios. Education in Scotland is the responsibility of the Secretary of State for Scotland, and there was no opportunity for Ministerial visits north of the Border, other than to a scientific establishment. Besides, English Ministers of Housing, Health and Education have had a certain reluctance to poach upon the Scottish Secretary's territory — quite apart from which they have more than enough obligations of their own to fulfil.

On her election as Leader of the Party in 1975, it was therefore obvious that Mrs Thatcher must make one of her first official visits as Leader of the Opposition to the one place where she had not been much, and was virtually unknown — Scotland.

Her advisers accordingly laid on a schedule for her in Scotland, and naturally the tour was spearheaded by the Shadow Secretary of State for Scotland, Mr Alick Buchanan Smith. During a euphoric and unexpectedly enthusiastic reception in a shopping precinct in Edinburgh, Mrs Thatcher had a microphone thrust into her face. 'Are you in favour of an Assembly here in Edinburgh, Mrs Thatcher?' insisted a bevy of reporters. Not wanting to be evasive in a crowd, and with her Shadow Scottish Secretary, a well-known pro-Assembly man at her side, Mrs Thatcher could be excused for saying 'Yes'. No new party leader likes to appear indecisive. This was a commitment which doubtless she now regrets bitterly. The episode, which has led to much agonised ambivalence within the Conservative Party, illustrates one of the difficulties facing modern politicians. Churchill, let alone Mr Gladstone, was never placed in this kind of impossible position, where at the drop of a hat, at a most unsuitable time, one has to make what can, in effect, be a long-term policy decision. The press can hound a public figure into forming opinions on subjects on which his or her views have simply not matured.

A promise once given, under whatever circumstances, cannot easily be retracted. Moreover, the political difficulties of Mrs Thatcher's position are compounded by her generally delicate relationship with her predecessor, who has selected a 'Pro-devolution' stance as one of 'his issues'.

Most Conservatives want the Bill to fail: but many of them are unwilling to be saddled with responsibility for its failure, or to use an old Scots expression, of having 'belled the cat'!

This is basically why Conservative policies have made so many twists and turns, recently a matter of nuance and inference rather than of hard fact. One solid event worth recalling is that in December 1976 Mr Buchanan Smith and Mr Rifkind resigned from the official Front Bench, after the Shadow Cabinet had decided to impose a three-line whip against the Second Reading of the Scotland and Wales Bill. The succession went to Mr Edward Taylor, who until his appointment had recently been against any form of Scottish Assembly.

The Liberals

Tracing the history of the Liberal Party's devolution policies is a much easier task than following the labyrinthine thread of Labour or Tory policy. They have had the merit of being consistent, at least in having the same slogans — proportional representation and federalism. If it is thought less than charitable to introduce the Liberals in this way, the unhappy fact is that when James Callaghan concluded the Lib-Lab accommodation in March 1977, prior to a vote of no confidence in the Labour Government, he asked David Steel, leader of the Liberal Party, for detailed Liberal views on devolution. The document which was hastily handed over to him turned out not to be native Liberal proposals at all, but based on the work of the Outer Policy Study Group, led by Professors James Cornford and Alan Peacock, working on a non-party basis with considerable assistance from Professor John Mackintosh, in favour of devolution. Unkindness, however, ought to be tempered by the fact that an Opposition party in Britain does not have the massive resources of the Government machine to work out detailed policies. So let us turn our attention to the Liberals, and do them the courtesy at this point of reflecting on their two favourite war cries on the subject of devolution.

Ever since the Second World War, the Liberals have been generally sympathetic to devolution, and the hiving off of power from central government. The structure of the Liberal Party is such that the Scottish Liberal Party and the Welsh Liberal party are more identifiable entities within the party than either the Scottish Labour Party and Welsh Labour Party, or even the Scottish Conservative Party or Welsh Conservative Party. Tendencies towards decentralisation of power to Wales and Scotland were reinforced by the not entirely fortuitous facts that the Liberals were successful in maintaining Parliamentary toe-holds in the Celtic fringes at times when they faced electoral annihilation elsewhere, and in particular that Mr Clement Davies, MP, a Welshman, led the party for many years, followed by a Scot, Jo Grimond, who was succeeded by a Devonian in Jeremy Thorpe, himself succeeded by another Scot, David Steel.

If the demand for a Federal Britain is the main object of the Liberals, the demand for Assemblies elected on the basis of proportional representation has been a secondary objective. Naturally enough, this demand is related to the position of the Liberal Party in the last half-century, and has occupied an important place in the Liberal platform ever since David Lloyd George went out of power, and Liberal representation in the Commons has borne an unsatisfactory relationship to the size of the Liberal vote in the country.

There is, however, a special and substantial argument for the Liberal demand, defeated in the House of Commons during the passage of the Bill, that the proposed Assemblies should be elected on some kind of proportional representation. In days when there was two-party predominance, and some 97 per cent of the electorate voted either for the Conservatives or for the Labour Party, the first-past-the-post system of election had considerable merit in terms of decisiveness of Government. Yet, few can say at the present time that Scotland is a two-party place. There are three parties, Labour, Conservative, and Scottish Nationalist, neck-and-neck in the opinion polls, and the Liberal Party following up behind. In a winner-take-all election, a party with little over one-third of the vote could have an overwhelming predominance in the Assembly. Furthermore, since the proposed Assemblies will be elected on a four-year fixed-term basis, a sudden gust of political opinion at the particular moment of election could create a quite unreal result, which would determine the political complexion of Scotland for the full term of the Assembly.

Liberals see their case strengthened by a growing public distaste for the politics of confrontation, which grows out of a two-party system, facing each other head-on across the gangway of a debating chamber. Rather they would have the Assemblies conducted in terms of hemi-cycle politics, familiar throughout Western Europe, with a system of coalition and compromise between three, four, or five political groups.

Though from time to time Jo Grimond made various Home Rule noises, the distinctive contribution of the Liberals to the devolution argument has been a demand for a Federal Britain. On 23 February 1976, Mr Russell Johnston, MP, Chairman of the Scottish Liberal Party, launched the formal campaign for Federalism. He asked for a Scottish Assembly with wide internal powers, which could not be vetoed by Westminster; the Assembly should have a 'final say' over matters devolved to it. Full and sovereign internal autonomy is in fact Federalism. The policy has been set out in a pamphlet aptly called, *Let's Govern Ourselves and Keep the Link*.

Indeed, Liberals look to Europe both for PR and for Federalism. They quote the recent official West German guide to their Constitution: 'The Federal system makes it possible to create large states, while preserving national autonomy, religious identity, and other characteristics, particularly of a cultural or ethnic nature. A Federal state makes possible a common foreign policy and a uniform economic and financial system, while at the same time allowing sufficient independence to the different population groups.'

The Liberal concept of Federalism runs into difficulties at two different levels, one simple and mundane, the other of an altogether deeper nature.

First of all, there is the objection of geographical imbalance. England, with more than four-fifths (83 per cent) of the population would be one Province; Scotland with 11 per cent of the population would be another Province; and Wales with 4 per cent would be a third; and Northern Ireland with 2 per cent would be a fourth. This would be a wholly unwieldy structure.

The only conditions in which such a structure would become a practical possibility would be if the English wished to establish legislative Assemblies in London, Bristol, Norwich, Birmingham, Manchester, Leeds, and Newcastle, as the Liberals suggest. But there is no sign of a desire to re-establish Wessex, Mercia, or any other such Province. Well might Harold Wilson observe that, 'Any such solution to this problem would at best be totally contrived and artificial, and at worst unworkable and unwanted.' At a deeper level, Mr Wilson also spoke for many when he claimed that Federalism would be 'artificial, arbitrary, and highly legalistic' and would be alien to our mature British democratic tradition, in which the sovereignty of Parliament is indivisible.

The official position of the Government was put by Mr Gerald Fowler, MP, then Minister of State in charge of the devolution unit in the Cabinet Office, when he spoke to the Regional Studies Association Conference on 17 October 1975:

Federalism of course entails a sharing of sovereignty and a formal division of powers and resources. This may work well in other countries, either because of their historically federal tradition, revealing their origin as nation states in the coming together of smaller principalities or republics, or in nations so large that some division of powers between territories geographically remote from one another is perhaps inevitable. It seems extremely unlikely that such a system would work well in a country the size of the United Kingdom, with no tradition of federalism, and where no separate state has existed outside the Union since 1707.

A nation and three sub-nations of grossly unequal sizes cannot be turned into a United States, or even a Federal Republic of Germany. Indeed, the German comparison which the Liberals like to make is false. The history of German Federalism, or more accurately, political fragmentation, goes back a long way. For hundreds of years people whose cultural and religious distinctions were wide apart were aware of being 'Germans', although no central German government, as such, existed. This of course is absolutely the opposite to the feelings of being Scottish or Welsh, while living under a separate British sovereignty.

German nationalism was a centralising force. Bismarck, Holstein, von Bülow and their contemporaries saw it as a socially progressive force, equating as they did bigotry, ignorance and feudalism with the existence of autonomous German small states and margravates. After 1871, hostility to the little states was transferred to the provincial kingdoms and authorities within the Reich, itself a Federation of a kind. It was the Nazis who finally made Germany into a unitary state.

The Allies in 1945 accordingly decided that a decentralised Germany was the only sort of Germany which would be anti-Fascist and democratic. At first, only conservative anti-Nazis agreed with them. The socialist and liberal-nationalist traditions were both centralising. The Allies had their way. West Germany was built up out of formally autonomous Länder. Some of them corresponded to units which had existed before 1933, like Bavaria or the city state of Hamburg. Others like Nord Rhein Westfalen were simply invented by the Allies. Today most West Germans accept the Federal structure and also accept the assumption that such a structure is a fundamental guarantee against dictatorship. It is clear, all the same, that to the extent that Federalism is effective, it is a generally conservative force. The only real power of the Länder, individually or collectively, is to impede or slow down central government. The Federal structure cannot be assimilated to a strongly interventionist and statist way of running society, which is the way in which most pro-devolution politicians in Britain consider that a government should carry out its responsibilities.

In the the three decades since the West German Constitution was created, the centre of Bonn has steadily gained in influence and control at the expense of the Länder. This has not changed the formal, constitutional structure of the Federation. Instead it has built up a kind of 'parallel' central government. More and more of the functions have come under the joint control of committees formed of representatives of the Länder, with or without the presence of a representative from the Bonn government at the table.

Higher education is one example. The second television network is another. Regional development is a third. Such matters are run by a collectivity of Federal states, which is by no means the same as the official Federal government. Centralisation is in fact being forced gradually upon West Germany by the growing needs of a modern society, and the spirit of the Constitution is gradually being eroded away. The entire *raison d'être* of the West German Federal system is diametrically opposed to the thinking which makes a number of Scots interested in Federalism. In Germany, the existence of provincial government is seen as a defence against radical change. In Scotland, the main justification of a Federal Scottish Parliament would be that it could do things which a London government could not afford or could not be bothered to do. Federalism is seen in Britain by some people, particularly Liberals, as a vehicle for change. In Germany, Federalism is seen as a brake on change.

The Basic Law in Germany specifies that one of the purposes of taxation should be to remove the differences in the standard of living between different parts of the country. Accordingly a complex formula of redistribution obliges rich Länder, like Bavaria, to part with revenue for the benefit of poorer regions, like the Palatinate. There is nothing approaching Regional nationalism in Germany that I could detect as a participant in the 1976 Federal elections. Here again there is a contrast. One of the assumptions which the Liberals in Britain make is that Scotland, in particular, would be justified in demanding some financial autonomy, because this would give her a far better deal than any British pattern of revenue redistribution.

West Germany is a 'classic' Federation, born of the wish to be closer together without being too closely governed. Federalism in Scotland is a moderate form of nationalism. It often amounts to the wish to get farther away from England without the traumatic upset of secession from England.

Those Liberals who have organised study tours of West Germany, in order to enhance their case for Federalism in Britain, ought to reveal that they have been advocating something similar only in name, but in reality very different from the West German model and ethos.

9

The Pressure Groups: I

In spite of all the ballyhoo, devolution is far less widely supported in Scotland than its supporters would like us to believe. In the next two chapters we shall be examining the attitudes and arguments — on both sides — of institutions, organisations and pressure groups, from manufacturing industry to the churches and from the legal profession to the mass media.

It is tempting to assume that particular institutions or pressure groups can be neatly labelled as being pro- or anti-devolution. Alas, to do so would be a gross oversimplification. The reality is far more complicated. Although it is hardly a crime to change one's mind on a subject as one learns more about it, many people are reluctant to withdraw publicly from positions they had taken up when they understood the issues less well. Feeling themselves to be the prisoners of their past utterances, they hold to their public positions out of an inflated sense of honour and loyalty. These are not qualities to be sneered at, but they may explain why it is sometimes virtually impossible to know exactly what some public figures and pressure groups feel on the subject.

Others, from whom little had been heard in the past, have made their opinions known on the perfectly reasonable grounds that they never believed devolution would get this far, but now that it has, the time has come for them to stand up and be counted. Some people refuse to commit themselves, preferring to see which way the wind is blowing. Others have fallen silent.

Naturally there are considerable differences of opinion within particular groups or organisations, and to make broad generalisations is to invite disagreement. Bearing this qualification in

mind, how do the major pressure groups feel about devolution
for Scotland?

Manufacturing Industry

Writing to *The Times* in December 1976, Lord Polwarth, a
former chairman of the Scottish Council of Development and
Industry, said that from his experience in finance and industry
in Scotland, England and overseas — and as a Minister of
State for Scotland for two years — he was convinced that 'an
additional layer of government can only damage, rather than
help, the prospects for economic prosperity and inward investment on which Scotland so much depends'.

He is by no means alone in thinking this. No pressure group
has opposed devolution longer than the men who run manufacturing industry in Scotland, the Scottish CBI and the Scottish
Association of Chambers of Commerce; and their initial
scepticism has developed into outright opposition as devolution
has changed from a vague daydream to a real possibility.
Businessmen and industrialists of all levels and seniorities — from
the nationalised industries to the local manufacturer, from
multinational corporations to purely Scottish industries — are
united in their opposition. If their doubts took some time to
incubate, this was at least partly because few industrialists ever
imagined that the politicians were serious about devolution,
and felt that there was little point in wasting time and energy
on a subject which would die a natural death anyway.

Until the spring of 1976, this was certainly the attitude of
Douglas Hardie, a medium-sized employer based in Dundee
and the current Chairman of the Scottish CBI. He has dismissed the proposal for an Assembly as a gratuitous burden on
industry at a time when the nation's breadwinners have more
than enough problems to cope with already. He is particularly
concerned about the complications facing medium-sized firms,
which could be tossed from Westminster pillar to Royal High
School post and back during their dealings with government
Departments.

According to Lord Weir, Chairman of the Weir Group:*

---

* In a personal statement to me.

The Scottish engineering industry, one of the largest employers in the West of Scotland, believes that the establishment of a separate Scottish legislative assembly must almost inevitably lead to the separation of Scotland from the rest of the United Kingdom. It views this eventuality with the gravest concern. Most large engineering firms depend upon a healthy home market to survive, for it means substantial and regular orders from government departments and government-controlled industries — the armed forces, water supply, road construction, transport and the like. It is seldom the practice of modern states to award this kind of contract to foreign firms. Therefore, recognising the limitations of future oil-based development in Scotland and the healthy number of competent British engineering firms based outside Scotland, the Scottish engineering industry could only regard the reduction of its domestic market by 90 per cent — which is what Scottish independence would mean — as a disaster of the first magnitude. The certain consequences for employment in an area of Scotland where jobs are already scarce do not need to be described.

He goes on to say:

Independence would present us with very serious problems indeed. And for that reason we are very opposed to the SNP's policy, which they really have not thought out very carefully.

We may be an extreme case in public sector work, but there are many other people in the same position.

Less than 5 per cent of our products in Scotland go to the home market, while about 45 per cent of our Scottish production goes to English public sector industries such as electricity, steel, water, coal and the Ministry of Defence.

This is the inherent nature of our business and with that in mind we would be dealing with a foreign government.

In all these fields we have established competitors in England. Self-interest being what it is we would expect to lose virtually all of that business right away.

To adjust our system under independence we would be placed somewhere between difficulty and impossibility. We might only survive by attempting some solution that would probably involve moving south.

We would have to consider very very seriously whether we would move from Scotland. Just now we feel there are positive things about being in Scotland. It is better being a big frog in a small pond. We get tremendous help and are well looked after by government departments.

If we went independent we would be employing about 2,000 people for whom we had no work and obviously this would spread widely through ancillary and related industries.

Businessmen quoted in a *Glasgow Herald* survey, published on 6 April 1977, included the following:

Mr. Peter Balfour, chairman of Scottish and Newcastle Breweries: 'We have a company with two thirds of its production in Scotland and two thirds of it marketed in England. If our products are going to be more expensive because of any fiscal arrangements then we are going to have to shift.

'If we are going to remain competitive with the English we would have to move, because England is by far Scotland's biggest customer.

'I would look on independence as being unfavourable to industry in Scotland. I would reckon that as many as 2,000 of our jobs could be affected.'

Mr. Gerald Elliott, managing director of Christian Salvesen, the transport, oil services and food group: 'With a lot of our activities in England any change in taxation would affect our competitiveness and make life very difficult. As a multinational we would have to consider moving our headquarters south.

'We employ about 1,000 people in Scotland and have a turnover of £90m. The majority of our business is conducted outwith Scotland.'

Mr. David Nickson, vice-chairman of Collins, the publishers: 'We have not formed a company policy on this, but I view the possibility of independence with the utmost horror and dismay. I have yet to meet anyone in any walk of industry who has a good word to say about the prospect.

'Our monetary exchange rates are inextricably linked with England. We have been the beneficiary over recent decades. Oil is only a short term stopgap which will last no more than a decade.

'The literary marketplace is sadly not in Scotland, but in London and Europe. A £1.50 Scottish pound would make our job harder. About 60% of our market is outside the United Kingdom.'

Sir Eric Yarrow, chairman of Yarrow and Co. and Yarrow Shipbuilders: 'As one of three specialist naval shipbuilders in the UK it is most important that work continues at the existing rate. The Ministry of Defence requires two thirds of our capacity.

'The rest is used for export orders. Any alteration in this arrangement would not only mean redundancy at Yarrow Shipbuilders but also among the many subcontractors in Scotland supplying us with equipment.'

It is understandable that those responsible for managing great industries should have displayed a circumspect reticence about indulging in public controversy on the issue of devolution. With the almost unique exception of Sir William McEwan Younger, the brewer, their private views are firmly opposed to an Edinburgh Assembly. Most of their companies operate on a United Kingdom basis, often within an international framework, and the last things they want to deal with are extra fiscal and commercial complications. Corporation tax and VAT make life hard enough as it is.

This is still more true of those who run the nationalised industries, and are anxious to avoid public confrontation with the government. Anything which threatens the economic unity of the United Kingdom must be contrary to their interests. Thus, when Michael Foot suggested in the House of Commons in 1976 that the Scottish sector of the British Steel Corporation should be more autonomous, the managers of BSC were furious and appalled. They agreed that there could be a case for a greater devolution of decision-making within the corporation and that it could make a good deal of industrial sense — provided it was done on a technical rather than a geographical basis. It could make sense, for example, to devolve more power to the Special Steels Division — but not to a Scottish division as such.

Exactly the same applies to British Rail, which obviously has to plan on a national basis. Successive chairmen have taken a discreet line on devolution, partly because — after seven minutes' discussion at their annual conference in 1976 — the National Union of Railwaymen is officially in favour of it. However, writing in a personal capacity in the *Transport Review*, Dave Bowman, President of the NUR and a Scot from Dundee, opposed a Scottish Assembly on the grounds that it could lead to separation, which would be disastrous for the railway industry.

Leaders of the nationalised industries are not alone in fearing that devolution could affect their ability to run businesses and plan their strategies at a national level — something that is increasingly important now that the economies of different countries are so closely integrated. One leading Scottish industrialist — recently retired, and therefore with none of the inhibitions affecting those who have to conduct delicate industrial negotiations with all sections of the community and all political persuasions — has spoken out in the most forthright terms about the effect devolution could have on the Scottish economy. Sir John Toothill was not only for some years the manager of the sizable Ferranti plant in Edinburgh, he also chaired the committee which produced the Toothill Report, which was published in 1962 and provided guidelines for Scotland's significant, if relative, industrial advances of the 1960s. Toothill does not mince his words. He believes that a Scottish Assembly is not only crazy, but probably harmful and dangerous to the best interests of the people of Scotland. And he has lent support to his views by becoming an active president of the 'Scotland is British' campaign.

Again, many industralists are worried that an Assembly would almost certainly add to the costs of industry. They are only too aware that one of the fundamental problems facing British industry is the burden which is placed on the shoulders of manufacturing industry by the non-manufacturing sector. Whereas there were 9,200,000 men and women engaged in manufacturing industry in Britain in 1962, by 1975 the figure had been reduced to 7,900,000.

Even allowing for the introduction of automatic, semi-automatic and labour-saving devices, this represents a significant fall in relative production potential. British industry now finds itself having to carry more administrative and service industries than that of any comparable industrial nation. In these circumstances, it is hardly surprising that Scottish industrialists should dread the introduction of yet another tier of government, with all the paperwork, bureaucratic delays and stifling red tape that would be involved. As we shall see in Chapter 11, their dread would turn to horror if the Assembly tried to finance itself by imposing Scottish corporation or income tax.

Although the nationalists like to pretend that Scotland has always received a raw deal compared with the rest of the United Kingdom, Scottish businessmen are fully aware that this is far from true, and that she has, if anything, received preferential treatment from successive Westminster Governments; and they fear that this would no longer be the case once Scotland had her own Assembly. In January 1976, Roger Scott, MP — now PPS to the Prime Minister — pointed out that in 1974 industry in England received only £13·1 per head per annum, as opposed to £28 in Scotland and £29·5 in Wales: once Scotland had her own Assembly, Ministers in London would find it far harder to discriminate in Scotland's favour at the expenses of the English regions — and the resulting sense of grievance in Scotland would merely increase sympathy for the separatists.

As we have seen in Chapter 4, the old myth that wages in Scotland are substantially lower than those in the rest of the country, outside London, no longer has any validity; the establishment of an Assembly would do nothing to iron out the far more considerable discrepancies that exist within Scotland itself. Industrialists fear that an Assembly with full economic powers of the kind demanded by James Sillars's Scottish Labour Party would mean that the whole system of United Kingdom national wage bargaining, so important to industries like engineering which operate at a national level, would come under attack. They have no more desire than the trades union leaders to see the pattern of national wage bargaining collapse: British industrial relations are complicated enough as it is, and the existence of a separate Scottish bargaining system would be

as repugnant — and as disruptive — to industrialists working
on both sides of the Border as specifically Scottish changes to
the tax laws. In either case, the net result might well be that
industrialists would decide to run down their Scottish operations
or build new plant elsewhere. And the political uncertainty
which would follow on from the establishment of an Assembly
could well discourage English or foreign firms from expanding
into Scotland.

Again, Scottish industrialists have a very clear understanding
of how central administration works in practice: a point made
with considerable force by Douglas Jay, a former president of
the Board of Trade, during the Second Reading debate on the
devolution Bill in December 1976:

> I also urge my Scottish and Welsh colleagues to understand
> two other rather sobering facts. Because Northern Ireland
> was separated administratively, during these years, those of
> us with responsibility for directing policy did not feel the
> same immediate responsibility for Northern Ireland as we
> felt for Scotland, Wales and the North East coast of
> England. As a result, when major English and American
> firms asked for advice from the Board of Trade on location,
> they were more often steered to Scotland and Wales than to
> Northern Ireland. Perhaps it was wrong, but that is how
> administration works; and it is one of the reasons there are
> so many major firms in Scotland and Wales and one of the
> main reasons for Northern Ireland having suffered very
> much higher unemployment in the past 30 years than
> Scotland and Wales [Hansard, 15 December 1976].

Mr Jay went on to make the equally sobering point that in
recent years there has been a remarkable lack of large-scale
native industrial enterprise in Scotland and Wales. The vast
majority of new projects which brought fresh employment
opportunities to both countries came from the Midlands or
South East England or from the United States. More significantly, many well-established Scottish firms, such as North
British Locomotives and Fairfields, had contracted or collapsed.
Not only would the establishment of an Assembly make future
overseas investments of this kind less likely: on account of the
likelihood of the Assembly paving the way for a separate state —

and therefore a smaller, tariff-complicated market — head offices in English firms would feel less responsibility for their Scottish employees in much the same way as Whitehall and Westminster would feel less responsible for providing jobs and financial help to Scotland as a whole.

A whole range of Scottish industries are now expressing anxiety about devolution, ample evidence of which was provided in the spring of 1977, when the Dundee Chamber of Commerce — representing 2,000 firms on Tayside — passed a unanimous resolution against the principle of an Assembly in Edinburgh.

Take, for example, the forestry industry. The private sector of the industry is extremely worried about devolution. Naturally enough, their initial fear is that the division of responsibilities between Westminster and a Scottish Assembly could in effect lead to separate forestry policies for England, Scotland and Wales: they believe that this would create severe administrative problems for the Forestry Authority, and weaken Britain's position when it comes to evolving a forestry policy within the EEC.

They go on to point out that the fragmentation of an already small industry along nationalistic lines would adversely affect its efficiency and viability. Costs would be increased, including the cost of the administration of government grants, with the result that there would be less aid available in real terms. There would be a distortion in the marketing of products, which would then affect the development of large processing industries. And the proposals put forward in the Government's most recent Bill, to the dismay of the Chairman of the publicly owned Forestry Commission, John Mackie, set forestry and agriculture further apart from each other by devolving one but not the other, at a time when the two industries need to be more rather than less closely integrated.

Similar fears are being voiced by industrialists on both sides of the border, from multinational corporations to purely local Scottish firms. They appear to be almost unanimous in feeling that yet another layer of governmental bureaucracy, with all the expense involved, would be a disincentive to industry; that devolution would inevitably make it harder for them to run their United Kingdom operations as a whole, and would do nothing to resolve the problems facing Scottish industries in particular; and that not only Scottish industry, but the Scottish work force and the people as a whole, would be the losers at the end of the day.

Financial Institutions

For generations now, Scottish financial institutions such as banks, investment trusts and insurance companies have been a by-word for probity and excellence throughout the United Kingdom; and since so high a proportion of their business is done outside Scotland, it is hardly surprising that those who run them should be fiercely opposed to devolution. As major producers of wealth — and the source of significant employment in Scotland — they can be expected to give an informed opinion on the cost of the exercise, and the implications of this for their own businesses.

THE INSURANCE COMPANIES

I. H. Stuart Black — Chairman of the General Accident Fire and Life Assurance Corporation, one of the largest composite insurance companies in the United Kingdom — told his Annual General Meeting in 1976 that it was hard to imagine that devolution, in whatever form, was not going to affect their pockets:

> As a leading Scottish Company, but with very extensive business both in England and world-wide, we must express our fears that additional costs, whether in the form of rates, taxes or any other way, will put us at a disadvantage with our competitors south of the Border and overseas. It would be even worse if legislation were to impose restrictions or controls, which imposed on us Scots, but not on the English.

Similar views were expressed by Ian Isles, the retiring General Manager of one of Scotland's oldest and largest insurance companies, Scottish Equitable, in March of this year. He pointed out that 86 per cent of the new business contracted by Scottish Equitable in 1976 came from England. He feared that an Assembly could lead to a separate Scottish government with its own currency, tax laws and financial regulations; in which case, his company might well be forced to move its 800 employees down to England, rather than risk losing its most profitable source of business.

Writing in his annual report, the Chairman of Scottish Equitable, Ernest Dawson, says that the Scottish Life Offices have examined the document entitled *Financial Management after Self Government*, in which the SNP suggests how an independent Scottish economy might operate. 'These proposals, if implemented, are bound to lead to adverse financial consequences for Scottish policy-holders,' he writes. 'We must therefore resist these proposals, too.'

Senior executives of Standard Life and Scottish Widows tell me that their minds boggle at the thought of operating in a different way in Scotland from the rest of the United Kingdom. They point out that altering or dismantling an operation within an existing unitary state in order to meet the special requirements of one part of it would be infinitely harder than starting from scratch and winning business in a foreign country.

SCOTTISH BANKS

Ironically enough, one of the many petty irritants on which the SNP has thrived has been the occasional refusal by English shopkeepers to credit Royal Bank of Scotland or Clydesdale Bank pound notes (in fact, this has only happened to me twice in the fifteen years that I have been an MP, spending a lot of my time in London). Since many Scots are only too ready to take offence and positively relish letting off steam over a grievance of this kind, a trivial annoyance has been made far too much of; it goes without saying that the picture on the note is fiscally irrelevant.

For those concerned with the purely monetary aspects of banking, the existence of Scottish banknotes is an irrelevant if agreeable anachronism, with no bearing on the very real problem of whether devolution might eventually lead to the establishment of a separate Scottish Treasury — as suggested in the Liberal proposals to James Callaghan at the time of the Lib-Lab agreement of March 1977 — and, sooner or later, separate exchange rates.

Scottish bankers regard the possibility of there being a

separate Scottish bank rate as the crowning absurdity. The very thought of having to rearrange their investment portfolios and subject their activities on either side of the Border to currency regulations makes them shudder with alarm. Until recently, senior bankers have assumed that no Government in its right mind would allow such a situation to come about. Recently, however, they have begun to realise that a pound sterling and a pound Scots are all too real a possibility. None of them shares the SNP's fanciful belief that the Scots pound would soar away on the wings of North Sea oil revenues — leaving the pound sterling hopelessly earthbound — to join the stronger currencies of Europe in the financial stratosphere; most of them take a very gloomy view of the prospects of the Scots pound, even assuming that Scotland shared in the oil revenues. They realise that, whatever the nationalists might claim, the Scottish economy would be even more dependent on that of England than that of the Irish Republic at present, and that the English would hardly be in the mood to bestow monetary favours on the Scots.

The taxation of share and equity holdings held by Scots in banks outside Scotland would obviously present appalling problems, and vice versa. Not surprisingly, Lord Armstrong — the Chairman of Midland Bank, and as Sir William Armstrong, head of the Treasury and Civil Service, and himself the son of two Scottish Salvation Army Officers — admits that he is dismayed at the thought of there being an Assembly in Edinburgh, let alone one which, as we shall argue in Chapter 11, could represent the first step towards the dismemberment of the United Kingdom. Quite apart from anything else, he points out that many of the best brains of Britain, who should be focusing their minds on how we are going to pay our way in the world, would be busying themselves for a decade or more on the unproductive business of dismantling the United Kingdom.

The SNP's Financial Policy

Since few people outside Scotland fully appreciate the drastic nature of the SNP's financial proposals, it may help the reader if at this juncture we contemplate the gist of SNP financial thinking.

SNP spokesmen have repeatedly emphasised their belief that

Scotland and England should have different currencies — a pound Scots and a pound sterling. From the SNP's point of view, separate currencies with different parities are a natural development from Scottish independence. It would be difficult for a Scottish Government to pursue a separate policy if its currency were geared to that of another country and to the decisions of a central bank, like the Bank of England, over which a Scottish government would not have the slightest influence. They draw support for this argument by pointing to the Republic of Ireland: to all intents and purposes, the Irish pound is linked to the pound sterling, and Irish politicians will ruefully admit that their economy is largely dependent on that of the United Kingdom, and that anyone with any wealth in Ireland keeps a close eye on the London Stock Exchange.

To those who lack financial expertise, the land of milk and honey envisaged by the SNP can be alluring. On the strength of Scottish North Sea oil revenues and a better-managed Scottish economy — and freed from the 'gross incompetence' of an English Treasury — the pound Scots will become stronger and stronger than the pound sterling, we are told; as a desirable currency it will swiftly climb past the French and Belgian francs, the Dutch guilder and the Danish kroner, past the American dollar itself to join the Deutschemark and the Swiss franc. This is sheer fantasy. Apart from a host of other considerations, such as the costs of extracting the oil and the weakness of many traditional Scots industries, the hard fact is that much of the Scottish market for goods is south of the Border. The Scots would find in many spheres that they were competing with one hand behind their backs, since no one in England would buy dearer Scottish goods — for which they would have to pay more if the value of the pound Scots were higher than that of Sterling — when they could get their own country's goods more cheaply. Besides, there would be such resentment in England that it is hard to imagine any English Government letting the Scots get away with it. No one has stated the position more bluntly than Mr John Drummond, a Scot who is a director of Shell UK: 'The way I see it, it's like Gowon and Ojukwu in Nigeria — it's these people out there in the sticks trying to get their hands on the Feds' oil.' Perhaps the comparison with Nigeria appears to be grimly facetious. Certainly there are differences, such as the resentment which existed in many parts of Nigeria against the Ibo people, which so far at least has not been felt towards the Scots by the rest of the United Kingdom. Yet the Biafra comparison is more relevant than most people might care to admit.

In January 1977 an interesting row which had been brewing up for some months came to a climax. The Associated Scottish Life Offices complained bitterly about the SNP's proposals for requiring international and English companies to set up independent groupings in Scotland. The Scottish Life Offices control at least £3,000 million of assets in Scotland, and had indicated that since so much of their business was in England or abroad, they might have to consider emigrating. This prompted the accusation in the *Glasgow Herald* of 10 January 1977 from the Conservative MP Mr George Younger that the SNP were economic illiterates, who wanted to dress up in tartan the prosperous insurance industry, one of the best of its kind in the world, and make it become inward looking and parochial.

The SNP's economic policy so worried the Scottish clearing banks — the Bank of Scotland, the Royal Bank of Scotland, and the Clydesdale — that they set up a working party to examine it in 1976. One of their conclusions was that a separate Scottish monetary system would not be able to operate effectively without a Scottish discount market. Replying to the clearing banks, Douglas Crawford, MP, the SNP finance spokesman, said that serious currency mismatching between the Scottish and London banks could occur. He claimed that, as it is, Scottish banks in London use Scottish deposits to finance lending in London, and that after self-government there could well be a surplus of pounds Scots in Scotland. The aim of the SNP would be to use these resources to eradicate social deprivation in the West of Scotland, and to create long-term and rewarding jobs in Scotland. To put it mildly, this is simplistic economic thinking and presupposes a degree of economic and monetary control which would set off a major flight of capital from a separate Scotland. Certainly there is a need to tackle the pressing problems of social deprivation in the West of Scotland — and on Merseyside and in the West Midlands — but stringent control of capital along the lines suggested is an improbable way of achieving such an admirable objective.

The Scottish Trades Union Congress

No organisation has been more effective in promoting the cause of an Edinburgh Assembly than the Scottish Trades Union Congress. If ever a tail wagged an enormous dog, that tail was the caucus of the STUC General Council: never, to parody Churchill, did so few commit so many in so short a space of time to so much about which they knew so little.

The relationship between the British Trades Union Congress and the STUC is extremely vague. Both in theory and in fact, the STUC can work out its own policies on matters affecting Scotland. In the case of devolution, the STUC caucus has been able to put pressure on individual unions in Scotland to persuade their United Kingdom national committees to support the Government's devolution proposals; and because most English trade unions are ignorant about and indifferent towards the whole subject, it has been possible to persuade unions at a national level as well to take a sympathetic line on devolution. No national trade union leader wants to stir up unnecessary rows with sections of this own membership, least of all over a subject which seems to be at best marginal and peripheral to the main work of the union. Thus, for example, Jack Jones has made it clear that he has no intention of quarrelling with the pro-devolutionary views of his Scottish colleagues in the Transport and General Workers' Union — and certainly not with those of Alex Kitson, the National Officer of his union and a strong advocate of devolution.

On top of all this, most unions are very often in the throes of some hard-fought election for some post of consequence, the participants in which are extremely anxious not to antagonise particular powerful blocks within the union — one of which is 'the Scottish vote'.

The Scottish Trades Union Congress has always been well aware of both these factors, and has exploited them in order to exercise a disproportionate influence over the Trades Union Congress as a whole. Devolution has seldom been discussed in any detail by individual unions at the national level: most members have hitherto had no strong views on the subject, and little effort has been made to consult local officers, let alone the mass membership.

Only very occasionally have local officers been able to influence TUC thinking on the subject of devolution. At the instigation of Ernest Leslie, Edinburgh Divisional Officer of the Amalgamated Union of Engineering Workers, and David Graham, a convener of shop stewards for the union at ICI Grangemouth, the Edinburgh Divisional Committee of the AUEW passed a resolution instructing its National Committee to ask the Government to withdraw the Scotland and Wales Bill. Their action had a significant effect, since it provided welcome support to those Labour MPs who defied Government pressure and their party whips to vote against the Guillotine on 22 February. It gave the Labour rebels reason to think that receiving a resolution of this kind from the second largest Division in Scotland could indicate a change of AUEW policy at the next national conference, which in turn could help persuade the Labour Party to think again. Over 1 million AUEW votes against devolution at the next Labour Party Conference — plus those of the Electrical Trades Union; the Society of Graphical and Allied Trades; the Association of Scientific, Technical and Managerial Staffs; the Union of Construction, Allied Trades and Technicians; and of many other unions which have come out against devolution — would be more than welcome to anti-devolutionists. And since unions can change their views on matters that they consider fairly peripheral to their real interests at alarming speed, a number of other unions might then follow the AUEW into the anti-devolution camp.

No trade union has opposed devolution more doggedly than UCATT, the building workers' union. Many of its members migrate between England and Scotland in the course of their work, and could be adversely affected by devolution; its General Secretary, George Smith, is a Scot working in England who shares the view of his Scottish National Officer, Dan Crawford, that devolution could lead to the disintegration of the United Kingdom; and in Eric Heffer and Tom Urwin — two of the union's sponsored MPs — UCATT possesses two formidable adversaries of devolution.

How, then, has it been possible for the 'caucus' to exercise such a disproportionate influence in favour of devolution? To understand the reasons for this, we must take a look at the recent history of the STUC.

The one man who was responsible for bestowing considerable authority on the STUC was Harold Macmillan, when Prime Minister. Macmillan was always very concerned about unemployment, not least as a result of his pre-war experiences as the MP for Stockton-upon-Tees during the Depression, and was anxious to do something about Scottish unemployment, which was persistently higher than in some parts of England. As a result, he worked hard to bring the giant steel works to Motherwell, Ravenscraig, and the motor industry to Bathgate and Linwood. Ever the party politician, he made sure that such credit as went to the 'Scottish working class' went to the STUC and their doughty General Secretary, the late George Middleton — for whom he developed a personal regard — rather than to the Labour Party. Ever since then the STUC have made a practice of enjoying access to the Prime Minister of the day.

Governments — and particularly Labour Governments — have been quick to sound out the views of the STUC; perhaps the high point of their influence was reached on 27 February 1975, when Harold Wilson and half his Cabinet — including Edward Short, the Deputy Prime Minister, Michael Foot, Eric Varley, and William Ross, the Secretary of State for Scotland — travelled up to the Excelsior Hotel at Glasgow Airport to spend two days meeting and talking to them. (But, although it was promised that this would become an annual event, it seems unlikely that there will be a repetition, at least in the near future.)

An element of confusion in the Prime Minister's mind together with bad advice was responsible for the 1975 outing. Harold Wilson seemed to think that he was going to devote precious time to the Scottish equivalent of the Finance and General Purposes Committee of the TUC — a contact which he very rightly prized highly, setting enormous store on the work of the TUC Labour Party Liaison Committee, which was by then meeting regularly on the first Monday of each month.

Although it would be unfair to describe the STUC as a stage army, it is a far less impressive body than the Finance and General Purposes Committee. As far as its day-to-day workings are concerned, it is for all practical purposes run by its General Secretary, a group of Clydeside union leaders and one or two

leaders of the Scottish miners. A number of these men have —
quite honourably and openly — voted for the Communist
Party all their working lives; whether they should possess a
quite disproportionate influence over a party for which they
have never voted is open to question. The caucus of the STUC
cannot feel as concerned about the welfare of the Labour Party
or of a Labour Government as a Jack Jones or a David Basnett;
its members favour devolution in the belief that they could more
easily achieve some of their political objectives in a Scottish
rather than a British context, and are quite happy to exert
undue influence on the Labour Party to this end.

Whatever the reasons for the STUC's favouring devolution,
it has provided Government Ministers with a convenient
weapon with which to fight those who oppose it; the fact that
— for example — the Scottish CBI opposes it can be met with
claims (albeit rather slender ones) that the trade unions are all
in favour. Nor should one underestimate the very natural desire
of Labour Ministers to give way to the unions on any matter
that does not appear to involve an immediate increase in public
expenditure, the concession of large wage demands or passionate
feelings on the part of the members of other unions. As we have
seen, devolution is unlikely to rank very highly among a Scottish
trade unionist's list of priorities, let alone among those of his
English colleagues (and the indifference, even apathy, of the
average Englishman towards devolution is something that the
government and pro-devolutionists have always been eager to
capitalise on, in the hope that the English will only realise
what's happened when it's too late to do anything about it);
supporters of devolution like to point to TUC resolutions in
favour of establishing an Assembly in Edinburgh, and the
Government has had no compunction about doing so; yet, as
Eric Heffer pointed out in the Commons last May, they were
rather less eager to take notice of union resolutions criticising
their economic policy, even though such resolutions would have
been preceded — unlike those concerning devolution — by
lengthy and well-attended debates. 'Why are they being so
selective over the question of devolution?' he asked.

Nor should it be forgotten that Conference resolutions —
whether at Labour Party or TUC Conferences — are inevitably
decided by a few men at the top of their respective organisations.

When people claim that the trade union movement in Scotland is in favour of devolution, they forget that the hundreds of full-time union officials who engage in day-to-day negotiations over pay, conditions and employment opportunities in the main do not believe that an Assembly at Edinburgh would help their members in any way.

10

The Pressure Groups: II

'The devo-traitors', screeched the *Scottish Daily Express* — which for the last two years has been printed and largely sub-edited in Manchester — after forty-three Labour MPs had stuck to their guns and denied the Government their Guillotine motion on the Scotland and Wales Bill. As one of those MPs, I have been lampooned as a traitor in the *Sunday Mail* — the Scottish equivalent of the *Sunday Mirror* — for opposing devolution on the grounds that it would not be in the best interests of the people of Scotland. Even the BBC in Scotland muttered darkly about the 'sabotage' of the Bill.

The media in Scotland have always been in the vanguard of those who favour devolution: not only do they claim to reflect public opinion, but they are — with one or two exceptions — strongly in favour of a Scottish Assembly and even a separate Scottish state.

The enthusiasm of the media for devolution can be explained very simply. The media thrive on news; and devolution is eminently newsworthy. Devolutionary moves make far better copy than the retention of the *status quo*; it is far easier and more enjoyable to write ferocious leading articles about the raw deal Scotland has received from London and slick, simplistic headlines about Scotland's oil than to discuss the less colourful and often extremely complicated issue of how Scotland can be better governed within the *status quo*.

The Press

One of the major problem with the press — at least as far as

opponents of devolution are concerned — is that because devolution is newsworthy, politicians and political commentators
south of the Border have tended to pay far more attention to
those newspapers which support it than to those which oppose
it: a situation that is aggravated by the fact that, despite its
extremely modest circulation, the fiercely pro-devolution
Scotsman is considered by many people in London to be the
most balanced, sensible and prestigious of Scotland's newspapers. In fact — as we shall see — Scotland's other three
'heavy' newspapers (the *Aberdeen Press and Journal,* the *Dundee
Courier* and the *Glasgow Herald*) do not share the *Scotsman's*
missionary zeal; and, like them, the *Sunday Post* — easily the
most widely read newspaper in Scotland — has given a pretty
balanced account of the arguments on both sides. But we will
begin by taking a look at those papers which have supported
devolution.

Ironically enough, the Scottish *Daily Express* and *Sunday
Express* have become far more stridently nationalistic since it
was decided that they should be printed in Manchester rather
than Glasgow. This may be to some extent a natural development following on from the much-publicised closure of the
Express's Albion Street plant in Glasgow, and the still more
widely publicised attempt by Robert Maxwell, Tony Benn and
Allister Mackie and the workers' co-operative to get the short-
lived *Scottish Daily News* off the ground. Less charitably, it's
quite possible that the *Express* believes that voicing fiercely
nationalistic views may be one way of preventing its circulation
from dropping any further, at least in Scotland. Of course a
newspaper has the right to express whatever views it likes: what
is objectionable about the *Express* is that it has led the way in
reducing the whole devolution argument to a matter of slogans
and counter-slogans. The slick catchword has become a substitute for thought.

The *Daily Record* is a very different kettle of fish. Not even
those who disagree with its views would deny that it has given
serious thought to the matter. The *Record* has established itself
in the honourable tradition of crusading newspapers over the
last decade, and its talented staff — some of whom are English
— have devoted their considerable skills to demanding a greater
say for Scotland. However, the *Record* claims that it does not

favour a separate Scottish state — nor is it prepared to concede
that this would, in fact, prove inevitable if the maximalist kind
of devolution for which it argues came into effect.

The basic snag about the degree of devolution demanded by
the *Record* is that it would never be acceptable in England —
evidence of which is provided by the very different line taken
by the *Record*'s sister paper, the *Daily Mirror*. It is instructive to
compare the editorials in the two papers on the morning
following the publication of the Government's White Paper,
Our Changing Democracy, on 27 November 1975. 'We were
PROMISED more now. We want more', screeched the *Record*
in two-inch type:

> because, Harold, your deal is just not good enough. It isn't
> enough. Not nearly enough. Scotland expected more.
> We want more. That is the Record verdict on the Govern-
> ment's much trumpeted White Paper on devolution, titled,
> "Our Changing Democracy" ... Let us state again, the
> Record does not preach separatism. Keep it Great Britain!
> But the Scottish people will still feel badly let-down. The
> sense of grave disappointment comes when we consider the
> proposed Assembly will be a body — without real economic
> powers, without real industrial powers, without real money
> raising powers — so where will the Assembly have power of
> its own? It sounds an imposing list — roads, transport,
> education, local government, health, social services, hous-
> ing. But these were all taken for granted. These could
> hardly have been refused. These do not give the Assembly
> teeth. UNLESS WE ARE TALKING ABOUT MILK-TEETH? ...
> Why shouldn't we keep some of Scotland's wealth
> generated in Scotland? HOW ABOUT WHISKY? Last year,
> all these nips and halves contributed £300 million to the
> Exchequer. Surely we could have a slice of that lot?
> Oh Yes, and the Oil, Of course it's Britain's oil. BUT WOULD
> IT REALLY BE GREEDY FOR SCOTLAND TO GET £1 from every
> barrel landed here?

Not surprisingly, the *Mirror*'s editorial took a very different
line:

> It's the least that could be offered and also the most —

that's the Mirror's verdict on the Government's plan to give more self-rule to Scotland and Wales ... To offer more would risk the break-up of the United Kingdom ... The Scots and Welsh won't have their own Army or Navy. Nor their own tax system. Nor control of economic policy. On one point the Government plan is rightly firm; North Sea oil belongs to Britain. It is not Scotland's private property. The oil is British oil, just as English coal and natural gas are British.

When I asked Geoffrey Goodman of the International Publishing Corporation how he could justify such diametrically opposed views within his publishing group, he blandly spoke about the virtues of editorial freedom. Fair enough: but it's hard to see why the Government should pay more attention to the views of the *Record* (cuttings from which are always being thrust into the in-trays of Ministers involved in the arguments over devolution) than to those of the *Mirror*.

If the *Record* has been a godsend to devolutionists on account of its wide circulation, the *Scotsman* has provided 'heavyweight' respectability and a rather misleading reputation as 'Scotland's national newspaper'. For many years now, the *Scotsman* has had a sober and level-headed reputation, and it's hardly surprising that politicians and civil servants in London should have assumed that its views represent those of Scotland as a whole. The truth of the matter is that the *Scotsman* sells only 70,000-odd copies a day — and those mostly in the Edinburgh area — and is probably relatively rather less influential in Scotland itself than in London government offices.

There are several reasons why the *Scotsman* has campaigned for devolution of the most extreme kind, as well as federalism and — occasionally — outright nationalism. In the first place, it is an Edinburgh paper, and as such it is not widely read in Scotland beyond the Lothians, South Fife and the Borders. An Assembly would, of course, be based in Edinburgh, so it's hardly surprising that the *Scotsman* should feel more enthusiastic about its establishment there than the *Glasgow Herald*, the *Dundee Courier* or the *Aberdeen Press and Journal*.

A second reason can be found in the paper's recent history. In the late 1950s, after the scholarly editorship of the late J.

Murray Watson, the *Scotsman* — then under the rather difficult ownership of the late Sir Edmund Findlay — found itself in something of a rut. In 1955, the paper was bought up by Roy Thomson — the first of the many British papers he was to acquire. The *Scotsman* was, for a time, Thomson's pride and joy. People in Edinburgh either liked Thomson, as I did, or they disapproved of him as a brash vulgarian; no one could deny that his acquisition of the *Scotsman* made it a more lively paper.

As is well known, Thomson then acquired Scottish Television (which — in a celebrated phrase — he described as a 'licence to print money'), before leaving Edinburgh for London, where he bought up *The Times* and the *Sunday Times*, as well as a host of provincial papers.

Not surprisingly, the *Scotsman* no longer enjoyed such a central place in Thomson's life after his move south; and its staff would have been more than human had they not resented this — and the fact that they received substantially lower salaries than their colleagues on Thomson papers in London. Thomson was, of course, well known for allowing his editors complete editorial freedom, provided their papers remained in the black, and he bothered not that the *Scotsman* was becoming increasingly sympathetic to devolutionist — and even separatist — ideas.

Throughout Alastair Dunnett's editorship from 1955 to 1972, the paper was broadly sympathetic towards devolution, but its editorial attitudes remained balanced. Mr Dunnett now looks after some of the Thomson Group's North Sea oil interests, and was rather more sceptical about the merits of the Government's Scotland and Wales Bill. His successor, Eric Mackay, makes no attempt to conceal his sympathy for maximum devolution and for views which border on outright separatism. For Mr Mackay devolution is a 'Cause', and it is quite honourable for editors to crusade in causes. Needless to say, the staff of the *Scotsman* includes many active members of the SNP and a brace of SNP parliamentary candidates.

Because, as we have seen, devolution is eminently newsworthy, and because the *Scotsman* carries far more weight outside Scotland than any other Scottish newspaper, pro-devolutionary views originating in the *Scotsman*'s offices become diffused throughout the world. Earnest German colleagues in the European Parliament often ask me about reports in the German newspapers that Scotland is going to become an independent state: one then discovers that a German journalist has visited the *Scotsman* office, or that an article by one of its talented writers — such as Neal Ascherson — has been syndicated in the German press.

The *Glasgow Herald*, on the other hand, has taken a far more moderate line towards devolution. There are several reasons for this. As we have seen, an Assembly would be based in Edinburgh rather than Glasgow, and neither the *Glasgow Herald*'s 90,000-odd readers — 98 per cent of whom live west of Falkirk — nor its journalists have the same immediate interest in its establishment.

Second, the *Herald* is part of the George Outram Group of newspapers, which came under the control of the Fraser group in the early 1970s. Owners, editors and staff have jealously retained the principle of editorial independence, in a style which is entirely to their credit.

Finally, the *Glasgow Herald* is — not surprisingly — far more attuned to the commercial interests of the community than the *Scotsman*, in much the same way as the *Financial Times* is in England. The *Herald*'s business editors have been extremely aware of the opposition of the business community to devolution (including the Glasgow Chamber of Commerce under the chairmanship of John Risk) and the paper very much reflects the views of this important segment of its readership.

The *Aberdeen Press and Journal* reflects the scepticism of the Grampian region towards devolution; Aberdeen has benefited enormously from North Sea oil, and has become a cosmopolitan oil capital in its own right, with little desire to show allegiance to Edinburgh. Similarly, the *Dundee Courier*, with saturation coverage of the Tay estuary and a larger circulation than the *Scotsman*, recognises no fealty to a possible Edinburgh government.

Local papers may well be as influential as national papers, and the fact that in eastern Scotland the anti-devolution case has had such a good hearing is due to the fairness shown by the owners and editors of the important Johnston and Outram groups. In the north-west, the radical and anti-devolutionist *West Highland Free Press* — for some years brilliantly edited by

Brian Wilson — gave space to the kind of controversy on which the Highlands thrive.

The Broadcasters

Like the *Scotsman*, BBC Scotland has shown a growing antipathy to London: whereas Scottish Television has been very balanced in its approach, BBC Scotland appears to have leant over backwards to emphasise its Scottishness.

THE BBC

Visiting Edinburgh to gather evidence for their report on the future of broadcasting, some members of the Annan Committee were rather taken aback by their experiences. A number of organisations, including the BBC, submitted evidence asking for a much greater degree of independence for broadcasting in Scotland; yet later, in private, some of those who had represented these organisations confessed that independence could be a disaster. And they were not just thinking about the calculation by John Gray, head of the BBC in Edinburgh, that if Scotland were to have its own BBC television service while maintaining the existing output of United Kingdom national network programmes, a television licence in Scotland would cost at least £120 a year: hardly a popular possibility, or vote-catcher for separatist MPs!

The situation at the BBC is complicated further by the fact that the head of BBC Scotland, Alistair Hetherington, returned to Scotland in 1975 after editing the *Guardian* in London for twenty distinguished years, full of missionary zeal to change BBC Scotland and make it more independent of London than it had been hitherto. The BBC's political producer, Matthew Spicer, and political correspondent, James Cox, are first-class professionals, who always endeavour to give all sides a full hearing.

SCOTTISH TELEVISION

Scottish Television (STV) has taken a far cooler attitude towards devolution. This is partly because senior management there has a shrewd suspicion that the whole subject bores most viewers rigid; and those in charge at STV tend to be home-grown professionals, such as Colin Mackay, with few of the messianic tendencies that afflict returned Scots or expatriate Englishmen working for the BBC. Furthermore, the relationship between STV and the Independent Television Authority in London is far less close and — as a result, no doubt — more harmonious than that between the BBC in Glasgow and Broadcasting House. Sad to say, it has proved all too easy to assume that a greater degree of local independence in broadcasting would benefit from political devolution, and to confuse two very different issues.

COMMERCIAL RADIO

Personalities are always enormously important when it comes to an issue such as devolution. Radio Clyde, with up to 1 million listeners, is one of the most successful commercial radio stations in Britain, and its boss is Jimmy Gordon, who has been a Labour candidate and STV's much-respected political commentator. Gordon is a man of stature who takes politics seriously and makes sure that all parties are given the opportunity to ventilate their views over the air in the political discussions chaired by Donald Dewar, a former Labour MP for Aberdeen South and an important supporter of devolution within his party.

The standard of political debate is equally high on Radio Forth, which is based on Edinburgh and has an audience of up to $\frac{1}{2}$ million. Radio Forth is run by Tom Steel, the son of a former Labour MP and an ex-Lobby Correspondent at Westminster. Like Jimmy Gordon, he has always made sure that the case against devolution gets a fair hearing — thus helping to offset the generally pro-devolution views expressed by the BBC.

Education

The Scots have always been justifiably proud of their educational system and of the respect which — at least until recently — has been accorded to education in Scotland. As early as the fifteenth century, Scotland could boast four universities — Edinburgh, St Andrews, Aberdeen and Glasgow — as against England's two.

Scotland's universities fall within the scope of the University

Grants Committee, which itself is the responsibility of the Department of Education and Science in London. Scottish schools, on the other hand, are controlled by the Scottish Education Department, which is responsible to the Secretary of State for Scotland rather than the Ministry of Education in London. The Scottish Education Department is also responsible for teacher-training colleges, technical colleges and other institutes of higher education.

The educational aspects of devolution have been more widely debated and studied than any other. This is hardly surprising, since academics are used to discussing ideas in the abstract, while trade unionists or businessmen are too busy coping with day-to-day matters to devote that much attention to matters that are not of immediate and urgent interest.

THE UNIVERSITIES

Under the Government's most recent devolution Bill, responsibility for the Scottish universities was to remain in London: but it may well be that the decision to retain the *status quo* was more a matter of political tactics — and pressure from Scottish academics — than of the highest conviction. For some politicians the universities are expendable in that it is quite possible that once the Assembly had come into being control of the universities could be granted to it simply in order to pacify separatist elements.

Back in 1974, the Scottish vice-chancellors rejected completely any suggestions that university education should be devolved or a separate Scottish University Grants Committee established. They have reaffirmed their position since then, and have received the support of the full British Vice-Chancellors' Committee.

The vice-chancellors maintain that the University Grants Committee has always acted as a highly effective buffer between the universities and the Government of the day, preventing the idiosyncratic views of a particular Government — or changes in Government — from having an unsettling effect on academic programmes. There is a great deal of truth in this: but it could reasonably be asked whether a specifically Scottish University Grants Committee could not perform a similar role equally well. The short answer is that an Assembly which was only just down the road from Edinburgh University, and within easy reach of the Universities of Glasgow, Strathclyde, Heriot-Watt, Stirling, St Andrews and Dundee would be far too close for comfort. One might well ask why London University should not feel itself to be imperilled by the proximity of Westminster: but the House of Commons has far less interest in meddling than an Assembly for whom control of the universities would be 'the brightest jewel in their crown'. The Scottish vice-chancellors fear that the Assembly would always be trying to find out how they were spending or mis-spending their finances: petty animosities and disagreements might well lead to reprisals, which would endanger academic freedom and initiative. Sustained political interference and a measure of economic control could lead to academic manipulation.

The dire effects of all this for research were suggested in graphic, if slightly exaggerated, terms in a letter written to me shortly before he died by the late Professor C. H. Waddington, FRS, of Edinburgh University, one of the fathers of modern genetics:

Someone may want to ask me, what do I think about Devolution, if it meant transferring the responsibility for University or Research Council financial support of my Department from London to Edinburgh?

(i) I am not a bit afraid of control on the basis of producing results of practical value. My lab has provided the Directors of both the ARC's [Advisory Committee on Research Councils] Poultry Research Institute and Animal Breeding Research Organisation; and we have a good claim to have been the most important influence on the development of the poultry (broiler and egg-producing) and turkey industries in this country through informal 'Round Tables' and operational research consultancies which would not have been feasible in Whitehall-controlled operations with direct governmental financing.

(ii) What I should be scared of is *any* controlling agency (St Andrew's House or Whitehall) sitting just outside my doorstep. If you try to build up a Department to something in the top class, the only hope is to do it where no one will notice it (e.g. north of the Border) otherwise somebody will quickly realise that you are getting too big for your boots and *stop it*. It has also been possible to do it in places like Cambridge, with backing from a sufficiently prestigeful Great Man, but even then only *outwith* the University. I am afraid I would prefer my funds to come from administrators as far away as possible — Brussels rather than London — and certainly *not* from people just up the street, who can drop in at any moment, and ask why I should be claiming so much more than the neighbour in Morningside they'd been having dinner with last weekend.

Sir Fred Stewart, Professor of Geology at Edinburgh and Chairman of the United Kingdom Advisory Committee on Research Councils, has expressed fears that the whole structure of academic research in the United Kingdom could be adversely affected if the Scottish universities were divorced from current research proceedings in the rest of Britain. The vice-chancellors also fear that if responsibility for higher academic as well as general education is transferred to the Scottish Assembly, that body or its education committee would not necessarily be ready to support the needs of the universities and university research against the demands of other areas of education in Scotland, which would be competing with the universities for scarce educational funds; and that there is no reason why an Assembly which had control of the Scottish universities should not run them down on account of their allegedly privileged status and past treatment. If they remained in the British context, the Scottish universities would retain the support of other universities in order to combat such moves by a national government; in a local Scottish context, they might well find themselves in a minority, with very scanty support from other educational institutions.

The vice-chancellors also fear that devolution of university education would create two separate and perhaps increasingly divergent university educational systems within the boundaries of the United Kingdom, with the result that the movement of students between different parts of the country would decline. The Scottish National Party have transformed this into a highly sensitive issue by harping on the alleged iniquity of school-leavers from south of the Border taking up places at Scottish universities, which they feel should have been reserved for Scots boys and girls, even though in many cases they were less well qualified than their English contemporaries. Once places are awarded on the basis of which part of the United Kingdom one was born or reared in, rather than by academic merit or promise, a unitary university system becomes quite impossible. It would be all the more intolerable in the current situation, since Scotland, with 10 per cent of the United Kingdom population, has 15 per cent of the student population, and Scottish universities received 15 per cent of the total finance available to universities in the United Kingdom. If there were to be discrimination against applicants, because they came from south of Hadrian's Wall, the advantage that Scotland has at present in terms of the total British tax-payer's expenditure on university education might well come under review.

If divergent university systems would restrict the mobility of students, and lead to parochialism, the effect on their staff would be even more serious. What non-Scottish member of staff at a United Kingdom university is going to be persuaded to join a smaller and different system, one-sixth of the size of that to which he is accustomed, and from which he might not easily achieve promotion to another system? It is altogether far too facile and simplistic to cite American or Continental universities, or to suggest that all the world can be the oyster of Scottish university academics. Permanent posts at American or European universities go to very few non-nationals. Even in times like these when academic jobs are scarce, and when proverbial beggars cannot be choosers, applicants of quality would reflect before opting for a job in one of the smaller Scottish universities. So long as indecision and doubt hang like a pall over the future of the Scottish universities, they will find it more difficult to attract teachers of calibre from all over Britain in the manner to which they have been used, and from which they have greatly benefited. An ugly foretaste of what could happen was provided when the late Professor Tom Cotterell, FRS, Principal of Stirling University, died prematurely and tragically. 'Why could they not appoint a Scot?' was heard from many quarters. In fact, the university did appoint a distinguished Scot, but he had, in his last post, been building up the Medical School at the University of Leicester, and had not

been working in Scotland. The moment that it seems that preference is being given to Scottish staff because they are Scots,
rather than because they are the best-qualified candidates for
the job in hand, a counter-reaction will set in. If English men
and women find that they are discriminated against in the
Scottish universities, questions will no doubt be asked, albeit
reluctantly at first, about the position of many hundreds of Scots
now working in English universities. Many academics and
others would be dismayed if they felt that this is what Britain
in the mid-twentieth century had come to.

While devolutionists might contend that things would only
come to such a sorry pass were there to be a separate Scottish
state, the reality may be that the same ill-effects would occur as
soon as the Scottish universities became responsible to an
Assembly. Hitherto, government Ministers have understood
this, and have said that they will resist change in the university
framework; on the other hand, if ever those calling for more
powers for the Assembly and stronger devolution measures get
their way, one has the distinct impression that responsibility
for the Scottish universities could become a negotiable subject,
if not even a pawn in the political argument.

The Association of University Teachers has been quite as
strongly against any change in the *status quo* as the vice-chancellors. On 8 February 1975, their Executive passed the following motion with one abstention, and the Association has not
altered its policy since:

We feel that it would not be appropriate for the AUT(S)
to comment upon the general political issue of devolution.
We are, however, concerned to safeguard fully the aims and
interests of the Scottish Universities and their staffs and
their students. In particular we feel that it is essential that
university autonomy and standards be maintained in such
matters as teaching and research, the admission of students,
the use of finance, and the appointment of staff, and that
there continues to be unhindered interchange of staff and
students within the United Kingdom.

We recognise that certain forms of devolution may continue to safeguard these aims and interests but in the
present state of our knowledge we believe that these will be

best preserved under the continued guidance of the United Kingdom UGC and the present relationship with the Research Councils.

A survey carried out in February 1975 by the Secretary of the Edinburgh branch of the Association of University Teachers showed that out of 398 members of staff questioned, 291 were strongly for the *status quo*, and 22 weakly for the *status quo*; 2 were indifferent, 13 were weakly for devolution, and 64 strongly for devolution. I am told that these latter 64, in favour of devolution, were strongly weighted towards departments of Politics, Sociology/Social Sciences and Scottish Studies. The only heavyweight academic to come out strongly for devolution is the Reverend Professor Dr John McIntyre, DD, of the Department of Theology at Edinburgh. It is significant that hardly any, if indeed any at all, of the senior scientists have come out in favour of a Scottish Assembly, and indeed most of them are ardently against such a move. In January 1975, after a fairly extensive discussion, the Senate of the University of Glasgow voted by 86 votes to 6 votes in favour of retaining the existing relationship with the University Grants Committee. There has been no indication that this view has weakened; on the contrary: by all accounts, it has strengthened.

THE SCHOOLS

Scotland has always retained her own educational system, and over the centuries Scottish schools have come to be highly regarded — though it must be admitted that this has more to do with the good start in life it provides for the talented pupil, the 'lad o' pairts', than with any special achievements as far as the average pupil is concerned. Universal education was introduced in 1872, two years later than in England.

Scottish education in the larger communities has been based on a system of senior secondary schools, equivalent to English grammar schools, and junior secondary schools, the equivalent to English secondary modern schools. In smaller towns and rural communities, the all-purpose academy often provided its pupils with an excellent education. Over the last two decades, senior and junior secondary schools have been successfully merged into comprehensives under the supervision of the

Scottish Education Department — which, as we have seen, is responsible to the Secretary of State for Scotland rather than the Ministry of Education in London.

The professional teaching associations in Scotland — the Educational Institute of Scotland, the Scottish Schoolmasters' Association, the Scottish Secondary Teachers' Association — have varied in their attitudes towards devolution, and it would be hard to draw any firm conclusions. Many of their members, however, are firm supporters of the SNP — particularly women teaching in primary schools. Many teachers tend to be sympathetic to 'radical' or 'left-wing' political parties anyway, and now that the Labour Party has become the party of Government, supporting a nationalist party in order to knock the Establishment may well be preferable in Scotland and Wales to supporting the International Socialists or the Communist Party: and support for the SNP may well have more to do with this sense of protest or such diverse cultural activities as Scottish country dancing than with any anxiety to see a separate Scottish state established.

Teachers in general appear to favour the Scottish universities coming under the control of the Assembly along with the schools, though it is hard to believe that they would be unduly upset if the universities successfully resisted such a move — or, indeed, if the Assembly never came into being.

Recently, however, a number of teachers' leaders have begun to realise that their members could be worse, rather than better off under an Assembly. The English would be far more vigilant about making sure that the Scots did not get more than their fair share of the cake, and the *per capita* share of public funds allocated to Scotland would almost certainly be lower than at present. The chances are that Glasgow Assemblymen demanding more houses would carry more weight in the Assembly than the teachers' lobby, and that the share of the block grant set aside for education — and for teachers' salaries — would be rather less than it is at present.

The Legal System

As we have seen, Scotland has a separate legal system. Scots Law, more akin to Roman Law than Anglo-Saxon Law, was given full recognition in the Act of Union. The Scottish judges, the Scottish Bar and Edinburgh legal society have a life of their own which chiefly impinges on the London court system in annual golf matches against the Temple Benchers.

As in every other country, Scottish lawyers are by no means immune from the very understandable desire to combine practice of the law with a political career. Now, an English-trained lawyer who is also an MP can get himself a position in London or, for example, become a recorder for one of the areas of England from which there is reasonably easy access to and from London. Not only does distance from Westminster make it difficult for a Scots MP to practise at the Bar in Edinburgh, even on an occasional basis; he is trained in a different system of Law, and cannot take on occasional work in London chambers. A seat in a Royal High School Assembly would tie in nicely with a legal practice in Parliament Square, Edinburgh. Understandably, and not dishonourably, a number of Scottish barristers have personal reasons for welcoming the idea of an Assembly in Edinburgh.

Quite apart from this, many barristers and others connected with the courts have become impatient with Westminster over a number of years on account of Parliament's failure to tackle various problems and areas of legislation, which they feel ought to have received more attention than they have. For example, only in 1976 was the vexed problem of changing the Scottish marriage and licensing laws legislated upon; the fact that it has been more difficult to obtain a divorce in Scotland than in England, and Sunday Drinking Hours Regulations, have been fruitful sources of controversy in Scottish politics for years past. A substantial number of practising lawyers were strongly in favour of reform, as a result of their every-day experience: those politicians who were against reforming the divorce laws and the licensing laws tended to be a little shy about arguing their case, for they were conscious that they might then be thought pre-judiced or reactionary, and so, rather than get involved in arguments, they tended to shrug their shoulders and claim that the desired reforms could not take place as a result of 'lack of Parliamentary time' for Scottish measures in the House of Commons. This was an excuse, not a reason, for failing to carry legislation which they did not want to see carried: but the fact that it was given simply served to inflame those lawyers who were strongly in favour of reform against the Westminster set-up. In fact, the spleen of the reformers would have been better ventilated against Willie Ross, the Scottish Secretary of State, and other Ministers and MPs who did not want to see these reforms made, than against the Westminster system itself.

If we add to dissatisfactions of this kind the understandable fact that many barristers are keen to see alterations and new developments in Scottish Law, it is not difficult to see how a powerful head of steam has been built up at the Scottish Bar in favour of an Assembly.

Not surprisingly, however, Scottish solicitors are far less in favour of an Assembly. They do not feel that they are as likely to benefit personally from devolution, and they are appalled at the thought of more laws being churned out, over and above those already in existence — all of which will add to an already grievous burden of work.

The administration of justice in Scotland at present is integrated; it is regulated and controlled by the court system itself and is free from Executive interference. The Scottish Judges have formally — and unanimously — declared that they want to keep it that way. They say that the power to make fundamental innovations in matters concerning the powers, jurisdiction and procedure of the courts, in any way which might disturb the broad relationship of these courts to one another and their relative standing as courts of the United Kingdom, should not be confided to a subordinate authority with responsibility for only one of the sources of the law which the courts will administer. The Scottish judges point out that this would in no way derogate from the powers of an Assembly to legislate on substantive law in devolved fields. They are critical of suggestions emanating from various sources, including government law officers, that some, if not many, of these powers of the court should be transferred to an Assembly, or to a member of the Assembly Executive or Cabinet. Were the Assembly Minister a law officer or a layman, such a move could be destructive of a system which has stood the test of time, and has kept the law virtually free and independent of the executive branch of government.

The second matter on which the Scottish judges have

strong views is the relationship or *vires* between the courts, the Assembly, and the Westminster Parliament. As this is a complex, if very important matter, I quote from the speech in the House of Lords of 27 January 1976, when the Lord Justice Clerk, Lord Wheatley, spelled out the unanimous and agreed view of the Scottish judges:

The idea that the ultimate decision on a matter of *vires* should rest with a Minister of the Crown is one that offends what we regard as all constitutional propriety.

In spite of the checks proposed while any Bill is going through the Assembly to satisfy the Assembly about its *vires*, and whatever checks may thereafter be made by a Minister of the Crown, there may be cases, even if they occur rarely, where the Assembly Acts exceed, at least in certain of their provisions, the powers devolved by the devolution Statute, or where conflict emerges between the provisions of the United Kingdom Statutes and Assembly Acts. It would seem contrary to sound constitutional principle and, one would think, wise public policy, that any person entitled to invoke the jurisdiction of the courts whose rights are affected by provisions which, *ex hypothesi*, are *ultra vires*, should be denied the protection of the courts. To admit the right of challenge would have the clear advantage of securing respect for the constitutional arrangements embodied in the devolution Statute, and may result in the development and acknowledgment of a body of principles governing the boundaries of the respective competences of Parliament and the Assembly.

Let me deal with two arguments levelled against this. The first is simply the question that *vires* being decided by a Minister would produce finality and not hamper good government. I think that what was said by my noble and learned friend Lord Kilbrandon was that maintenance and oversight of a judicial system in constitutional terms should be a function of the sovereign power, and that power after devolution will still be the Queen in Parliament. To give that function to a delegated body with limited powers which do not embrace the wide spectrum of the work of the courts would not only offend against that principle but might well lower, or appear to lower, the status of our courts in comparison with comparable courts in England. From the practical angle, the judicial system of Scotland must continue to be, in terms of structure, inter-related jurisdiction and procedures, both suitable for and capable of discharging the whole responsibilities of the system; that is, the administration of the whole law applicable to Scotland, which will consist, as I have said, of United Kingdom law, our common law, Community law and Acts of the Assembly in the devolved fields.

The court system in Scotland at each of its levels, and the jurisdictional and procedural relationship between the courts of different levels, can be considered properly only in the context of the totality of the functions it must discharge. The Court of Session (that is, the High Court judges), by acts of sederunt, prescribes the procedure for civil causes of all kinds in the Court of Session and in the sheriff court. The High Court of Justiciary (that is, the High Court judges), by acts of adjournal, regulates for all the criminal courts of Scotland on all matters of procedure not otherwise prescribed by Statute. In their capacity as judges of appeal these same High Court judges have constantly under review the work of all the courts in Scotland. They are accordingly, I would suggest, in the best position to see the work of all the courts in to see whether procedural changes are necessary [Hansard, 27 January 1976].

THE LAW COMMISSION

On 29 June 1976, the Scottish Law Commission, a high-powered Standing Committee under Lord Hunter, which was reviewing the Law of Scotland, published their memorandum on the White Paper *Our Changing Democracy*, on the assumption that there was going to be an Assembly. While welcoming the proposal that most aspects of private and criminal law should be devolved, the Commission regretted the many vague exceptions which remained in the Scotland and Wales Bill. For example, it was proposed that Westminster and Whitehall should retain control of most of the commercial and mercantile law of Scotland, and matters relating to 'law and order' and 'law enforcement' in the field of criminal law. As the House of Commons was subsequently to discover during the attempted passage of the Scotland and Wales Bill, it never made clear how much of the criminal law was to be devolved, how much was to be left to the courts, and how much to Westminster. Indeed, this was one of the many rocks upon which the Bill eventually foundered. The general suggestion of the Law Commission was that matters concerning state security should be reserved to the United Kingdom Parliament, while local maintenance of law and order and consequential criminal law and legal proceedings should be devolved to the Assembly. 'There is a difference', the Commission claimed, 'between providing for the defence of the institutions of the state against attack by organised groups of terrorists, and arranging for the arrest of a person, drunk and incapable, on a Saturday night.'

The Law Commission says that there is a strong case for the Minister in charge of law enforcement being responsible to the Assembly. On the other hand, both the White Paper and the Scotland and Wales Bill envisaged the Secretary of State for Scotland retaining powers over the police, and being responsible for answering questions arising from police matters in the Westminster Parliament. Yet whatever the Law Commission's learned opinion may be on this point, the kind of situation which could develop if a law Minister were responsible to a Stormont-like Assembly, and not to the United Kingdom Parliament, is absolute anathema to many Scots who are aware of developments in Ulster. If, as the Law Commission hopes, law enforcement is devolved, then responsibility for the Public Prosecutor and the procurator fiscal service — the equivalent of the magistrates' system in England — would have to be invested in the Assembly. So also would responsibility for the administration of the Scottish courts as a whole, including administrative tribunals.

The Law Commission has registered disapproval of the suggestion that dual membership of the Assembly and other bodies, such as Westminster or Regional authorities, should be possible: and since a number of MPs have indicated to the press that they would like to stand for the Assembly while retaining their Westminster seats, this could present a very real problem.

The Law Commission observes that dual membership could lead to real conflicts of constitutional responsibility in the all-too-likely situation of there being disagreement between Westminster and a Scottish Assembly.

Farmers

The views of Scottish farmers on devolution can be expressed quite simply. They are appalled at the extra expense and administrative work that it would involve; and they are extremely worried about responsibility for agriculture being divided between Edinburgh and Westminster, particularly as far as the Colleges of Agriculture are concerned.

As far back as January 1975, a unanimous decision was taken at the annual meeting of the Ayrshire branch of the National Farmers' Union — the second largest in Scotland, which includes, ironically enough, the constituencies of Jim Sillars of the Scottish Labour Party and the ardent devolutionist David Lambie — rejecting devolution as 'too costly'. Among those who spoke at the meeting was John Caldwell, from Kilmarnock, which is in ex-Secretary of State William Ross's constituency: many farmers fear that the post of Secretary of State would eventually be abolished following the establishment of an Assembly, and that the interests of Scottish hill-farmers and those who farm what is, by English standards, somewhat marginal land would no longer be represented in London.

The official NFU position is that agriculture in its broadest sense must remain the responsibility of Westminster. They dread the creation of grey, borderline areas of undefined responsibility, and the uncertainties which the collapse of the present arrangements would inevitably cause. The Council of the Scottish Colleges of Agriculture is particularly anxious to retain the present integrated system of teaching, advisory and investigative work, which has stood the test of time and is, they claim, eminently suited to the structure and needs of Scottish agriculture.

The Scottish NFU is broadly representative of the farming community in Scotland. Its own anxieties are very much reflected by particular branches of the industry. Take, for example, the large-scale arable farmers who specialise in growing seed potatoes on the red soil of East Lothian, almost exclusively for the English market. They dread the possibility of this trade being hindered in any way. Much the same applies to the farmers of Berwickshire, Roxburgh, Selkirk, Dumfries and Kirkcudbright, many of whom have close working relations with a large, cross-Border co-operative known as West Cumberland Farmers.

The Milk Marketing Board and the Egg Marketing Board are also, in effect, large-scale co-operatives. As government bodies they cannot pronounce publicly on government policy in a field outside their own spheres of activity: however, they have made it clear in private that their whole complex operation would be hindered by devolution — particularly if the process eventually led to a variable rate of exchange between the pound Scots and the pound sterling.

Fishermen

Like the farmers, the trawler-owners foresee a brighter future for themselves if Scotland remains inside the United Kingdom, at a time when the industry is facing problems such as the Cod War with Iceland, the establishment of the 200-mile limit, and the overfishing of certain waters both by our EEC colleagues and by Eastern European countries. Ironically enough, on the very day that the White Paper *Our Changing Democracy* was published, the Scottish Trawler Owners' Federation successfully completed their amalgamation with the British Trawler Owners' Federation: and their main reason for doing so was a belief that Scottish fishermen would stand to benefit if their case was argued at Brussels along with that of their English colleagues — in much the same way as British trawlermen realised that they were more likely to obtain satisfaction in the negotiations with Iceland if they allowed the EEC Commissioner, Mr Gunderlach, to speak for the Community as a whole.

Medicine

Until recently, most of the medical profession in Scotland safely assumed that devolution would never get off the ground, and they need not bother themselves too much about it. Like their

English colleagues, their complaints have become rather more vocal over the past couple of decades or so — but these generally concern matters which are common to the profession on both sides of the Border.

Scottish junior doctors working in hospitals sometimes complain that they tend to earn less than their English colleagues: this results from better staffing levels in Scotland, so that although they may earn some £320 p.a. less than their English counterparts, they can console themselves with the fact that their average working week is some seven hours shorter. However, this has not prevented nationalist politicians from exploiting the pay differential.

Now that a Scottish Assembly has become a real possibility, doctors in Scotland are proving to be as hostile to devolution as Scottish academics. Like some of the more perceptive teachers, they are worried that their salaries might suffer: but what worries them even more is the possibility of the Assembly's setting up a Health Committee, which would then insist on taking over the responsibilities of the Regional Hospital Boards, and interfere to an unacceptable extent: to the disadvantage of the doctors and their patients.

In terms of staffing and provision, the Scottish Health Service compares favourably with that in many regions of England. Scottish health activities are largely centred on the concentrations of population in which the four medical schools — Edinburgh, Glasgow, Dundee and Aberdeen — play an important role in determining the pattern and quality of health care, training graduates whose numbers far exceed the medical services of Scotland. The Royal College of Physicians pointed out in an official submission to the Government in January 1976 that any change in the Scottish Health Service which could give rise to the product of peculiarly 'Scottish' qualifications would operate to the disadvantage of Scottish medicine. The College's concern was that it was important to maintain standards which would ensure that the health services of Scotland are no less efficient, no less well-financed, and no more encumbered with administrative bureaucracy than those of other parts of the United Kingdom. They expressed concern at the proposal of a Health Committee of a Scottish Assembly whose members would offer suggestions to and oversee the work of the

Executive Department, and who, elected along political lines, would advise the assembly on the legislation and financing of the health services in Scotland with a wide remit to cover policy on such matters as family planning, transplant surgery, abortion, private practice and the control of nursing homes. Since this Committee would have responsibility for Health Boards and other nominated bodies, the physicians say that the effects of such changes would be to introduce an additional politically based tier into the administrative structure of the Scottish Health Services; they say that it is:

not apparent how such additional tiers can do other than detract from their efficiency especially when they have yet to settle, following the major reorganisation of 1974. Since then the new Health Boards have been formulating their policies to suit best the composite health needs of their areas, and the requirements of the four Scottish medical schools in collaboration with the Health Department, and in a pattern correlated with that of the UK NHS. The superimposition of a policy-making body, whose aim will be to promote Scottish as distinct from UK interests, must surely complicate many administrative considerations, and the uncertainty of added directives to ensure purely Scottish aspects of health care may well result in the Scottish people receiving a service less efficient than that they presently enjoy.

The College of Physicians express concern that conditions of service in Scotland could conceivably become different from those operating elsewhere in the United Kingdom. For example, say the physicians, if family planning, transplant surgery, or private practice — most of which are potentially emotive issues with political connotations — were to be the subject of alteration of policy by the Assembly, a situation could arise in which the pattern of health care for 5 million Scots might differ radically from that in the remainder of the United Kingdom. 'The conditions of service in Scotland could thus be materially changed, and could prove less attractive to the quality of professional staffing which the Scottish health services have long enjoyed.' And what many doctors realise is that in order to justify themselves, and their existence in a Scottish Assembly,

Members of the Royal High School will try to change conditions for the sake of change. This, after all, is their *raison d'être*.

As medicine becomes increasingly specialised, co-operation
between hospitals and research centres up and down the country
becomes more and more essential. Any disruption of the present
system could be detrimental to the workings of the National
Health Service. (As it is — to take a couple of examples —
hepatitis and tropical disease patients from the North of England are normally treated in Edinburgh, while Lowland Scots
go to Newcastle for renal transplants).

Still more serious, according to Dr Clifford Mawdsley, the
distinguished neurologist, would be any disruption or fragmentation of research, particularly in the highly sophisticated
— and expensive — frontiers of medicine.

The Conservation Groups

The Scottish Wildlife Trust feel very strongly that the proposed
legislation, at least as it is presently framed, is unsatisfactory in
the way in which it deals with nature conservation and the
Countryside Commission for Scotland. Under the 1972 Act,
the duties of the Countryside Commission for Scotland include
the conservation of areas of natural beauty, which are construed
as also including 'the conservation of features of geological and
physiographical interest therein and of the flora and fauna
thereof'.

Responsibility for the conservation of natural beauty and
amenity (under Schedule 6 of the Scotland and Wales Bill,
Group 10, Environment) is to be devolved to the Scottish
Assembly and Executive but 'not including the conservation of
features of geological and physiographical interest, and of flora
and fauna'. These particular items are not to be devolved.

I am a Member of the Council of the (United Kingdom)
Fauna and Flora Preservation Society, and know at first hand
that experts in the field believe that this non-conformity between Scotland and England presents real difficulties. For
example, the Countryside Commission for Scotland — having
a devolved function — will be financed by a Scottish Assembly.
It is therefore to be expected that the funds allowed to the
Commission will not include any sums for the conservation of

excluded environmental features, which are not a responsibility of the Assembly; the net effect, forecast the Wildlife Trust, will be a curtailment of the activities of the Countryside Commission and an unbalancing of its functions. Enormous trouble was taken at the time when the Countryside (Scotland) Act was framed in 1972 to make sure that a balance was struck.

The importance of nature conservation in the Scottish scene is widely recognised and undeniable. Many of the finest nature areas in Britain are to be found in Scotland, and nature conservation in this part of the United Kingdom deserves the fullest support.

The Scottish Wildlife Trust demand 'the strongest links with the UK Government'. They say that the curtailment of the functions of the Countryside Commission for Scotland is 'clearly a step in the wrong direction'. It appears to them that the authority of the Nature Conservancy Council may be adversely affected by the Scotland and Wales Bill's proposals to devolve to the Assembly responsibility for the revenue of the important countryside bodies, which it is proposed will be represented by head offices in Scotland, whereas the Scottish Office of the Nature Conservancy Council will only have regional status.

The root of the matter is that flora and fauna, birds and beasts, do not recognise Hadrian's Wall, and it is absurd to suppose that they should! Moreover, like many other bodies whose sphere of activity is not seen as central to the economic, political and electoral policies of a Scottish Government, the environmentalists fear that they would do far less well financially than at present. Since the amount of money available from central government would be limited to the block grant, those spheres of activity which command the greatest electoral dividend would probably be given priority. In a smaller national context, this tendency would be exaggerated; in the broader context of the United Kingdom as a whole, where the pressures are not so immediate, a wider view could be adopted.

The Church

THE CHURCH OF SCOTLAND

On balance it is probably true that, so far at least, the Church of Scotland has been in favour of an Edinburgh Assembly. Within the ranks of the Church, not least among ministers, there is a whole range of viewpoint — some not concealing their support for the Scottish National Party, others seeing it as a hideous parody of patriotism, and a party of tawdry greed.

Introducing his last report as Convener of the Church and Nation Committee before the General Assembly of the Church of Scotland in 1975, the Reverend William Johnston reminded the Assembly of the Kirk of its consistent demand for more power over Scottish Affairs to come to Scotland, but only within the British framework. For Mr Johnston, centralisation on Westminster meant less than justice for the needs of Scotland — though, like others who have taken this line, he did not specify exactly what he meant by this. He felt that there were forces which inevitably bound the economies and lives of Scotland and England together, making separation disastrous. He was afraid that voices were becoming increasingly strident in the debate, 'and many of them made dismal and alarming listening'. Mr Johnston told the Kirk that some supported devolution as a means of obtaining power for themselves, while others opposed it, for fear of losing their power. All such were playing power politics for what they could get out of it. But, said Mr Johnston, 'devolution should not just be about power and politics: it is about the spirit and goals of our national life'.

In this important contribution to the Annual Conference of the Kirk, Mr Johnston asked, 'Is it to be a Scotland that is divided into partisan groups, each wanting to get as much as possible for themselves? Is it to be a country that is never going to get anywhere because they are too busy arguing about where they are going?' But current Kirk policy is that an Assembly in Edinburgh should get a special share of the North Sea oil revenues, a special voice for Scotland in the European Economic Community, and for a maximalist amount of devolution.

THE EPISCOPAL CHURCH

The Episcopal Church is the Church of England's Scottish branch, and in the nineteenth century very much catered for English husbands or wives living in Scotland, who were reluctant to adhere to a different communion. It has always tended to be fairly wealthy, if small in numbers, and because of its English connection it has understandably — and no doubt wisely — been reticent on the subject of devolution, and has had little influence on discussion about it.

THE ROMAN CATHOLIC CHURCH

The attitude of the Roman Catholic Church is altogether different, though no policy proposals have, or are likely to be, published. A large number of Catholics, clergy and laity, view with increasing unease, bordering sometimes on dismay, the arrival of an Assembly. Many Catholics are strongly against independence for Scotland, not only because they think that it is unnecessary, but because they suspect that it may prove harmful to them, even dangerous. Many are against 'devolution' because they fear that it must inevitably lead to Independence, and look twenty miles across the water to Ireland, where most of their forebears came from two or three generations ago.

Incidentally, there is a degree of religious-based voting in Scotland, which goes far beyond anything familiar in England. Indeed, Dr Henry Dricker, Head of the Scottish Government Unit at Edinburgh University, makes the interesting assertion that religion is a better indicator of voter intentions than class. Dr Dricker refers to a survey conducted in Glasgow after the February 1974 election asking people how they voted. Of Roman Catholics, 79·3 per cent said that they had voted Labour, a higher percentage than any class indicator would give; 11 per cent said they voted Conservative, 6·9 per cent SNP, and 2·8 for other parties. Of the Church of Scotland vote, only 34 per cent were Labour supporters — less than the Labour proportion in Scotland as a whole — 38·2 per cent Conservatives, and 24 per cent Nationalists. Glasgow may not be exactly representative of the rest of Scotland but this situation does provide a potential for division which would be most unpleasant if it were continued and exaggerated, or somehow institutionalised in the party division between Labour and the SNP.

Women

It is always difficult to make generalisations which, by their very nature, cannot be proved or disproved. Nevertheless, some of us who have been opposing SNP candidates at elections over the past decade have a hunch that significantly more women vote for the SNP than men.

Two kinds of circumstantial evidence lend support to this view. Time and again while canvassing we have been told, 'You have my vote, but the wife will be voting for the SNP. I can't talk her out of it!' Very rarely have I come across a woman who tells me that she'll be voting Labour, but that her husband will be supporting the SNP.

Second, opinion polls have shown that women tend to feel more strongly than men that 'Scots should have more say' in the running of their own affairs.

There are several possible explanations for this. First, as we have said before, voters tend to vote *against* rather than *for* political parties. Many women are understandably angry about interminably rising prices — and because they do the daily shopping they are far more aware of them than their husbands. As a result, they tend to spurn the two major political parties out of protest — to the advantage of the SNP.

Second, some women vote for reasons that have more to do with social status than with politics. There is a great deal of evidence to suggest that women moving from Glasgow to the new towns of East Kilbride, Cumbernauld and Livingston have switched their votes to the SNP, as a now respectable alternative in just this way: certainly the SNP has done extremely well in the new towns, winning local government control of Cumbernauld in particular.

Third, some women tend to be more emotional about their politics than men — and Scottish nationalism has an extremely romantic aura about it, if only for 'cultural' reasons. For example, they have been astute enough to capitalise on the cultural traditions of Scotland, and they have produced some very attractive silver jewellery in the old Scottish style. This may seem an extremely trivial matter, yet the trivia of politics often prove invaluable in whetting an individual's appetite for and interest in the subject, as is so evident in the American political scene.

Perhaps it is no coincidence that women have rapidly risen to the top of the party. Before anyone had ever imagined that Mrs Thatcher might one day lead the Conservative Party, Mrs Ewing had become the first SNP MP, followed briefly by

Margo MacDonald in 1973, and by Margaret Bain in 1974. Female leadership has not been restricted to the House of Commons. I gather from party members that Margo Mac-Donald, Mrs Jannette Jones — a Regional Councillor in Strathclyde — and Miss Isobel Lindsay — a junior Vice-President of the SNP — exercise considerable policy-making authority within the party hierarchy. The possibly ill-judged gibe that the SNP is a 'woman's party' has more than an element of truth to it.

Young People

As a group within the community, many young people take their politics as seriously as their elders, if not more seriously. Yet by any objective criterion, the SNP have been conspicuously successful in attracting support from the young: and not all of this comes from the more thoughtful element. Part of their success is due to the simplicity of their message; part is due to the fact that after so many years in power at Westminster and at local government level, Labour has become identified with the Establishment. Most young people are by nature anti-Establish-ment: the SNP has provided an outlet for them, and has bene-fited enormously as a result.

The SNP have also produced vast numbers of badges and other trinkets, which the unsophisticated are attracted by (and it should not be forgotten that they can now vote at eighteen, rather than twenty-one). One's first vote is an important occasion, and to win the support of first-time voters can prove extremely fruitful for a political party: it may even be possible to win a voter for life, since few people like to admit, even to themselves, that they have made a mistake. The SNP claim that their support is bound to increase over the years as older voters die off and a generation which has always voted SNP moves into its thirties. However, in this they may well be over-optimistic: it's common enough for people to shift their alle-giances — generally towards the right — as they grow older, and it would be surprising if many who blithely vote for the SNP as a form of protest — or because they don't really believe that the SNP could ever come to power in Scotland, and therefore a vote for them can't do any harm — do not have second thoughts as they grow older and realise that their votes could bring about the disintegration of Britain.

'Scotland is British'

One pressure group which has played an important part in the shaping of events is the 'Scotland is British' campaign. In the summer of 1976, when it became evident that no political party was going to act as a focus for anti-devolution feeling in Scotland, George Lawson, former MP for Motherwell, Mr Archie Birt of the Transport Salaried Staffs Association, and Mr Adam Fergusson, the well-known contributor to *The Times*, started to galvanise into action a number of individuals in public life in Scotland, from all shades of political opinion.

Not surprisingly, the fiercely pro-devolution *Scotsman* attacked the group as 'a collection of individuals who represent no organisations, neither political parties nor unions. It comprises some political has-beens, a few industralists and trade unionists': to which Mr Lawson pointed out that with all the political parties committed to devolution, 'there was no option for disfranchised Scots but to speak up for that large collection of individuals who think as we do'.

The Chairman of 'Scotland is British' is Sir John Toothill, former manager of Ferranti, and the man who was responsible for bringing its major plant to Edinburgh. The Vice-Chairmen are Mr Dan Crawford, Scottish Officer and Executive Council Member of the Union of Construction, Allied Trades and Technicians, and Viscount Weir, Chairman of the Weir Group and a director of the British Steel Corporation. Other members of the 'Scotland is British' Campaign Committee are David Graham, Chairman of the Central Scotland Section of the Amalgamated Union of Engineering Workers; Mr William Blairford, Scottish Officer and Executive Council Member of the Electrical, Electronic, Telecommunications and Plumbing Union; Sir Charles Wilson, former Principal of Glasgow University; Sir George Sharp, Chairman of the Convention of Scottish Local Authorities; Lord Polwarth, past President of the Scottish Council for Development and Industry; Mr Bruce Weir, QC; Mr David Edward, QC, Treasurer of the Faculty of Advocates; and, in their representative capacity, Mr Douglas

Hardie, Chairman of the CBI in Scotland, and Mr William Jack, Chairman of the Association of Scottish Chambers of Commerce. Though the *Scotsman* may sneer at these people as a 'collection of individuals', the truth is that they represent a large cross-section of Scottish life, and that people so disparate in other regards should have come together to defeat the devolution Bill reveals a great deal about the real state of opinion in Scotland.

11

The Slide to Independence

To their credit, supporters of the SNP have always had a far more realistic and far-sighted attitude towards the establishment of an Assembly in Edinburgh than their pro-devolution opponents; they have campaigned for devolution on the very reasonable grounds that the Assembly, in itself an uneasy compromise, would be unworkable, and that the resulting frustration and sense of grievance on the part of its members would inevitably push them into demanding a still greater degree of autonomy for Scotland and, eventually, complete independence from the United Kingdom. Far from satisfying nationalist aspirations, an Assembly with limited powers — not least in the crucial area of finance — would only create new problems and aggravate old grievances. Ironically enough, its very existence would bring about the situation it was designed to avoid.

As a subordinate Parliament in a unitary state, the Edinburgh Assembly would soon find itself in an impossible position. As we have seen, it would remain financially dependent on Westminster; and despite the Government's neat, theoretical distinction between 'devolved' and 'reserved' areas of legislation, it would in fact be impossible to separate specifically 'Scottish' issues from those affecting the United Kingdom as a whole. Conflict between Westminster and the new Assembly would be inevitable, particularly if the governments in London and Edinburgh were of different political persuasion; members of the Assembly, from all points on the political spectrum, would be more than human if, having once tasted power, they did not come to resent the limitations imposed upon them and to demand greater power for themselves. It's hard to believe that many of those who blithely advocate the setting up of a Scottish Assembly cannot have thought out the full implications of such a step. A Parliament is, by definition, a very different kind of institution from a local authority or even a Regional authority, and inevitably arouses far greater expectations both in its members and those who vote for it: an unworkable and essentially frustrated Assembly is a recipe for disaster. It is to the impracticability of the proposed Assembly and its potentially fraught relationship with Westminster that we must now turn.

The Assembly is a Constitutional Impossibility

A fundamental error on the part of those who advocate an Edinburgh Assembly — whether out of self-interest, political expediency or a genuine belief that to do so is to align oneself with the mainstream of enlightened thought — is the assumption that it is possible to establish a subordinate legislative assembly in a unitary Parliamentary state like Britain: and that an Assembly in Edinburgh can be thought of in much the same way as existing elected bodies such as local councils or Regional authorities.

The truth of the matter is that the proposed Assembly represents an unsatisfactory and impracticable half-way house in a unitary state which is doomed to failure. Clearly if the United Kingdom is to remain in existence Scottish and Welsh voters must continue to be represented at Westminster — and we shall be examining the formidable and often farcical problems this will raise later in this chapter. If drastic changes are called for — and I do not believe that they are — then the establishment of Scottish and Welsh Assemblies must have one of two different results: either Britain becomes a Federal state, with a written Constitution setting out the powers and scope of the Assemblies and Parliament, as the Liberals suggest, or — and this is the long-term aim of the SNP and Plaid Cymru — the United Kingdom is dismantled, Scottish and Welsh voters are no longer represented at Westminster, and Scotland and Wales take their place as fully independent nations. To assume that there is a realistic third alternative is to inhabit the realm of fantasy.

But why, it may reasonably be asked, should Britain not

become a Federal state? After all, West Germany — whose post-war economic record is so enviable by British standards — is a Federal state. And why should Britain not have a written Constitution, in common with the United States and most West European countries?

The Chairman of the Public Health Committee of the European Parliament, and member of the Bundestag in Bonn for the city of Brunswick, Dr Hans Jahn was a leading member of Chancellor Adenauer's Private Office in the late 1940s and 1950s when the system of the Federal Republics was set up by the British and the Americans in the aftermath of the Second World War. He tells me that at that time the motive of the occupying powers was to hinder the resurgence of a powerful unitary military state in Germany. But he claims that Dr Adenauer and his entourage realised at a very early stage that decentralisation was likely to make Western Germany more and not less efficient. During the War, the Germans experienced the inefficiency of centralised Berlin government; a quarter of a century later, few people would care to deny that the Federal system of government has been one of the main factors contributing to the West German economic miracle. So why not transpose it to Britain?

In general terms, one should always be cautious about the feasibility of transplanting a system which has worked well in one country into the different conditions of another.

More specifically, the German system is fundamentally different from a British scenario in which only Scotland and Wales would be comparable Federal states. To pursue the German analogy, it is as if Schleswig-Holstein and Baden-Württemberg were alone to have their own subordinate state legislatures, while at the same time being over-represented in a Bonn Parliament which was responsible for the government of the rest of the Federal Republic. This would be intolerable to other Germans, particularly if the Schleswig-Holstein and Baden-Württemberg representatives determined the complexion of the Government in Bonn, and were able to deal with matters for which they were not responsible in their own provinces.

Second, the German states were for the main part ancient kingdoms, like Bavaria, or margravates or Hanse cities, with a proud separate history. Only Nord Rhein-Westfalen is an artificial new land. The Scottish and the Welsh situations are perhaps broadly comparable: the English position is not. Because England is so much more heavily populated than Scotland or Wales, the Federation would be completely out of balance; nor is there any identifiable demand for subordinate Parliaments in Norwich for East Anglia, Winchester for Wessex, Birmingham for Mercia, Manchester for Lancastria or New-castle for Northumbria — all areas which, in terms of popula-tion, are comparable with Scotland or Wales. Bavaria and Nieder Sachsen are larger than the other German states, but are easily containable. A Federation in which the English made up 83 per cent of the population, the Scots 11 per cent, the Welsh 4 per cent and the Northern Irish 2 per cent is just not workable. There is no demand for the dismemberment of England itself nor is there any likelihood of such a demand materialising. This is very different from saying that there is no demand for decentralisation. There is — and in the final chapter I shall deal with the virtues of decentralisation which do not involve the creation of legislative assemblies.

The *sine qua non* of a Federal system is a written Constitution. In the absence of a written Constitution and a Supreme Court, which would interpret such a Constitution, a Federal state would find itself enmeshed in interminable internal difficulties, and disputes as to the frontiers of power. Now there is no reason why Britain should not in theory have a written Constitution. In practice, it would mean altering our way of government far beyond the confines of the Scotland and Wales Bill. And even if such a radical change were to take place — for which there is little obvious demand in England — would it really solve the problem of Scotland and Wales? The SNP demand nation-status, with all the trappings of a separate army, navy, air force and diplomatic representation which accompany nation-status. Exactly the same factors which would help to make any devolution settlement unstable would operate in the case of a Federal solution. For a Federal solution to work, there would have to be a unanimous desire to want to make it work. And it is this that is manifestly lacking in the Scotland of the 1970s.

Nor is it possible to pretend — as so many politicians would understandably like to — that an Assembly in Edinburgh would be little more than a glorified county council and that its establishment need cause no alarm to anyone on either side of the Border. (All too often one gets the impression that politicians who favour devolution hope to persuade an apathetic English electorate that devolution represents little more than tinkering with Welsh and Scottish local government and therefore need be of no concern to them, whereas — as we shall see — its implications are enormous, not only for Scotland and Wales, but for the United Kingdom as a whole.) An elected Assembly with legislative power is neither more nor less than a Parliament; it is not a local authority. Local authorities, whatever their size, have no power to make or alter the laws they apply; they take decisions at a purely administrative level within the limits laid down by the law, which is not made by them, but by Parliament. Nor do local authorities attract the feelings of patriotism and emotion invested in a Parliament, which acts as a focus of national pride. An Assembly of the kind proposed for Edinburgh, whatever the limitations on its power and whatever its innate implausibility, is a very different kettle of fish from even the grandest local authority. It is both misleading and unrealistic to pretend otherwise.

Given that the Assembly is — for all its limitations — an altogether different political animal from a local authority, how can it function effectively in a unitary state in which the Westminster Parliament remains the supreme legislative authority? The answer is that it cannot possibly do so, and that conflict, bitterness and resentment can only follow its establishment; and the fact that so much store has been set on the proposed Assembly by devolutionists can only exacerbate these feelings. Expectations which have been raised and are then thwarted are the stuff of life of those who claim that the best solution is for Scotland to make a clean break with its history of the last 250 years. We must now examine the areas of conflict between London and Edinburgh — and of thwarted expectations — in greater detail.

As in so many areas of life, money is at the root of the problem. As we have seen, it has been suggested that the Westminster Parliament should grant the Scottish Assembly an annual block grant, the size of which would be decided in London; it would then be up to the Edinburgh Assembly to decide how the money should be spent in those areas which had been devolved to it. Financial dependence is humiliating and frustrating at the best of times, and especially for those with great expectations; and if there isn't enough to go round it's natural enough to blame whoever holds the purse strings. The obvious answer is to allow the dependent to make his own money and pay his own way — in other words, for the Assembly to raise its own taxes inside Scotland; but as we shall see, that is easier said than done.

Throughout history, Parliament's struggles for power have almost always centred on the control of taxation and money. Money was at the root of Charles I's conflict with Parliament, and the American War of Independence; and it would bedevil the Scottish Assembly's relations with Westminster. As we will see, it has hitherto proved impossible to suggest an acceptable form of revenue-raising for the Assembly. For three years now, able Ministers and ingenious civil servants have racked their brains to discover one, and they have all failed — not for want of the necessary expertise, but because there is simply no way of raising revenue for a subordinate Parliament within a unitary state which is acceptable to a sensitive and democratic electorate.

The result is that the Assembly will be totally dependent on its annual block grant; and however skilfully and persuasively the Scottish Executive may present its case to the Prime Minister and the Chancellor of the Exchequer in London, the size of the grant will be determined by the United Kingdom Treasury and endorsed by the United Kingdom Cabinet. And exactly the same would have applied had the exchequer board which was suggested by the Kilbrandon Committee been accepted. From its inception the Assembly will be in a financial straitjacket; for all the government claims about the Scots having freedom of choice, the Assembly's room to manoeuvre would be extremely limited, particularly in these tight economic times. Assembly members would naturally come to resent their dependence on Westminster. Not only would they complain about the size of the grant, and blame their inability to push through their electoral promises on the parsimony of London; they would also resent the fact that their ability to decide how the money should be spent would in fact be extremely limited, particularly in the early years when hopes were at their highest (most Government programmes, from roads to school buildings, are decided years rather than months in advance). However first hand the knowledge of its members about the problems of Scotland, the Assembly's scope for making any early changes or improvements on the way money is spent in those areas for which responsibility had been devolved to it would be extremely marginal.

Not only would Scottish politicians and those who elect them feel frustrated and resentful: ironically the chances are that Scotland would end up worse off than it is at present. Despite the age-old belief that the Scots are England's poor relations, the Scots — rightly or wrongly — receive more than their share of United Kingdom public expenditure at present. Out of every £100 of public expenditure per person, someone in Scotland currently receives £119, someone on Humberside £87. And for as long as Westminster and Whitehall feel fully responsible for Scotland, public expenditure will continue to be allocated on a basis of both political judgment and need. But if the Scots had their own Assembly, Government Ministers in London would come under tremendous pressure — particularly from those areas of England whose need is as great as that of Scotland — to make sure that the Scots do not get more than their fair share of the cake when the annual haggling over the size of the block grant comes round. The North-East of England, for example, would almost certainly feel that the Scots were trying to get the best of both worlds at the expense of the rest of Britain: the regions of Britain would be only too aware of the progress of the negotiations, and they would expect a government that was now more responsible for their needs than those of the Scots to strike a hard bargain. If as a result the Scots got less — perhaps substantially less — per head then they do at present, all the political parties in Edinburgh would inevitably complain that the Scots were being done down by the English, and that a far greater degree of independence was essential for Scotland. And even if the Chief Executive and his Cabinet — displaying a superhuman degree of political honesty and statesmanship — refrained from blaming the London Government for their failure to squeeze as much money out of the Treasury as they might have liked, it is inconceivable that the Leader of the Opposition in Edinburgh would be equally reticent. It would be only too tempting for him to promise to remove the limitations imposed on the Assembly by the Scotland and Wales Act once he was returned to power; and once promises of this kind have been made it is awkward to go back on them. The likelihood of Scottish independence would be brought that much closer.

The old adage that 'he who pays the piper calls the tune' is as true in public and governmental life as in any other sphere of activity. When devolution was first discussed it was naturally assumed that the Assemblies in Edinburgh and Cardiff would — and should — be granted significant revenue-raising powers of their own. Anyone with any experience of local government will agree that a local authority which was not responsible for raising at least a part of its own finances through rates or some equivalent tax would soon manifest a hideous lack of financial discipline. An authority that was wholly reliant on central Exchequer funds would dream up all sorts of weird and wonderful schemes for the benefit of its citizens; and if the money were not forthcoming, the councillors would naturally enough shift the blame on to Westminster. It is essential that those who enjoy the benefit of local services and amenities should directly bear at least part of their cost; otherwise one might as well opt for a wholly centralised state.

Experience of the European Parliament — which has only limited control over the EEC budget and no power to raise its own taxes within the member countries — points to the same conclusion. The Plenary Session of the European Parliament blithely passes a mass of resolutions, each the result of months of painstaking work by the various Committees of the European Assembly meeting in Brussels. This would not be the case if — like national MPs — members of the European Assembly had to face their electors and justify every item towards which they were expected to contribute their taxes. It is seductively easy to make promises of the wildest and most extravagant kind where other people's money is concerned.

It is one thing to say that Assemblies in Edinburgh and Cardiff should have revenue-raising powers — coming up with concrete proposals is a very different matter, and no satisfactory or plausible solution has yet been found. Let us now examine the various proposals that have been put forward.

A LEVY ON THE RATES

The original — and most favoured — suggestion was that the Assembly should introduce a levy on the existing rates. This appeared to be a relatively simple solution, with the advantage that residence in Scotland could be easily differentiated from residence in the rest of the United Kingdom.

The objections to a levy are as follows. In the first place, gearing the Assembly's finances to any system of rating would make it seem little more than a glorified appendage of Scottish local government. This was a major objection among those who took a grandiose view of the Assembly's role.

A more serious objection lies in the highly controversial nature of the rating system itself. However well it may have worked in the past, it is doubtful whether either domestic or industrial rating remains a fair or sensible way of raising public money: it tends to be regressive, and to bear most heavily on those who can least afford it. There would be little point in linking the Assembly's finances to a system that would eventually be discarded.

However, the conclusive objection to a levy on the rates is a political one. The Convention of Scottish Local Authorities fully recognises that any significant increase in the rates would be seen as their responsibility, and they refuse to be saddled with the odium of large-scale rate increases in order to help central government finance the Assembly. Councillors throughout Scotland are outraged at the suggestion that they should become, in effect, the Assembly's tax-gatherers; and they also realise that, in effect, such a scheme would enable the Assembly to raise money by starving local government. Even without directly levying a surcharge on local rates it seems as though the Assembly would be able to increase the rates merely by withholding part of the rates support grant to local authorities, and practising a form of 'oblique' taxation by not paying out part of its block grant to local government. Such considerations led Dr Cecil Stout — the distinguished Director of Finance for the City of Edinburgh District — to his conclusion that:

> there is probably no satisfactory half-way house between financial dependence and complete financial indepen-

dence. Complete financial devolution really means separatism. Independent tax raising for the Assembly is ruled out as long as the economic and political unity of the United Kingdom is regarded as inviolate [*Scotsman*, 7 January 1976].

NORTH SEA OIL REVENUES

Basing their policy on the work of Professor James Cornford, Lord Crowther Hunt, Professor Alan Peacock and other members of the Outer Circle Policy Unit, the Liberal Party suggest that royalties brought ashore in Scotland at a fixed United Kingdom rate should be an additional source of revenue, to bring up the Assembly's independent resources approximately to the level of the block grant. The Liberals contend that this would avoid the difficulties associated with natural resources in general, and would not affect the decisions of the oil companies about the landing of oil, if the rate were constant. They point out that calculations of yield are difficult, given unpredictable fluctuations in prices and rates of depletion. Estimates for the United Kingdom yield for 1980–5 at 1975 prices give the proceeds from royalties for the United Kingdom at an average of £650 million per annum. The Liberals say that a substantial proportion of these royalties derives from oil brought ashore in Scotland and thus might give an approximate yield of £400 million per annum for the Assembly. Together with the proceeds of a Scottish personal income tax this would give a total of £1,400 million per year, compared to an estimated block grant of £1,300 million. Yet, earmarking revenues from natural resources from one part of the United Kingdom for use in that area presents a problem of principle (see p. 274).

LOCAL INCOME TAX

Any politician, whether local or national, knows that the public feel particularly strongly about their rates. The dull thud of a rates demand dropping through the letter box somehow seems to irritate people far more than a demand from H.M. Inspector of Taxes; any steep rise in the rates is accompanied by a shrill public outcry and much gnashing of teeth at ratepayers' meetings and in the local newspapers. Given people's sensitivity on this score, might it not be more acceptable to raise money for the Assembly through a local income tax collected through PAYE? Collected along with United Kingdom income tax, a local income tax could perhaps come to be regarded as merely part of the Scottish taxpayer's overall tax burden, and its impact obscured in a way that a levy on the rates could never be.

It is hard to believe that most Scottish voters would remain passive for very long when they realised that they were paying an additional tax for the supposed benefits of devolution. Supporters of devolution — as opposed to a separate Scottish state — tend to think again when they realise how it could affect their own pockets.

It has been suggested that, by some means or other, an amount equivalent to that which the Scots would pay in local income tax should be made up to them by some kind of rebate from United Kingdom income tax. Quite apart from the fact that such a proposal would be extremely unfair on the rest of the country — why should the English in effect subsidise a Scottish Assembly? — the administrative complications involved are hideous to contemplate. Driving H.M. Inspectors of Taxes to a nervous breakdown hardly seems the most sensible way of financing an Assembly — all the more so since one of the causes of nationalism has been the top-heavy burden of bureaucracy and administrative costs. Quite apart from which, the skills of the tax inspectors are desperately needed in so many other areas.

Income tax is assessed by a person's place of work, and not by residence; and over 60 per cent of all firms operating in Scotland including American-owned multinationals are registered in London.

At first glance, it might appear to be a relatively simple matter to make sure that PAYE should be levied simply at the place of work of all those earning their living in Scotland, and that it would be of minor consequence whether a company was registered in London, Zurich, Minneapolis or wherever. In fact, the position is much more complex. The PAYE system can only operate efficiently if all the tax affairs of a single company are dealt with by the same tax office. Thus a building contractor, like Wimpey, operating in all parts of the United Kingdom, would concentrate its dealings with a single office. As Member of Parliament for West Lothian, my main business is with the tax centre at East Kilbride, serving the whole of Scotland: however a substantial part of my work concerns offices at Southampton, Walsall, Salford and Newcastle which look after the affairs of major employers in the West Lothian area. I am told authoritatively by the Inland Revenue that disentangling the scheme would be a colossal task. The Inland Revenue reckons that to collect a supplemental income tax in Scotland would cost more than one-fifth of the tax raised — an intolerably high figure. They informed the Layfield Committee that in order to operate local income taxes throughout the United Kingdom, they would need to employ an additional 12,000 civil servants, and that as many people again would have to be enrolled in the private sector of industry; to operate a local income tax in Scotland alone would mean employing an extra 2,500 skilled civil servants. When one considers that both Britain's major political parties are committed to reducing the size and expense of government bureaucracy, and that a good part of our economic problems stem from the fact that the narrowing base of manufacturing industry and agriculture has to support far too heavy an administrative and non-productive load, it does seem both frivolous and irresponsible to swell the ranks of the bureaucracy in order to gratify a political whim. Scottish electors may feel that Scotland should have a greater say in the running of its own affairs; they certainly do not want to have to pay for an expensive and cumbrous extension of government bureaucracy.

CORPORATION AND PAYROLL TAXES

A Scottish corporation tax and a Scottish payroll tax can be bracketed together for our purposes, since they are both open to the same objections. What would be the result if the yield from such taxes — or from a surcharge on the existing taxes on industry — were to be allocated to the Edinburgh Assembly? The simple answer is that it would be extremely damaging to Scottish industry and investment, and therefore to employment and the well-being of the Scottish people in general. Industrialists and their accountants would quickly discover that these additional taxes meant that their overall costs were higher in Scotland than in England, and that it would not be in their

interests to expand their activities in Scotland, let alone set up
new plants there.

Again, it has been suggested that, in order to offset this,
Scottish employers could be given a rebate from their contribution to United Kingdom corporation tax. Once again we
have to consider the practicality of this. Tony Christopher, the
Secretary of the Inland Revenue Staffs Association, threw up his
hands in despair at the very thought of what would be involved
for his members. Corporation tax presents enough problems as it
is, without adding a Scottish element to it. And some United
Kingdom firms have made it clear that they would rather run
down the Scottish side of their operation than have to treat their
accountants for nervous strain, even if the actual amount they
ended up paying to the Treasury and the Scottish Assembly was
no greater than that paid at present to the Exchequer. There is a
limit to the amount of time-consuming paperwork that any
government can ask of industry, and many businessmen feel
that this limit has already been reached with VAT.

How could firms like Coats Patons or the House of Fraser,
which have huge Scottish and English operations, identify those
elements in their activities which would be subject to Scottish
corporation tax and those which would not? To suggest
that business concerns should add to their already existing
problems by paying different taxes on different aspects of their
operations in Scotland and England is nothing short of lunacy.

A SCOTTISH VAT

Those politicians who glibly claim that there could be what they
inelegantly term 'a Scottish element to VAT' cannot have
attended a Commons Finance Bill Committee Stage during the
past seven years. To raise a specifically Scottish VAT would be a
monumentally complicated affair not only for the Inland
Revenue — absorbing the time and energies of many of its
most skilled tax officials — but for businesses of every kind,
particularly those trading on either side of the Border. It is
hardly surprising that a proposal put before one of the Government's Cabinet sub-committees whereby the Assembly would
be enabled to raise an additional £300–400 million through
differing rates of VAT between England and Scotland was
stillborn!

Any scheme for using VAT to finance the Assembly would almost certainly run foul of EEC regulations, under which no regional variations in VAT will be allowed after 1980. Brussels is committed to harmonising VAT rates throughout the Community in order that the Community — with the approval of a directly elected European Parliament — will be able to raise part of its own budget from each member state's VAT. A fresh disparity in VAT rates in order to finance the Edinburgh Assembly would not be tolerated by our Common Market partners.

SALES TAX

Well aware of how important it is that a Parliament should be responsible for raising its own revenue, Lord Home has suggested that the Assembly should be financed through a Scottish sales tax.

The most immediate side-effect of such a tax would be observed on Sir Alec's own doorstep in the Border country — still mercifully customs-free and frontier-free. If it were to serve any real purpose, a Scottish sales tax could hardly be a token or minimal tax; and naturally enough, shoppers from the Scottish side of the border would take to nipping across to England to do their shopping — which would hardly be to the advantage of their own shopkeepers and traders. (Border people are used to travelling long distances, and most of them feel that they have more in common with the North of England than with Edinburgh, which lies across the Soutra Hills. If devolving power and decision-making to those affected were really the aim of the exercise, no Government in their right mind would link the Borders with Edinburgh. There would be an administrative centre in Berwick-on-Tweed, covering the eastern Scottish Border country to the north and North Northumberland to the south.)

A more serious objection to a Scottish sales tax is the effect it would have on investment and employment through the retail price index. Moreover, any differential taxation of this kind would make it impossible for any government to operate an effective counter-inflation policy throughout the United Kingdom.

Towards the end of 1975, serious consideration was even

given to suggestions that the excise duty of spirits should be increased in Scotland in order to finance the Assembly. This would mean in effect that the price of a dram of whisky in a Scottish pub or a bottle of whisky at the off-licence would be higher than in England. Only a Scottish politician with suicidal tendencies could put his name to such a proposal!

It has also been suggested that there should be what Chris Baur, then of the *Financial Times*, on 8 October 1975 called a ' "supplemental" tax, raised conceivably through value added tax, vehicle licence or other excise duty mechanisms. The assumption is that such taxation autonomy for the Assembly would, in practice, be too unpopular to use'.

Mr Baur has a high reputation for accuracy, and his paper saw fit to print his story on its front page. From my own first-hand knowledge, I know that it was being argued in Government circles that the Assembly should be given such unpopular taxation powers that they would never dare to employ them; responsibility for the Assembly's lack of financial muscle would then reside fairly and squarely on its own Members. Fortunately it was realised that the scheme was an entirely cynical exercise which could well have backfired, and it was duly dropped.

Charging more for vehicle licences in Scotland was in itself a non-starter. Quite apart from the fact that many people on the Borders would register their cars in Berwick or Carlisle, Scottish resentment at having to pay more for a licence than the English would have run very high. Public outrage over this might well have rendered insignificant the considerable controversy that has taken place over the years — fuelling nationalism in the process — over the tolls paid by motorists using the Forth, Tay and Erskine road bridges. The fact that there is a similar toll on the Severn Bridge is conveniently forgotten: much ill-will is generated by the fact that Scots should have to pay to cross over Scottish water while the English pay nothing to use the many miles of English motorway.

Legislative Confusion

The sheer impossibility of finding an acceptable and practical way of raising money for the Assembly has meant that those who favour devolution have had to resort to the altogether unsatisfactory annual block grant, with all its attendant miseries. But financial lack of clout is not the only disappointment in store for the newly elected Assemblymen. As we have seen, the Assembly is by its very nature an uneasy hybrid which is unlikely to satisfy anybody and the division of powers between Westminster and the High School offers little hope of its being a success. It is, in effect, being suggested that the Edinburgh Government should carry into effect — and produce secondary legislation for — legislation originated by the Government in London, which may well be of a totally different complexion. The problem is aggravated by the fact that the Edinburgh Government would be responsible for administering many of the social services without being in a position to control or even influence the economic policies which would produce the resources to fund these services. Here again, some of the social services would be the responsibility of Westminster, while others — such as housing — would be controlled from Edinburgh: an artificial distinction which completely ignores the fact that one cannot differentiate between 'Scottish' national issues and the perennial interaction between the two.

Even the Kilbrandon Commission — which, as we have seen, was influential in persuading leading politicians from both the major parties to take seriously the question of devolution — emphasises that there should be no break in the chain between legislation on the one hand and the application of administrative decisions on the other: they should form part of a continuing two-way process, with ideas being translated into action, the experience of which should lead to fresh ideas, fresh laws and fresh action. It is now suggested that two different bodies should each make part of the law. The Edinburgh Executive will have to try to translate Westminster's intentions into practice, though — given electoral cycles and the Assembly's four-year term — it may well be totally out of sympathy with what has been proposed. And even if it were not, the scope for confusion and resentments would still be very wide. The creation of fresh legislation will become divorced from administrative experience, and will be sucked into a morass of political conflict.

We will return to this question of the conflict between Westminster and the High School when we consider the position of the Scottish MPs at Westminster later in this chapter;

enough has been said to indicate that the whole subject is a political minefield.

The Assembly Members

Not surprisingly, the 150 Assembly Members — whether in Government or in Opposition — would rapidly become disillusioned and resentful. Imagine their sense of disenchantment on reaching the Assembly direct from the hustings, full of enthusiasm to create a New Scotland, only to discover that, at least to begin with, the most they could hope to achieve was to make one or two marginal changes of emphasis: perhaps from spending on roads to spending on education, or vice versa. Hardly would the first Queen's Speech have been concluded before indignant Assembly Members would be on their feet complaining about their own impotence and interference from Westminster.

Their sense of grievance would, of course, be shared by the electorate, who would soon begin to ask their Assembly Members why they had not succeeded in doing this, that, or the other on their behalf. Such complaints would be all the more bitter since — alas — few proposals have been quite so oversold as the Scottish Assembly. Like North Sea oil, it has come to be regarded in some quarters as a universal panacea for all the ills of Scotland: expectations have been aroused which cannot possibly be fulfilled.

Assembly Members would be more than human if they did not try to shuffle the blame off on someone else: and the Government in London is the obvious scapegoat. It is not hard to imagine the eloquent, self-pitying speeches tumbling from the lips of disappointed Assembly Members to the effect that if it weren't for the parsimony of the Treasury and the Cabinet — dominated as it inevitably is by English MPs — they would have been able to implement every clause of their party's Assembly election manifesto. If they only had the power and the resources they needed, how easily they could have carried out their promises! Every school that is not built, every antiquated hospital that is not modernised, every road that is not built will be blamed on sinister men in Westminster, latter-day Gnomes of Zurich who are determined to 'do us Scots down' and pinch the oil revenues which are the birthright of every native Scot.

Nor can one assume that such complaints would be restricted to SNP and nationalistically inclined Assembly Members. Once an institution like a Parliament has been brought into being its Members will — understandably enough — fight tooth and nail to acquire as much power as possible for it, whatever their political inclinations and however sceptical or even hostile their initial attitude may have been. Those of us who have watched erstwhile anti-Marketeers in action in Strasbourg or Luxembourg have soon realised that there are no more doughty warriors for the rights of the European Parliament than those who have previously opposed the very principle of Britain's belonging to the EEC. Not only would the SNP and sympathetic politicians such as John Mackintosh and Jim Sillars demand greater power and financial autonomy for the Assembly: Labour, Liberal and Conservative members would also come to believe that any Assembly of which they were members must be important enough to warrant the additional power and responsibility demanded. A greater and greater share of power will be expected: conflict with Westminster would become inevitable.

Scots MPs at Westminster

But the touchy subject of the Assembly's relationship with Westminster and Whitehall does not end there: we have yet to examine the role of the Scottish MPs at Westminster. What exactly will this role be? To what extent could they involve themselves in Scottish affairs which — theoretically at least — were the concern of the Assembly? How many MPs should Scotland have at Westminster? What would be the role of the Secretary of State and what should his relationship be with the Chief Executive of the Scottish Assembly?

If the United Kingdom is to remain in being, then there can be no question but that the Scottish constituencies must continue to be represented at Westminster. (On a less elevated level, no Labour Government would be prepared to sign away what has been — until the SNP mounted its challenge — an electoral birthright in the form of a mass of safe Labour seats, particularly in the mining and industrial areas of the country. Without these safe Scottish — and Welsh — seats, Labour Governments would be rather less frequent than they are at present.) Yet once the Assembly had come into being, and was legislating for those areas that had not been reserved to the United Kingdom Government, the position of the seventy-one Scottish Westminster MPs would become awkward and invidious. Their credibility — like those of their counterparts in the Assembly — would be deeply suspect, simply because there would be so many areas of concern to their electors on which they could not pronounce. Imagine the scene at the hustings:

> *Voter:* What are you going to do about housing and rents?
> *Candidate:* Sorry, that's nothing to do with me — you'll have to ask the High School.
> *Voter:* What about schooling then?
> *Candidate:* Don't ask me — try your Assembly Member.

And so on. Hardly a recipe for content.

Understandably enough, Scottish voters may well ask themselves exactly what their MPs can do at Westminster (and once direct elections to the European Parliament have been introduced it will become rather more difficult for a Scottish MP to claim that he devotes himself to foreign affairs!). Scottish voters may well react by expecting their MPs at Westminster to give up all their time and energy to extracting as much money as possible out of the Treasury so that the Assembly has a large enough block grant to provide the schools, houses and hospitals for which it is responsible. The success of Scottish MPs — and of the Secretary of State for Scotland — would be judged by their ability to squeeze the Exchequer; and this in turn would breed the most intense resentment against the Scots amongst English MPs and voters.

The feeling of being 'done down' by the Scots would undoubtedly filter through to all levels of government — including Downing Street — making relations with the Scottish Chief Executive and his Cabinet edgy, to put it mildly. Nor would it be possible for the British Prime Minister to take a relaxed attitude towards it for long, since sooner or later some incident would inevitably occur which would persuade the English regions — and particularly those, like the North-East or

Merseyside, with serious problems of their own — that the Scots were getting more than their fair share. Then the pressure would really be on. Cosy relations between Downing Street and Charlotte Square — or wherever the Chief Executive decided to take up his official residence — would become impossible.

There are four possible answers to the problem of Scottish and Welsh representation at Westminster; and not one of them can be reconciled with Britain's continued existence as a unitary state:

1 The first possibility is that Scottish and Welsh voters would not be represented at all at Westminster: in other words, all political power in Scotland and Wales would be transferred to the Assemblies in Edinburgh and Cardiff. This is of course the solution advocated by the SNP and Plaid Cymru. However, if there is to be a United Kingdom Parliament, this argument is obviously impracticable.

2 The second possibility is that Scotland and Wales should continue to be represented on the same basis as at present. But would this really be acceptable — and for how long? As we have seen, Scotland is significantly over-represented per head of the population at present (as is Wales, though to a lesser extent); if there were Scottish and Welsh Assemblies, this would become even less defensible than it is at present. How could one defend a situation in which the Northern Irish electorate — which no longer has its own Parliament at Stormont — had 12 Westminster MPs, each representing 85,000 voters, while Scottish voters had 71 MPs, each representing approximately 52,000 voters as well as their own Assembly looking after education, housing, health and various other devolved matters? And it is the gut issues of politics, such as housing and education, which decide elections.

The fact that retaining the *status quo* in relation to the number of Scottish MPs at Westminster is official Government policy does not make it any more acceptable. We would have the absurd situation in which Scottish and Welsh MPs could continue to legislate on subjects which had been devolved to the

Assemblies in their own countries. They would not be responsible to their own constituents for such legislation, nor would they be answerable to the English voters who would be affected by it.

Under the present proposals Mr Jo Grimond could vote on:

Local government reform in London, but not in Lerwick
Bankruptcy laws in Birmingham, but not in Bressay
Development of tourism in Devon, but not Dunrossness
Fauna and flora in the Fylde area of Lancashire, but not Fair Isle
Fire precautions in Fulham, but not in Fetlar
Freshwater fisheries in the Folkestone area, but not in Foula
Hospital facilities at Halifax, but not in Herma Ness
Injury and disability in Ipswich, but not Isbister
Maintenance of marine works in Margate, but not in Muckle Flugga
Marriage laws in Manchester, but not in Mousa
Police laws in Penzance, but not Papa Stour
Public holidays in Poole, Dorset, but not Pool of Uirkie
Roads in Rochdale, but not in Renwick
Schools in Sheffield, but not in Scalloway
Social welfare in Salford, but not Sullom Voe
Safety of reservoirs in Suffolk, but not Sumburgh Head
Water services in West Bromwich, but not West Burra
Young offenders in York, but not in Yell.

My own position is exactly the same — I could vote on policy and money for:

Arts in Alnwick, but not in Armadale, West Lothian
Aerodromes at Heathrow and Gatwick, but not Edinburgh Turnhouse
Buildings in Bath, but not in Bathgate
Burial laws in Blackpool, but not in Blackridge
Betting, bookies and gaming in Blackburn, Lancashire, but not Blackburn, West Lothian
Building control in Bolton, but not in Broxburn
Bridge maintenance regulations in Bradford, but not in Bo'ness
Land use in Leicester, but not in Livingston New Town

Licensing laws in Liverpool, but not in Linlithgow
Severn Bridge at Bristol, but not the Forth Road Bridge, South Queensferry
Shop hours in Swindon, but not in Stoneyburn
Water supply in Wolverhampton, but not in Whitburn
Waterways in Winchester, but not Winchburgh.

Scottish and Welsh interference in purely English affairs would be strongly resented, particularly since the participation of these MPs could well be decisive in deciding whether such legislation was introduced or not. Scottish and Welsh MPs could furthermore decide the political complexion of the Parliament at Westminster: to add insult to injury, this could happen after an election which had in part been decided on the issue of how autonomous the Edinburgh and Cardiff Assemblies should be.

Neither of the alternatives mentioned so far can be reconciled with the continued existence of the United Kingdom as we now know it. Equally, there is no comfortable half-way house between these two extremes. And let us now examine two other possible solutions to the problem of Scottish and Welsh representation at Westminster:

3   A third possibility is that Scottish and Welsh representation at Westminster should be reduced — a solution that tends to attract pro-devolutionists who pride themselves on being realistic.

    Scottish over-representation at Westminster is something that needs to be dealt with in any event; but reduced representation still does not solve the problem of irresponsible participation in other people's affairs. It is no more acceptable that 57, 50, 35 or 10 MPs should vote on matters for which they have literally no responsibility than that the existing 71 should do so.

    Incidentally, reducing the number of Scottish MPs at Westminster would, of course, defeat the entire purpose for which many Labour MPs — worried at SNP victories, and frightened of losing traditional Labour fiefs in Scotland — devised and supported devolution in the first place, namely to preserve the numerical level of Labour representation at Westminster.

4   The final possibility is that Scottish and Welsh MPs should speak and vote only on those matters — the reserved areas — which had not been transferred to the Assemblies in Edinburgh and Cardiff. This would put them in the same position as the 'in and out members' as they used to be called during the debates over Gladstone's 1893 Home Rule Bill. This too is indefensible. Apart from the fact that they would inevitably be thought of as second-class MPs, the fundamental difficulty — which bedevils the whole devolution issue — is that it is virtually impossible in a unitary state to distinguish one set of topics from another. Social topics — which might theoretically be the preserve of the Assemblies — and overall economic policy are inextricably intertwined: every Budget debate, for example, includes discussion of 'devolved' areas such as the level of housing subsidies, school meals and similar contentious social issues as well as of 'national' issues such as wages policy. As the economies of the world's nations become increasingly interdependent, there are few debates on foreign policy in general — and on such issues as foreign loans, the EEC or the International Monetary Fund in particular — which do not refer to their implications for domestic and social policies.

All this would put the luckless MPs from Scotland and Wales in an absurd, even impossible, position. Given all the good will in the world — which does not, and is never likely to exist — one cannot have Members of the same Parliament with different functions and different limitations. Is it really likely that any Government with a majority of under fifty would ask its Scottish MPs to refrain from voting on crucial issues which did not theoretically concern them, particularly if it was not clear whether the vote in question concerned a 'national' or a purely 'English' issue? Rules would have to be drawn up whereby one could decide on which issues the Scots and the Welsh could and could not vote: yet, as we have seen, it would be almost impossible for the Chair to pronounce satisfactorily on this. Defence, for example, may well seem to be a subject of 'national' interest, yet it is astonishing how often such matters as educational or housing expenditure are debated along with the level of defence expenditure — and rightly so! The Speaker would be put in a highly invidious position — and he would inevitably be drawn into the hurly-burly of party politics.

If there is to be an entrenched separation of functions between Westminster and the Assemblies the United Kingdom should become a Federal state in which all the parts have equal rights in relation to the centre.

The Role of the Judicial Committee

Everything we have said so far points to inevitable and all too frequent clashes between Westminster and the Edinburgh Assembly over the division of responsibilities between them. How could these conflicts be resolved?

Perhaps the only tenable answer to this problem is to set up a Judicial Committee of the Privy Council. Such a proposal seems entirely reasonable at first glance: who is better equipped than the judiciary to give a disinterested opinion? To counter the inevitable, if unfair, argument that Her Majesty's judges are divorced from the realities of life, the Judicial Committee should also include Privy Councillors with years of political experience behind them. However, the presence of judges on the Judicial Committee would bestow on it legitimacy, and a reputation for impartiality, in the public mind.

To expect judges from the English High Court and Senators from the College of Justice in Scotland to settle demarcation disputes between the High School and Westminster raises some very fundamental issues. The strength of the British judicial system lies partly in its record of uninvolvement in party politics, something for which it has been much admired in the rest of the world: yet it is now suggested that judges should become involved in trying to resolve arguments over the most delicate and sensitive matters of political power — and any dispute which comes before the Committee is bound to be one which arouses extremely strong feelings.

Let us take an imaginary example. Suppose a Tameside type

of row over education developed somewhere in Scotland (as
one very nearly did in Leith in 1976). Should a local education
authority be forced to go comprehensive against its will? It is
by no means clear from the most recent devolution Bill whether
the authority for dealing with such a situation should reside
with the High School or Westminster. The Assembly in Edinburgh might well take the view that comprehensive education
ought not to be enforced, while the Government in Westminster — which could well be of a different political complexion —
might insist that it should. To imagine that Westminster would
meekly give way is to ignore political reality. Scottish supporters
of the Westminster point of view, perhaps belonging to the
same party as the Westminster Government, would hurry to
present their point of view in London and demand that the
Government should overrule the Assembly. If, on the other
hand, a left-wing Assembly in Edinburgh tried to force independent schools in Scotland to go comprehensive — and the
Conservatives were in power in London — it is hard to imagine
Edward Taylor, MP, not leading an indignant delegation
begging Mrs Thatcher to do something about it.

Such an issue would then be referred to the Judicial Committee; and whatever verdict they reached, however convincing
their arguments, they would inevitably alienate at least one
political faction, and possibly every party to the dispute. However objective their judgment might be, it would be seen as a
political act — and disputed as such. If Britain needs a Supreme
Court like that in Washington — and the written Constitution
that goes with it — we ought to say so: but no such provision is
made in the Scotland and Wales Bill, nor would it be at all
proper to do so. Our political traditions are very different from
those of the United States: all we would be doing is to drag a
reluctant High Court into the most acrimonious political
arguments. Michael Foot and other left-wing MPs all used their
powers of invective to attack Sir John Donaldson for presiding
over Mr Heath's short-lived Industrial Relations Court: yet
his political role was far less invidious than that now proposed
for the judges serving on the Judicial Committee.

Suppose a Minister at Whitehall thought that a Scottish Bill
lay outside the competence of the Assembly. Now it is possible
that in any given case a friendly approach through 'usual

Parliamentary channels' could work, and a compromise be reached. It is much more likely, however, that, once the Bill had been published, the Assembly would not be prepared to concede that they had exceeded their powers and withdraw the Bill in order that the matter under consideration could be dealt with from London. Such an admission is a lot to ask of even the most amenable politicians and the most accommodating political organisations, let alone those who have come to power out of a desire to 'bash Westminster'.

The Whitehall Minister would either have to give in to the High School or refer the matter to the Judicial Committee. It doesn't require much imagination to picture the headlines in the Scottish press — much of which has always been stridently pro-devolution — if the Judicial Committee refused to give the Assembly a hearing: if they did, the whole law-making process would grind to a halt while the Committee heard evidence and deliberated. Dickens's Circumlocution Office would be as nothing to it!

The judges themselves are appalled at the prospect. The Judicial Committee would be being asked to do something which judges in the United States and other countries, as well as in Britain, have always regarded as falling outside their province: to pronounce in the abstract on hypothetical issues without having the advantage of evidence or argument from actual cases and before the practical consequences of their decisions can reasonably be foreseen. To make matters worse, it seems that a ruling by the Committee in favour of a particular Scottish measure would not be intended to bind other courts in deciding whether the measure was or was not within the Assembly's competence. It is quite possible that the very same judge could be party to one ruling in the Committee and a contrasting ruling at a later stage when called upon to interpret the actual effects of the same measure.

Nothing could be more calculated to bring British justice into disrepute. It is not the business of judges to concern themselves with hypothetical situations. Government Ministers may claim that they are pioneering novel forms of government. Maybe they are: but it is equally probable that no other Government has been as unwilling to face up to the implications of such slapdash proposals as far as they affect the courts. Their proposals

have little or nothing to do with good government, but a great
deal to do with what they mistakenly think of as political imperatives.

The Role of the Secretary of State

The role of the judges is inextricably tied up with that of the
Secretary of State for Scotland, whose continued existence
would complicate relations between Westminster and the
Assembly still further. The Scotland and Wales Bill suggested
that the Judicial Committee should be given the power to decide
whether or not an Assembly Bill is *intra vires* or not: yet if the
patient reader plods on through its jargon he will find that in
Clause 45 the power of veto is returned to London, based solely
on the discretion of the Secretary of State supported by a
majority in Parliament. If he acts in this way, and in reality he
is bound to, there is no need for the Judicial Committee to give
its own views on the matter. And as if this were not enough for
Assembly members to stomach, the Bill then gives the Secretary
of State the power to order the Scottish Government to act or
desist from certain acts. He will also be able to veto Statutory
Instruments and planning decisions. There would be at least
thirty-seven clear situations involving supposedly devolved
areas in which the Assembly could only act with the consent,
approval and acquiescence of the Secretary of State.

The role of the Secretary of State would be an extremely
tricky one as far as his relations with his Parliamentary and
Ministerial colleagues in London and with the Edinburgh
Assembly were concerned. The mind boggles at what would
happen if a future incumbent had the curmudgeonly qualities
of some of his recent predecessors. The 1974 Labour Party
election manifesto faithfully promised that, should an Assembly
be created, the Secretary of State would still remain in the
Cabinet: the chances are that he would become less and less
acceptable both in Scotland and to his Labour Party colleagues.

In Scotland itself, the Secretary of State would come to be
regarded as a kind of High Commissioner in London, whose
responsibilities and obligations could all too easily conflict with
those of the Chief Executive. Prime Ministers inevitably like to
conduct really crucial business themselves: any Scottish Chief

Executive worth his salt would want to negotiate directly with 10 Downing Street, and would resent being upstaged or by-passed by the Secretary of State. The prestige of the Secretary of State would inevitably be reduced in Scotland. Until now, he has always been a central figure in Scottish life, with a 'digni-fied' — in the sense in which Bagehot used the word — as well as a purely political role. Much of this would now be assumed by the Chief Executive.

Equally, the Secretary of State would carry far less political clout into the Cabinet. His colleagues would soon discover that it made more sense for them to discuss basic economic and social issues, whether theoretically devolved or not, with the Chief Executive and his Cabinet. The Secretary of State for Scotland would be under pressure to surrender his seat in the Cabinet to the holder of another portfolio, or it might be decided to reduce the size of the Cabinet. No longer would Scotland be rep-resented at the Tuesday and Thursday Cabinet meetings; and even if the Secretary remained in the Cabinet on sufferance or as political window-dressing, he would be largely ineffective.

Relations between the Chief Executive and the Cabinet in London might theoretically be easier if both Governments were from the same political party or of the same ideological com-plexion. This might not in fact be the case, particularly if the setting up of the Assembly had been accompanied by bitterness and recriminations: and prickly, contentious issues like the distribution of oil revenues would present problems however theoretically amicable relations might be. Relations are unlikely to be exactly cosy even if both administrations are formed by colleagues of the same party.

But in fact — as Sir Harold Wilson has always foreseen — the chances of party colleagues occupying both Downing Street and Charlotte Square are fairly slim, given that there always tends to be a natural reaction against the party of Government, particularly in the middle of its term, and that Westminster and Assembly elections would almost certainly be held at different times. If, for example, a Labour Government in London was proving unpopular, the reaction against Labour would in-fluence the course of elections for the Assembly, making it more likely that a Conservative administration would be returned in Edinburgh.

Conclusions

The fundamental flaw in the proposals set out in the Scotland and Wales Bill is that those who have advocated devolution in both the major political parties have, as we have seen, been almost exclusively concerned with saving their own political skins. Too busy watching the nationalists over their shoulders, they have groped from one desperate expedient to another and cobbled together a dog's breakfast of a Bill as a result.

An acid test of the Government's proposals is to ask oneself whether, should it be in a position to implement them, they are likely to be operating in their suggested form in five or ten years' time. Everything we have discussed in this chapter suggests that an Assembly of the type that is proposed would be unworkable, and that — as the SNP have always maintained — it would represent little more than a staging-post on the way to full independence.

According to the SNP's official spokesman on devolution, the Government's Bill is the 'road' to full independence, while Neal Ascherson of the *Scotsman* feels that the Assembly, with all its contradictions and incompatibilities, could well be a kind of pod within which independence would ripen. Perhaps the situation was best summed up by Donald Stewart, MP for the Western Isles and Parliamentary Leader of the SNP, when he compared the process of getting a legislative Assembly in Edinburgh to heaving a huge boulder up to the top of a hill. Once it had reached the top, it would then run down hill under its own momentum — towards independence.

Those pro-devolutionists who claim that they are anxious above all to preserve the unity of the United Kingdom — and argue that this can only be achieved by granting devolution to Scotland and Wales — should ask themselves why it was that the keenest supporters of the Bill in the House of Commons during the four-day debate on the Second Reading were those on the Scottish and Welsh nationalist parties' benches.

12

The Unrealities

In the last chapter we suggested that devolution represented an unworkable and unrealistic half-way measure, and that far from satisfying or assuaging nationalist aspirations it would tend to convert even those Scots who had hitherto opposed it to separatism, and make Scottish independence and the break-up of the United Kingdom merely a question of time. We will now examine some of the arguments against devolution which have not already been discussed in that chapter and in Chapter 10.

The Irrelevance of Devolution

Perhaps the most shocking aspect of the whole devolution saga is that so much time and energy should have been wasted — and continues to be wasted — on an issue which is utterly peripheral to the real problems facing the country as a whole and Scotland in particular. At a time when Britain's long-standing economic problems have made her a source of pity and embarrassment to her friends, her political leaders have preferred to tinker around and make constitutional but entirely marginal alterations to existing institutions, instead of tackling the fundamental issue of the economy.

'Bringing government closer to the people' is one of those easy panaceas which sound attractive but in fact may provide politicians with an elaborate excuse for shying away from difficult and unpopular decisions. As we will see later in this chapter, devolution would not in fact bring government any closer to the people; and it is hard to believe that many of those who have suddenly discovered themselves to be devolutionists in the last few years are concerned that it should. But what matters here is that few of those who advocate devolution even go so far as to suggest that it would do anything to solve the problems which are common to Scotland and to the rest of the United Kingdom: the low investment, antiquated industrial plant, low productivity per man, poor industrial relations, unemployment, unreliable delivery dates and the rest of the gloomy litany which has become so familiar to us in the last fifteen years or so. Solving the country's economic problems would do far more for the average worker in Scotland than providing him with an unnecessary and unwanted Assembly would ever do. Britain's ability to compete with her European partners, with the United States and with Japan is weakened with every day that passes: yet the Government prefers to waste priceless time dreaming up expensive and impractical schemes like devolution.

A Bureaucrat's Delight

To their credit, the Government have been sensitive to charges that devolution would lead to a swelling of the bureaucracy; for there can be no doubt at all that the establishment of an Assembly would be a red-letter day for bureaucrats (and Constitutional lawyers). At a time when the Prime Minister has given top priority to helping manufacturing and productive industry and reducing public expenditure by central and local government, it would be surprising if the Government were not at pains to protect themselves from accusations of doing exactly the opposite by setting up Assemblies in Edinburgh and Cardiff. Yet the contrast between the way in which local authorities and the proposed Assemblies are treated is striking. For example on 22 July 1976 the Prime Minister was busy assuring the House of Commons that

> In the case of an individual authority that breaks the limit, the Government will be taking powers to withhold not just any excess over the £6, but the full amount of the settlement. If an individual local authority seeks to finance an evasion of the limitation by manipulation of its capital finance, the Government have made clear that they will

use all their existing powers to control, case by case, that authority's borrowing, including access to the capital market [Hansard].

Yet that very same day notice was given of a very substantial rise in the estimates for converting the Royal High School in Edinburgh and the Coal Exchange in Cardiff.

On 14 December 1976, the Shadow Secretary of State for Scotland, Edward Taylor, asked the Secretary of State, Bruce Millan, if he thought it would serve any useful purpose to employ 1,000 extra civil servants in Scotland in order that there should be more people available to tell local authorities that they should employ fewer home helps for the elderly and fewer road-crossing attendants. Mr Taylor claims that 80 per cent of the estimated 2,300 extra civil servants required to service a Scottish Assembly would result from there being a separate Executive — something some Conservative pro-devolutionists do not want.

As a result of devolution the Scots will not only be suffocated by bureaucrats; they will also be the most overgoverned people on earth. In the 1960s areas of Glasgow and Edinburgh were represented by one MP and two Town Councillors; by 1978, they could be represented by a Member of the European Parliament, a Westminster MP, two or possibly three Edinburgh Assembly Members, three Regional Councillors and six District Councillors.

The Government have two basic answers to these accusations, both equally weak. The first — given on several occasions by Harry Ewing, MP, Under-Secretary at the Scottish Office with devolution responsibilities — is that one cannot pay too high a price for democracy. This is to confuse the quantity of democracy being offered with its quality.

The second is to claim that most of the civil servants needed are in existence already, and that they will simply be transferred to meet the new circumstances. Quite apart from the fact that there is a widespread feeling that the Civil Service is overstaffed as it is, if this were remotely true (and the Civil Service unions doubt if it is) it would not solve the problem of civil servants' dual allegiance to a Scottish Government and to Westminster, which may well be even more acute than has been anticipated.

Duplication of work and the conflict of loyalties within the Civil Service is an even more serious problem than the actual costs involved. There would inevitably be many borderline cases where civil servants working for the Assembly encroached upon or came into conflict with their equivalents working for the United Kingdom Government, and vice versa. And it is very doubtful whether civil servants can be answerable to two sets of masters. The very essence of the Civil Service is that it is loyal to the Government of the day, whatever the political complexion of that Government. If devolution came about, the role of many civil servants would be very similar to that of attempting to serve both God and Mammon. Probably they would opt to give priority to the Assembly or to Westminster according to how they see their career prospects.

It could be — as Dr James Kellas of Strathclyde University has argued — that civil servants working for a Scottish Assembly would feel that they no longer owed any allegiance to Whitehall, and that a 'wall of silence' would be raised between the two Governments, bringing the passage of information between them to a halt. The effect of this on the already shaky British economy — on both sides of the Border — hardly bears thinking about.

Incidentally, it is worth remembering that the Scottish Office already employs more people than the notorious 'Brussels bureaucracy' for the whole of the EEC. Obviously its responsibilities are very different: it does not alter the fact that Scotland now has more civil servants than any other part of the United Kingdom, including South-East England, and that — quite apart from its expense — a further dose of bureaucracy is something the country can well do without.

Bloated Bureaucracy?

It is strongly suspected that devolution will breed significantly more bureaucrats than any Government source has officially admitted. The 1977 Scotland and Wales Bill acknowledged that Scotland would need an extra 990 civil servants if there was an Assembly. Wales, which has less administrative devolution at the present time, would need 1,300 extra civil servants. Yet, no mention is made of several governmental United Kingdom bodies, which would lose their English head, and need to grow a new one in Scotland and Wales. For example, the Countryside Commission, based at Cheltenham, has a Committee for Wales with a staff of 6. The Bill proposes a whole new Countryside Commission for Wales, with a strength of 25; there would be no balancing decrease in English staff. Again, the Scottish and Welsh out-stations of the British Tourist Authority will be empowered to supplement the authority's advertising overseas. Both the Welsh and Scottish Tourist Boards have plans to put a Scottish and a Welsh representative into at least some of the authority's 21 offices abroad.

Then take the case of the British Airports Authority. The present position is that the Authority runs three airports in England — Heathrow, Gatwick, and Stansted — and four airports in Scotland — at Glasgow, Edinburgh, Prestwick and Aberdeen. It is proposed to devolve the Scottish four, which will lose their London expertise and back-up. No reason is forthcoming; it can only be assumed that Government Ministers have been frantically casting around to find every conceivable task for the Assembly, however inappropriate, in order to give the Assemblymen something to do, and to justify their plans. In January 1977, an official spokesman for the BAA actually put it thus: 'We would imagine that if Scottish airports became autonomous, they would have to duplicate head office planning, personnel, engineering, design, and finance functions.' Let it be said that these same functions occupy a London staff of 750, for seven airports. Professional opinion says that the four Scottish fields, comparably serviced — and modern regulations require comparable servicing, if there is not to be the risk of a Tenerife-type disaster — would need a new Edinburgh staff of about 400. Nor should it be supposed that the 750 in London would be reduced.

In the calculation of 990 extra civil servants, no estimate could be made of the detailed shape of a devolved Scottish Assembly. How many Members of the Scottish Cabinet would there be, each with an office to staff? How many subject committees would there be in an Assembly, each with its staff? What hours would the Assembly sit — a very important factor in determining the numbers required? Nor does Westminster experience suggest that the Scots Assembly members would be any more concise than English MPs!

The basis of Whitehall's calculation of 990 extra civil servants assumed only those governmental tasks which are done in Scotland already. No allowance is made for any attempt to improve the service. Yet, notionally, what is the point of the change, unless it is to improve the service? 'It's bound to require new ideas, and thus generate more paper,' said Campbell Christie, Deputy General Secretary of the Society of Civil and Public Servants, 'so you'll need more people to write the paper!' One wonders whether in fact the figure was not dreamed up out of thin air, and in a similar vein of thought to those chain-store managers who label many items at 99 p., since they think it is more attractive than crossing the £1 threshold.

The Civil Service Department have pointed to what could be a more serious matter, and one which greatly bothers some senior civil servants. Under the Scotland and Wales Bill, the cost of the extra staff will be borne by the Scottish and Welsh administrations out of their block grants from Westminster. The Assemblies might well be tempted to lower recruiting standards, in comparison with the United Kingdom Civil Service, or even try to save money on pay scales. The Civil Service Department and professional associations think that one could not go far down that road without reaching a position absolutely contrary to current Government policy — namely, separate Civil Services in Scotland and in England. If it came to that, the Scottish Civil Service would have to run its own personnel services, which the devolution White Paper of 1975 identified as a particularly costly item. Any advance on governmental accountability would be more than offset by the rise in cost and chaos in the government machine.

The Government's soothing claim is that the problem of the payment of additional civil servants is nicely contained within the Scotland and Wales Bill by the mechanism of the block grant. If, say the Government, the Assemblies in Edinburgh and Cardiff choose to spend a lot of the block grant on extra officials, then, too bad, they will have that much less to spend on welfare benefits or grants to industry. But such a suggestion does not come within the realm of reality. By no stretch of human nature will the Assemblymen see the position in that rational light. They will unquestionably demand a duly increased block grant on the grounds that if the Westminster

Government has willed certain constitutional arrangements, then Westminster must also will the money to pay for the staff changes which result. Possibly, in the ordinary process of bargaining, part of the claim will be conceded, and the extra cost will be met by United Kingdom taxpayers. It might be reasonably held that if functions are transferred to Scotland and Wales, the number of people engaged on those functions in England ought to diminish. From the examples already discussed, and from my conversations with the Chairman of the Forestry Commission, the signs are that the English numbers — where people have contracts — will not diminish.

The trouble is not that civil servants are lazy or inefficient, but that they produce nothing. The truth is that Britain must have more people working in the productive sector of the economy than in the service sector. The Prime Minister has underlined this point more effectively than any statesman in recent years. That is one reason why his commendation of the Scotland and Wales Bill is disingenuous. The measures he commends are certain to help proliferate non-productive jobs.

One answer to this problem is to write firm staffing figures into a devolution Bill, and require the Assemblies to return to the House of Commons whenever they need an extra member of staff, or an extra post. Yet the pro-devolutionists would argue with some justice that the assemblies would then have their hands so tied in advance as to make the whole process of devolution a pointless sham. At the end of the day, perhaps the real choice is indeed between wastefulness and going ahead with a charade, and recognising the pointlessness of the whole caper. Certainly, if staffing were allowed to grow like Topsy, this in itself would be reason enough for rejecting the whole devolution exercise.

Devolution and Local Government

A fundamental misapprehension on the part of those who favour the setting up of Scottish and Welsh Assemblies is that devolution is the same thing as decentralisation, and that it would somehow bring government 'closer to the people' making it less remote and more receptive to local points of view. 'Decentralisation' and 'participation' are of course fashionable political panaceas at the moment and to some extent, rightly so: yet it is extremely unlikely that devolution would in fact have the desired effect at all. The government of Scotland and Wales would become more, rather than less, centralised and regional and local government would be the losers: and since, as we shall see in the next section, different parts of Scotland have different requirements, local needs would be less sensitively treated than they are at present.

Before examining this argument in more detail, it might be worth reflecting on the future of local government in Scotland should devolution come about. As I see it, there are three possible alternatives:

1   The present Regions and Districts of Scotland — established in 1974 following the recommendations of the Wheatley Committee Report — would be retained intact. If this were the case, my own constituency would have to elect and help pay for Community Councils, West Lothian District Council, Lothian Regional Council, the Convention of Scottish Local Authorities, the Edinburgh Assembly, the Westminster Parliament and the directly-elected European Parliament, as well as the EEC Commission in Brussels. As suggested in the last section, this would make them just about the most overgoverned people on earth.

2   There should be some forty to fifty all-purpose authorities below the Assembly. This means an equal number of separate police forces, fire brigades, education authorities, water authorities and planning departments, each with its own administrative and managerial structures. This would certainly not provide a cheaper or more effective form of government. Whatever one's views on the Wheatley Report, it was generally — and rightly — agreed at the time that there were far too many authorities exercising major local government responsibilities. Putting the clock back to the pre-Wheatley days does not bear thinking about — quite apart from the sheer cost of the exercise.

3   The new Regions established after the Wheatley Report — Strathclyde, Lothian, Borders, Dumfries and

Galloway, Central, Grampian, Fife, Tayside, Highland, Orkney and Shetland, and the Western Isles —
should be done away with within a decade of their
having been set up. Superficially this has its attractions
since, like all new government organisations, the
Regions have had teething troubles, made worse by the
fact that they came into existence in a time of economic
difficulty. It is extremely frivolous to suggest — like
some MPs who should know better — that the Regions
should be done away with at a stroke. It is all too easy to
attack the Regions for their undoubted faults: yet the
Scots themselves would quickly realise that if they were
abolished decision-making in such areas of immediate
and real concern as education and housing — for which
the Assembly would rapidly assume more and more
authority — had in fact been taken further from them.

Those who favour abolishing the Regions have suggested
that responsibility for the day-to-day running of the police, fire
brigades, education, water, planning, etc., should be transferred
from the Regions to the Assembly, leaving administration of
minor local government services to a single-tier local government structure. A single police force for the whole of Scotland
would then be created — a proposal which many people view
with apprehension and alarm given the volatile state of Scottish
politics at the moment, and has little support among the police
themselves. Responsibility for the everyday administration of
schools from Stranraer to the Shetlands would be centred on
Edinburgh. This would be centralisation with a vengeance, the
very opposite of bringing decision-making closer to the people.

The Regions are sometimes criticised on the grounds that
local government has become remote from the people, yet it
must not be forgotten that the Regional authorities are demo-
cratically elected bodies: and if they seem remote, how much
more so would an Assembly that was effectively controlling
large areas of local government be!

One of the great fallacies of the whole devolution debate is
the superficially seductive but mistaken assumption that all
governmental decisions are likely to be that much better for
having been taken at as local a level as possible. Of course it is

important that local affairs should be dealt with at a local level. It is good that there should be a local rent office where people's problems can be sorted out, face-to-face, by authorities who are informed about and sensitive to local problems. It is a good thing if the local education authority offices are within reach if one has children at school. For these reasons it is essential that local issues should be dealt with — as they are at present — by local authorities rather than centralised on an Assembly. On the other hand, in a highly complex and increasingly integrated industrial economy it is essential that decisions of national importance — the management of the economy, foreign affairs and so forth — should be taken at a national level: in other words, by the Government in London. To emasculate Scottish local government in order to centralise the running of local government on Edinburgh would be in no one's interests.

There is no doubt that local government in Scotland as elsewhere has had an extremely bad press in recent years, and this is something which the SNP have benefited from, in local and national elections. Hardly a day goes by without some local authority or other being accused of profligacy or malpractice of some kind: and the media delight in stories of their alleged wasting of enormous sums of money on totally unnecessary manpower or equipment. The implication is that the same services would be cheaper and better if they were provided by somebody else, presumably a private entrepreneur or a national public authority — the only alternative being that local authority services should not be provided at all, to the enormous disadvantage of the less well-off members of the community.

Despite the constant criticism, the reorganisation of local government in Scotland has made the effective political control and direction of local authorities more feasible. The Wheatley Commission was particularly anxious to restore a degree of independence to local government, and free it from the close direction of central government Departments: this has been achieved, and the management of local government vastly improved as a result. Inevitably a major reorganisation of this kind has had its problems: it is unreasonable to expect Regional councillors and officials to adapt themselves to the changes overnight, and equally unreasonable to expect them to participate in yet another major upheaval.

Abolition of the Regions seems to offer a neat solution to those pro-devolutionists who are sensitive to the charge of over-government. But District authorities could not be expected to assume responsibility for the functions of the Regions, which would have to be transferred to the Assembly — in other words, to the state. In fact it would spell the beginning of the end for local democracy and local government in Scotland.

Edinburgh and the Isles

One of the great virtues of the post-Wheatley reforms is that they recognised that Scotland is made up of different regions, all with their own — and often very different — priorities and problems; and that the most sensible way to deal with them would be at the Regional level. Scotland is only a coherent entity as far as the Church of Scotland, the law, primary and secondary education and, of course, football, are concerned. The needs of the Borders are very different from those of Glasgow — indeed, as we have seen, if devolution was really concerned with good government rather than with trying to appease vague notions of 'national identity', the natural unit for decision-making on the Borders would be centred on Berwick-on-Tweed and include North Northumberland. In Anglo-Saxon times, Northumberland stretched well up the east coast of Scotland — always assuming that historical precedent is anything to go by, as nationalists claim it is! Even such a small — if contentious — issue as the licensing laws makes more sense if operated on a Regional basis to take account of local susceptibilities: the Western Isles take a very different attitude towards the vexed issue of Sunday opening of pubs from the Edinburgh and Lothian Regions!

This whole issue has of course been highlighted by the Shetland Isles' well-known opposition to an Assembly in Edinburgh, which has proved a godsend to anti-devolutionists and to those anxious to deride the SNP. The Shetlands were under Norse rule for 700 years, Scottish rule for the next 200 years, and have been under British rule for the past 250 years. They have made it clear that, while they do not dislike the Scots, they are different from them. 'Inverness is a town with which we have little or no contact,' says James Jamieson, Vice-Convener of the Shetland Islands Council:*

> We do not wish to become involved in a question of devolution for Scotland, since we feel that such a matter is for the people of Scotland to decide. We, however, see no advantage to Shetland in such devolution and would like to avoid its application to Shetland.

Orkney holds similar views, though its opposition is less tinged with Scandinavian irredentism. The Councils of both Orkney and Shetland feel that the Assembly's chief concern would be with alleviating unemployment in the industrial belt of Scotland, and that too little consideration would be given to outlying areas. They also fear that an Edinburgh Assembly would be far more likely to interfere with their powers, under the 1975 Shetland Isles Act, than Westminster — not least as far as the oil reserve funds are concerned. Although Shetlanders would like to be paid compensation from North Sea oil revenues for the disruption caused them, they are not at all possessive about the oil itself, which they regard as British oil and for the benefit of Britain as a whole.

They are quite happy for the British Government to use North Sea oil as a collateral for the British economy, and they have made it quite clear that, if the Assembly comes into being, they would prefer to retain their links with London. No doubt aware of such feelings in his own constituency, Jo Grimond, himself a Federalist with leanings towards an independent Scotland, felt obliged to table a Parliamentary question to the Prime Minister asking for a guarantee that any devolution legislation would take into account the special position of Orkney and Shetland. As he told *The Times*, 'Many people in the North of Scotland fear centralisation on Edinburgh and Glasgow almost as much as London'.

This feeling that Edinburgh would want to interfere more than Westminster, while at the same time being less concerned with the outlying regions of the country than with the industrial belt, is not restricted to the Shetlands and the Orkneys. The

* Speaking at Newcastle on 7 January 1977 at the Tyne and Wear County Council Conference on Devolution.

Assembly would, inevitably, be dominated by Members representing urban and industrial constituencies: Highland and Grampian Regional councillors are convinced that the problems affecting their areas can be far more effectively and understandingly dealt with from Inverness and Aberdeen. Whereas London is quite happy to let the Regions settle down, and possibly to devolve more powers to them, such as licensing, Regional councillors fear that Edinburgh would not only interfere, but that the existence of an additional layer of government would eventually lead to the abolition of the Regions. That would by no means be to the taste of the outlying areas.

Scotland's Interests Suffer

We must now turn to the question of Scotland's relations with the rest of the country following devolution, and to two issues in particular: the fact that Scotland would no longer receive preferential treatment from Westminster to provide jobs and stimulate its economy; and the fact that — particularly if the Edinburgh Assembly tried to take an over-possessive attitude towards the oil revenues — there would almost certainly be an English backlash which could prove harmful to Scotland's real interests.

Many of the economic arguments against devolution, both from the point of view of Scotland and from that of the United Kingdom as a whole, were discussed in some detail in Chapter 9. We saw there that industrialists and financiers on both sides of the Border are convinced that devolution would not be in the interest of the economy, and there is no point in our going into these arguments again. On a more general level, though, it is fairly safe to say that once Scotland had an Assembly of its own — albeit one whose responsibilities were limited to 'devolved' subjects, thus excluding the general management of the economy — politicians at Westminster would feel far less inclined to bear Scotland's interests in mind than they do at present, and far more likely to lend an ear to those regions of England with problems similar to those of Scotland.

As we saw in Chapter 9, Scotland has tended to receive more than its fair share in terms of Regional aid, government incentives and so forth: both the major parties have been anxious to woo the Scottish electorate, and the presence in the Cabinet of the Secretary of State for Scotland has heightened governmental awareness of Scottish problems and needs. We suggested earlier that the role of the Secretary of State would almost certainly be reduced once a Scottish government had come into being, and that even if he remained in the Cabinet he would carry far less weight than before; English politicians in particular could be forgiven for feeling that having asked for devolution the Scots should bear the consequences, and that once the annual block grant had been agreed upon it was up to the Scots to make the best of it. Devolutionists could argue that no sensible British Government would want to risk pushing the Scots into demanding full independence — and losing however many Scottish seats their party still held at Westminster — by neglecting their interests, and that rather than run such a risk they would be more anxious than ever to look after Scotland's interests. This is to ignore the fact that other parts of the country would be competing for increasingly scarce resources, and since these would not have their own Assemblies London would feel more directly responsible for them; and since, as we have argued, the Assembly would only be a very temporary staging post on the way to full independence, such developments could well be anticipated anyway on the purely political level.

Perhaps the simplest thing would be to illustrate my point with one or two examples. The first of these concerns what was known as the 'Linwood affair' in Scotland, and the 'Chrysler crisis' in the rest of the kingdom. In the autumn of 1975, John D. Riccardo, the President of Chrysler's parent corporation in Detroit, pointed the proverbial shotgun at the British Government and threatened that unless immediate government aid was forthcoming he would close down Chrysler's British operations, and in particular the Linwood plant in Renfrewshire, which employs some 6,000 people. A closure would have had disastrous consequences in an area already scourged by heavy unemployment.

As is well known, the Cabinet was deeply divided over whether the Government should in fact agree to bail out Chrysler, particularly since the Company's British operations had been notoriously badly run. Both the Chancellor of the

Exchequer, Denis Healey, and the Minister of Industry, Eric Varley, opposed giving aid to Chrysler, yet the arguments of the Secretary of State for Scotland, William Ross — which were essentially political rather than economic — carried the day, and Mr Riccardo's terms were agreed to. Had the Linwood plant not been situated in Scotland, it is improbable that the government would have taken what looked like, in strictly economic terms, an unwise decision; it is unlikely that Scottish considerations would weigh as heavily should a similar situation arise after devolution.

My second example occurred six months later, in the sweltering summer of 1976. It was widely believed that the Government had struck some kind of bargain with the SNP in return for votes at a crucial stage in the Shipbuilding Bill. Despite strenuous denials by Labour Ministers and the SNP, many MPs and others realised for the first time the extent to which a small nationalist party operating within the context of a unitary state could exercise an influence out of all proportion to their support in the country, and hold the rest of the United Kingdom up to ransom. The issue was revived in the autumn of that year. For some months the highly competitive rig-building yard at Graythorpes, Teesside, had been begging for orders to replace work completed ahead of schedule. No Government help was forthcoming. Then, at the end of 1976, another yard, the American-owned Marathon on Clydebank, ran into similar trouble. Within days, the Government had decided to come to the rescue with £14 million. The decision may have been justified, but it looked suspiciously as though Marathon was being given favourable treatment on grounds of geography and nationality rather than of technical competence.

North-East England was understandably incensed. More than any other issue, the Marathon episode prompted the Tyne and Wear County Council to stage its huge demonstration against the whole concept of devolution. The English backlash had begun in earnest.

The English Backlash

Although — as we have just seen — the Scots stand to lose in the long run from devolution, the English regions would inevitably feel that, with their own Assembly and Chief Executive as well as the Secretary of State looking after their interests in the the Cabinet, the Scots were trying to have their cake and eat it. The result could be what Eric Heffer has described as 'the ugly face of English nationalism'; and for the constituent countries of the United Kingdom to be at sullen loggerheads with one another would be to the benefit of no one.

Britain would still remain a country of regions following devolution; and some of these have problems which are quite as deep-seated and stubborn as those of Clydeside and far worse than those of the rest of Scotland, which is relatively well off. In terms of income per head, the south-west of England is very much worse off than Scotland; three regions, East Anglia, North-East England and Northern Ireland are worse off; while most of the others are in roughly the same position. Few others are in the privileged position of London and the South-East. How could a large-scale redistribution of income from the rest of the country to Scotland take place without invidious distinctions being made? (It had been suggested that, if Scotland kept a sizable proportion of the North Sea oil revenues, the block grant could then be that much lower: yet to do so would involve costly and Byzantine accounting operations, and inevitable accusations that Scotland was trying to hog all the benefits of the oil.)

We will be examining the elusive grail of North Sea oil in the next section. It is worth pointing out, though, that if the Scots insisted on taking an over-possessive attitude to it, the English could be forgiven if they turned round and claimed that English coal, natural gas, china clay and so forth were to be used for the exclusive benefit of England rather than of the United Kingdom as a whole. Once the revenue from one part of a unitary state has been 'hypotheticated', to use the Great George Street jargon, for use in that part only, other parts will claim the same rights — to the benefit of no one, least of all the bemused and battered British economy.

For years now the Scottish coalfields have been kept going by the more productive Yorkshire, Nottinghamshire and Derbyshire fields. Would the English be prepared to go on subsidising Scottish mines — and the jobs that go with them — if the Scots refused to share the benefits of North Sea oil? Would British

Gas now face demands that natural gas found off the coast at Blackpool and Yarmouth should therefore be earmarked for the exclusive benefit of North-West England and East Anglia?

For those of us on the Left, who believe in a measure of redistribution of wealth from the relatively well off to the less well off, the transfer of oil revenues to Scotland is still less acceptable. How could one justify the distribution of such income, say, from Mr Heffer's poorer constituents in Liverpool to well-heeled Scots who would benefit simply because they happened to live north of the Border? (The huge army of Scots living south of the Border would presumably not stand to benefit: but that is another matter.)

The English backlash was predictable enough, though it took some time to get under way. This was partly because of Harold Wilson's 1974 appointment of Edward Short as his devolution supremo. Short was a Newcastle MP: North-East England has always been particularly sensitive about Scottish devolution, and it was assumed that Mr Short would keep the interests of the North-East to the fore. In this they were mistaken; as we have seen, Mr Short threw himself into his new job with messianic zeal. Encouraged by his lieutenants Gerry Fowler at the Privy Council Office and Harry Ewing at the Scottish Office, he adopted an increasingly maximalist approach to devolution; yet, because of his ties with the North-East, his old political neighbours and colleagues failed to realise how ardent a convert he had become.

Gradually the regions came to realise that they might well stand to lose from devolution, and resentment against the Scots began to build up. The possible break-up of the United Kingdom became that much more likely.

Oil

The discovery of North Sea oil provided Scottish nationalists with the break they so desperately needed. It gave them electoral credibility; it provided them with emotional and patriotic rallying force: the slogan 'It's oor oil!' conjured up a tantalising vision of a rich, independent Scotland which would cut itself free from the economic and political decrepitude of the rest of the country.

The nationalists are not alone in looking to North Sea oil for an answer to some at least of Scotland's problems. As we saw in the last chapter, some of those who would like there to be a financially self-sufficient Assembly in Edinburgh have seen taxation of the oil revenues, possibly through variations of the Petroleum Revenue Tax, as the answer to their problems. For example, Professor Thomas Wilson, of the Department of Political Economy at Glasgow University, has tentatively suggested in the *Three Banks Review* that the Assembly should be given part of the oil revenues in place of grants in aid, thus giving it 'a substantial source of revenue under its own control'. And during the Second Reading of the Scotland and Wales Bill, David Steel, the leader of the Liberal Party, suggested:

> The international oil companies are well used to dealing with different revenues being taken by different layers of government. This is done in Australia, Canada and the United States, and it should be possible to devise a scheme whereby one of the oil revenues is levied by the Scottish Assembly and not directly by the United Kingdom Treasury [Hansard, 13 December 1977].

Yet however attractive and commonsensical such schemes may seem to be, the simple fact is that until a self-sufficient level of production had been reached, the large-scale revenues which North Sea Oil would yield on present price-cost relationships would amount to a tax on the whole of the United Kingdom. For one part of the United Kingdom to appropriate them and spend them wholly or substantially for its own benefit would constitute a transfer of income from other parts of the United Kingdom to Scotland.

This aspect of the matter tends to be overlooked since most people, very understandably, feel that a new resource such as North Sea oil must represent an unequivocal addition to the country's wealth; and that if the large financial surpluses which, on present prices, would result from its exploitation were secured by Scotland this would not be at the expense of the rest of the country since they would represent new income. The reality is far more complex.

Whole volumes have been devoted to the problems of pricing oil; however, the situation can be summarised as follows. Even if the United Kingdom is roughly self-sufficient in oil by 1980, the inconvenient truth is that as far as our oil consumption is concerned we shall be worse off over the next decade than we were in the autumn of 1973, before the first world oil crisis. Man hour for man hour, North Sea oil will cost us more than Middle East oil cost us then. We shall, I agree, be better off than we are now, but that merely reflects how far we have been pushed backwards by the actions of OPEC in the last four years.

The potential revenues from North Sea oil will not arise from 'value added' production, in the generally understood use of the term, nor from any kind of 'superior rental value' of North Sea reserves, but from the prices decided on at OPEC meetings. Once we were self-sufficient, it would be economically irrational not to charge ourselves OPEC prices for our own oil. But the resulting financial surpluses would derive from monopoly profits, largely extracted from ourselves throughout the United Kingdom and equivalent in most respects to the proceeds of a tax: and they would not in any sense represent a source of new real income relative to our position before 1973.

Again, it must be realised that substantial oil revenues will only directly accrue to an independent Scotland. However, Denzil Davies, MP, writing as a Minister of State at the Treasury, has reminded us that the SNP always seem to assume that if Scotland broke away from the rest of the country, the division of oil revenues and the national debt would be settled on their terms: and in particular that Scotland would get all or most of the oil revenues. In fact any financial settlement would have to be the result of negotiation, and would depend on the economic and financial situation at the time.

Even if London meekly allowed the Scots to appropriate North Sea oil revenues, and they turned out to be the crock of gold so many people assume they will be, this might not be an unmixed blessing for Scotland. An independent Scotland, with its own monetary system and substantial revenues from exported North Sea oil and gas, might well present very real problems for existing export industries such as engineering and woollen textiles.

All nation states are under enormous pressure nowadays to adjust their industrial structure to both deficits and surpluses on their balance of payments. In a deficit situation, a country must try to increase its exports and reduce its imports; yet no sooner is it in a surplus situation than it comes under pressure from its trading partners to reduce its exports and increase its imports — much as Japan and West Germany are today. Naturally a surplus situation is much to be preferred; the country is negotiating from a position of strength, and in practice it has the option of not adjusting its balance of trade unless it suits it to do so, and in particular, of not cutting back on its exports. The snag is that it cannot spend its payments surplus internally but must use it to build up foreign assets. Large foreign assets are obviously well worth having but they do not bring about those things — such as massive urban and industrial regeneration — which are so urgently needed in Scotland.

The crucial question is whether we are prepared to dismantle the Union for the fleeting and dubious advantages of a greater share of the oil revenues. It is worth remembering that North Sea oil reserves are not inexhaustible, and would probably be depleted within three or four decades; once the bonanza was over, Scotland might well repent her impetuosity if England set her face against extending to her the benefits she had enjoyed in the days of the Union.

Nor should it be forgotten that the enormous sums that the British Government has poured into the exploration and development of North Sea oil have been contributed to by British and not merely by Scottish taxpayers; and it is extremely unlikely that English and Welsh taxpayers would be prepared to write off their investment in what has always been seen as a British enterprise simply in order to placate Scottish nationalism. Would it really be possible for Scotland on her own to raise sums of this kind in future, let alone pay back the rest of the country for the amount invested to date? Developing North Sea oil is a highly complicated and extremely expensive business, in which the British government and multinational oil companies are deeply involved; North Sea oil is essentially a British asset, and should remain as such. It is extremely unlikely that disputes between Scotland and the rest of the country over oil could lead to civil conflict, but it must not be forgotten that the relatively sudden discovery of large quantities of oil has led to acute political troubles in some states, Biafra being an obvious example.

The EEC

Great play has been made by the SNP and by James Sillars and the Scottish Labour Party about the possibility of Scotland having its own representative in the Commission at Brussels and in the crucially important Council of Ministers — as well as on other international bodies such as the United Nations. There are two obvious flaws to daydreams of this kind: would our colleagues in the EEC be prepared to admit Scotland? And if they did, would Scotland be any better off as a result?

As we saw earlier, Britain's EEC partners are incredulous about the possibility of part of a member state hiving itself off and asking for separate membership. Their reasons are not entirely disinterested: they fear that, if the principle of Scottish membership were conceded, it would encourage separatist movements within their own countries and hasten the disintegration of Europe into an almost medieval patchwork of small, weak, theoretically independent states.

Nor is it at all likely that Scotland would benefit from separate representation, however heartening it might be to national self-esteem. The smaller members of the EEC have always found that their own interests tend to be subordinated to those of the Big Four member states, who tend to decide the really important issues of EEC policy between them. Scottish interests — from regional development to the fishing industry — are likely to be far better served if Britain represents them.

Nationalism as a Protest Vote: Don't Trust the Polls

Deciding exactly why an electorate votes in a particular way is an almost impossible exercise, and to claim that it would not have voted the way it did had it known exactly what it was voting for or if the crunch had come is to open oneself up to charges of wishful thinking and ignoring the hard evidence of election results and opinion polls; yet for all that, I am quite convinced that British politicians have been quite unnecessarily panicked into jumping on to the devolutionary bandwagon by what is essentially a protest vote, by opinion polls which fail to ask the right questions, and by a press which — for its own reasons — has often tended to be stridently pro-devolutionist.

This is by no means to deny that many of the issues on which the SNP has fought and won elections do not have some justification as well as considerable appeal throughout the country, or that it has had some great successes in both local and general elections. Yet, as we saw in Chapter 10, a vote for the SNP has remained a protest vote aimed at the two major parties rather than a vote for Scottish independence, and has been taken far too seriously by politicians at Westminster. If the Scottish electorate were really faced with the possibility of an independent Scotland — with passports at Berwick, currency controls at Gretna, friends and relations in England becoming foreigners, and the industrial and commercial chaos which would inevitably ensue — they would desert the SNP in thousands and return to their original political allegiances.

It is true that the SNP have done well in local elections. For example, they won a dramatic victory in a Regional election at Bo'ness, West Lothian, in spring 1976. Predictably enough, it prompted a leading article in the *Guardian* — headed 'The Bo'ness Monster' — to the effect that British politicians must take note and give the Scots this, that and the other in order to head off the SNP challenge. From my own first-hand knowledge, the voters of Bo'ness would have been astonished to be told that they were passing judgment on the future constitutional arrangements of the United Kingdom. The issues involved were essentially internal to a small town of 12,000 people. Nor can Regional Council Elections — or even Parliamentary by-elections — tell us a great deal about the real views of Scottish people on their future relations with the rest of the country.

Again, legend has it that the SNP enjoyed massive electoral successes in 1974. To an extent, the legend is correct (though only in the February General Election did it gain a Labour seat). Since many floating voters tend to vote against rather than for parties, their successes were not altogether surprising: the untried alternative always has an appeal of some kind. But few voters in 1974 really imagined that they were voting for an SNP Government, and to that extent voting for them was a luxury in which they could afford to indulge themselves — and putting the wind up the established parties is always an agreeable occupation. It is one thing to vote SNP in the hope that by doing so you will shake up those who — rightly or wrongly — you feel have made a bad job of government or become over-complacent, or in the hope that an SNP MP would form part of a Scottish ginger group in the House of Commons: it is a completely different matter to do so if there is every chance of an SNP Government coming to power.

Public opinion polls have been equally misleading: academic pundits and newspapermen have been far too quick to leap to conclusions on the strength of replies given in the abstract to questions which do not spell out the full implications of what is involved. Until at least the end of 1976, most people in Scotland were confused, bored and bewildered by the whole subject of devolution. Despite daily coverage by the press and the BBC in Scotland, a *Scotsman* poll revealed that devolution came twenty-eighth out of thirty-one subjects listed; and that among young people, who are supposed to be interested in and enthusiastic about devolution (many of these same young people vote for the SNP), devolution fared no better.

The trouble is that the really important questions have never been put to the Scottish people. Most of them would say that they would like a greater say in their own affairs, and therefore that they favour, in a vague way, devolution. Yet if one pointed out that an Assembly in Edinburgh would necessitate yet more elections, they might well feel rather less enthusiastic on the grounds that they have far too many elections as it is. Their enthusiasm would wane still further when it was pointed out to them that they would have to pay for between three and four times as many representatives as they have at present, as well as more departments of state, twice as many Ministers and at least an additional 2,500 civil servants. When they also realised that a vote for the SNP could mean a vote for the disintegration of the Union — with all the benefits it has brought the people of Scotland — it becomes less than likely that all but the most passionate nationalists would fail to change their tunes.

Sir Harold Wilson in particular was always far too susceptible to the findings of opinion polls and temporary political developments and fluctuations: with the result that British politicians have been stampeded into supporting devolution — which, as we have argued, will give the nationalists what they want in the end — for the flimsiest of reasons.

Nationalism and the Myth of Scottish History

Myths about a nation's history should be treated with considerable caution at the best of times: if they also incorporate an unjustified — and wholly unhistorical — sense of national grievance, they should be handled with especial care. Like the Irish, the Scots have a strong and pervasive sense of history, yet all too often they prefer the romantic myth to the complicated truth; and one of the great myths which the nationalists have exploited to the full is that in which the sturdy but out-numbered Scots, throughout their history, have been oppressed and done down by their English neighbours to the south.

No one could deny that England and Scotland have from time to time come into conflict with each other in the course of their history (but only a bigot would claim that justice was invariably on one side, ruthless self-interest on the other), and it is only natural that Scots should take Cup Tie-like pride in Bannockburn and Stirling Bridge. Knocking the English in a genial way is a harmless, time-honoured national pastime (particularly at Wembley or Twickenham, Hampden or Murrayfield); but to deliberately resurrect and inflame old antagonisms and to exploit an extremely dubious interpretation of Scottish history simply in order to make political capital in the 1970s is unforgivably irresponsible. Be that as it may, myths about the way in which Scotland has been maltreated by the English continue to be believed — and to be exaggerated and diffused by the inflammatory oratory of the SNP, which realises only too well that people often prefer to believe the exciting myth to the humdrum and occasionally squalid truth (not least teachers in primary schools in need of a heroic and bloodthirsty story). It is high time that such fairy tales were finally scotched, and in the remainder of this section I will be casting a somewhat sceptical eye at the half-truths which so often pass for Scottish history and tradition.

Unlike the Irish, the Scots have never been forcibly conquered and settled by an alien people; even the Roman legions were birds of passage here. The union between the two countries was a gradual and voluntary process, entered into by both England and Scotland for their mutual benefit. As Professor Trevor-Roper has pointed out, the Union of the Crowns in

1603 — whereby a Scottish king assumed the throne of both countries — was preceded by nearly a century of deliberation; and the Act of Union in 1707, whereby the Scottish and English parliaments were both dissolved and a Parliament of Great Britain set up in their place, by half a century of discussions (as the sixteenth-century Scot, John Mair, put it, 'if it be said that the Scots would thereby lose their name and kingdom, so would the English, for the king of both would be called King of Britain').

Ironically enough, Scottish nationalists now look back to the period between the collapse of the Pax Cromwelliana, when the first short-lived British Parliament was established, and the Act of Union as a kind of golden age. Professor Trevor-Roper is not so sure, describing it as 'the darkest age of Scottish history'. The truth of the matter is that Scotland was — as it had been throughout so much of its history — violent, feud-ridden and torn apart by religious strife and dogmatism. The characteristic of this period was the Scots' lack of tolerance for one another. However nostalgic SNP supporters may wax about the Scottish Parliament of the time, it had extremely shallow roots — having been in existence only for a matter of decades — and its passing was mourned only by a few minor lairds and self-important burgesses of Edinburgh unable or unwilling to attend the new Parliament in London. It was a minor pork barrel, distinguished for its venality even by the standards of the time: nor, of course, were the working people of Scotland represented in it in any way.

One of the great SNP heroes from the late seventeenth century also turns out on closer scrutiny to have feet of clay: the legendary Andrew Fletcher of Saltoun (after whom the SNP's Andrew Fletcher Society is named in pious memory). Fletcher advocated the use of domestic slaves in order to bolster the sagging Scottish economy, patriotically suggesting that the Highlands should be conquered and their clans reduced to slavery. To be fair to the lady, when Margaret Bain, the SNP MP for East Dunbartonshire, proudly informed the House of Commons during discussion on the Scotland and Wales Bill that she and her party were in the proud tradition of Andrew Fletcher of Saltoun, she like many of her colleagues showed herself to be conveniently ignorant of the more sordid truths of Scottish history.

By the early 1700s Scotland's economy was in a critical condition. The Darien scheme, a desperate attempt to stimulate Scottish trade, had failed miserably. England was becoming increasingly important as the principal market for Scottish goods, so what could be more natural than for the Scots to suggest the unity of the two countries? Provided that they could keep their legal system and their Church, they were quite happy to lose their Parliament in the process. Those who like to pretend that Scotland was bullied or bludgeoned into partner-ship with an overbearing England should remember that the Scots were far keener on union than the English — having far more to gain from it — and made all the running in the years preceding the Act of Union in 1707. Scotland wanted union for essentially economic reasons, England in order to strengthen the defences of Britain as a whole; their interests were mutual and compatible, and have remained so ever since. And some of the shrewder Scots of the late seventeenth century realised that religious bigotry and conflict were more likely to be contained in the context of the wider state.

It is hardly surprising that the real golden age of Scotland should have followed the Act of Union. The eighteenth century saw a remarkable and unprecedented flowering of Scottish talents in the arts, learning, science and commerce. Edinburgh New Town was built by Robert Adam, the first planned new town to be built in Europe since Greece and Rome; it pioneered the first fire brigade in Europe, and its university was to attracf Charles Darwin and other scientists to Edinburgh in the next century. The city became known for a while as the Athens of the North, and Scottish philosophers like Adam Smith and David Hume had a European influence. Edinburgh was no longer a claustrophobic, provincial capital; opened to the influences of England she became one of the glories of eighteenth-century European civilisation. And union with England offered — as it always has done since the hungry Scots, administrators and civil servants, accompanied James VI on his way south in 1603 — innumerable opportunities for Scots to make their marks, as Sir Lewis Namier and Richard Pares have eloquently demonstrated; and often their fortunes, as well, south of the Border. Boswell and Smollett are only two of a long list of Scots to flourish in the years that followed the

Union. Since 1707 Scottish people have made an immense —
and disproportionately large — contribution to the political,
commercial, scientific and cultural life of Britain, to the benefit
of all its constituent parts. To sacrifice all this, and to bring into
conflict two countries which have lived side by side with such
outstanding success and have become so mutually interdependent would be a tragedy of the worst kind.

The early years of the union were disrupted by the Jacobite
revolts of 1715 and 1745, and the '45 in particular has been
viewed through rose-tinted — and sadly distorting — spectacles
by romantic enthusiasts for Scottish nationalism. For all his
legendary appeal, Bonnie Prince Charlie was only interested in
Scotland as a means of recapturing the British Crown for the
Stuarts; he wanted to be King of Britain in London, and not
King of Scotland in Edinburgh. His army was made up almost
entirely of Highlanders, yet most of the great clan leaders
opposed him while Lowland Scots were uniformly hostile; a
substantial proportion of 'Butcher' Cumberland's army con-
sisted of Scots, and after Culloden he was awarded the freedom
of Edinburgh and an LL.D. by a grateful Glasgow University.

The truth of the matter is that we Scots have always been
more divided amongst ourselves than pitted against the English.
Scottish history before the union of the parliaments is a gloomy,
violent tale of murders, feuds and tribal revenge: the remembered events of 1577 when a Macleod force raided the Macdonald island of Eigg, trapped 395 people in a cave and killed
the lot, or again when the Campbells, fixing on the guests,
slaughtered the Macdonalds in the massacre of Glencoe of 1691
— a matter about which in the next four years the much
vaunted Scottish Parliament did nothing. Only after the Act of
Union did Highlanders and Lowlanders, Picts and Celts begin
to recognise one another as fellow-citizens. For centuries peoples
of the Lowlands and the East coast (whose native tongue was
Lallans, a dialect of English) regarded the Gaelic-speaking
Celts of the Highlands as barbarous Irishmen; as Macaulay
himself — a Highlander — pointed out, 'a Macdonald or a
MacGregor in his tartan was, to a citizen of Edinburgh or
Glasgow, what an Indian hunter in his war paint is to an
inhabitant of Philadelphia or Boston.' Just as the present day
SNP likes to blame on the English shortcomings which are so

often the direct responsibility of the Secretary of State for Scotland and his advisers and civil servants in Edinburgh, so romantic historians have preferred to assign guilt to the English rather than to their fellow-Scots for a host of grievances, from the Glencoe Massacre to the Highland clearances.

As we have said, the Scots remained a divided people until well after the Act of Union. Once the Highlanders had been pacified and their distinctive way of life largely broken after 1745, 'Their character miraculously changed,' writes Professor Trevor-Roper: 'From idle, illiterate, thieving rogues they became, in retrospect, romantic and picturesque.' This false, nostalgic idealisation 'owed much to the mythopoetic powers of Sir Walter Scott' and it made possible the creation of a Scottish national identity. A Lancashire ironmonger devised the tartan kilt; Queen Victoria moved to Balmoral; tartan was draped 'mystically, figuratively, over all Scotland from the Tweed to the Orcades'. And it is to this entirely synthetic myth of Scotland that romantic nationalists benightedly refer.

Scotland has preserved her own identity and character throughout 270 years of fruitful and mutually rewarding union with England. We have no need for misleading, belligerent myths with which to bolster our self-confidence. We must not barter away centuries of experience in the hope of recovering a land that never was.

13

The Irish Parallel

The whole devolution debate has been haunted by the spectre of Ireland. It has taken place against a background of near civil war in Ulster, the very existence of which as a political entity separate from the rest of Ireland is all too vivid evidence of the failure of successive generations of British statesmen to solve the 'Irish Question'; and it has been widely if somewhat nebulously feared that the troubles of one Celtic country could well be repeated in another unless the Scottish people are given a greater degree of self-government.

Parallels with Ireland are, as we shall see, almost entirely unhelpful and misleading: but comparisons continue to be made, and it is essential that we should examine them here. There are three different if interdependent arguments involved. The first is that if benighted anti-devolutionists persist in denying the Scots a measure of Home Rule — in much the same way as the Conservatives and Liberal Unionists denied Home Rule to Ireland from 1885 to 1914 — moderate Scottish opinion will be forced to support the SNP, just as frustration over Home Rule made many previously moderate Irishmen turn to Republicanism out of sheer desperation. The second argument is that if the Scots are frustrated they may well decide to emulate the violent methods employed in Northern Ireland, not only by the IRA but also by the Protestants of Ulster, many of whom are of Scots origin and have a close relationship with Scotland. The third argument is that — whatever its faults, and however much it may have been resented by the Catholic third of the population — for over fifty years Ulster enjoyed devolution of the kind now proposed for Scotland and Wales while remaining an integral (if disputed) part of the United Kingdom, and that it is absurd and unfair to deny something similar to Scotland, which is not only historically a full-fledged nation (unlike Ulster) but has few of the particular problems which made Stormont rule ultimately unacceptable and impractical.

We must now examine each of these arguments in turn.

The Home Rule Parallel

Speaking at Inverclyde in March 1976, Roy Jenkins, the then Home Secretary, specifically compared the present situation in Scotland with that of Ireland at the time when Gladstone was struggling to push his successive Home Rule Bills through Parliament in the face of mischievous Conservative opposition:

> I have become increasingly concerned that we may be at a stage in relations between Scotland and the rest of the United Kingdom rather like those with Ireland in the eighties of the last century — except that events now develop at a pace more suitable to the jet age than to the railway age. And I have a strenuous desire that these events should not be allowed to repeat themselves, with the same effect, either on the health and course of British politics, or upon the integrity of the United Kingdom.

Mr Jenkins is both a moderate and eminently reasonable politician and a widely admired historian of the politics of the nineteenth and early twentieth centuries in Britain; and his fears are shared by many of those who favour devolution from a belief that it would strengthen, rather than weaken, the unity of Britain. Speculating on the might-have-beens of history is seldom a very profitable business, but it is perfectly feasible to argue that politicians like Randolph Churchill who deliberately played the 'Orange Card' in order to frustrate Home Rule were indirectly responsible for the Easter Rising, the Irish Civil War and the eventual separation of Southern Ireland from the United Kingdom, and that had Home Rule been granted the Republican cause might have died the death and a united Ireland would still form part of the United Kingdom. But to go on from there to apply the same arguments to the situation in Scotland is a shade far-fetched; and even if one accepts the

Irish analogy, the establishment of an Assembly which, by its very nature, would satisfy no one is hardly likely to provide a satisfactory solution. Professor John Mackintosh, the MP for Berwick and Professor of Political Science at Edinburgh University, is one of those who argue very persuasively from the Irish analogy to the effect that to deny Scotland an Assembly would be to drive moderate opinion into the arms of the SNP: to which one can only repeat that — as the SNP themselves well recognise — an unworkable half-way-house in Edinburgh will in fact create rather than dampen down a sense of political frustration and have exactly the opposite effect to that intended; and that those who passionately advocate an Assembly will be hard-line members of the SNP already, so that a denial of devolution is far less likely to spawn a fresh generation of nationalists than its implementation.

Unlike the English, both the Scots and the Irish have a keen sense of history; and it is to the history of the two countries that we must first turn in order to find out why the Irish and Scottish situations are not as comparable as many advocates of devolution would like us to believe. As we have seen, the relationship between England and Scotland has essentially been one of partnership (whatever romantic nationalists may say to the contrary), whereas that between England and Ireland was that of a colonial power and a conquered people; and as a result, there is no firmly embedded republican or nationalist tradition in Scotland, no hereditary sense of grievance or persecution. With the arguable exception of Lord Mountjoy in Elizabeth I's reign, no English leader has encountered success in Ireland: Henry II, Henry III, the other Plantagenets, Henry VIII, Charles I, Strafford, William of Orange, Mr Gladstone, Mr Asquith and, in our own time, Mr Heath and Mr Wilson — they all failed. The history of England's relations with Ireland was — and remains — a long chain of disasters in a way that those with Scotland have never been; and so deep was the sense of grievance and resentment in Ireland, and so strong the feeling that they were being ruled by an alien people, that even if Home Rule had been conceded it may well be that the Republican tradition would, in the end, have triumphed. As Professor Trevor-Roper has pointed out, in Scotland 'there was no expropriation, no persecution, no disfranchisement'; there has been no history of oppression by the English remotely comparable to that which occurred in Ireland (and episodes like the Highland Clearances were, as likely as not, the work of fellow-Scots). By no conceivable stretch of the imagination can the Scots claim to come from an oppressed race. The position of the Scots within the British Empire was one of considerable power and influence: while it is true that the ruling Anglo-Irish families produced a disproportionate number of British military leaders, the position of the Scots was always far more secure and far more equal than that of the Irish in relation to the English.

One basic difference between the two countries is that there has been no history of English settlement in Scotland. It is impossible to understand the bitterness of Anglo-Irish relations unless one takes into account the system whereby from the time of the Norman invasion of Ireland until the seventeenth century, Englishmen (and, ironically, Scots in Ulster) were given the best and richest land in the country, and the expropriated Irish Catholic peasants driven into the hills and bogs of the west. Scotland never had a comparable agrarian problem.

As Professor Trevor-Roper points out, 'In each country there is a distinction between Saxon (or Norman) and Celt; Ulster against the rest of Ireland, the Lowlands against the Highlands of Scotland.' But, here again, the situation is very different in Scotland. Difference between the races have been smoothed out: there is no sense of racial difference or racial antagonism within the country, of one race having unjustly subdued and dominated another.

Nor is there a comparable religious problem of the kind that continues to bedevil the Irish situation. There is no clear racial identification — as there was, and still is, in Ireland — of Protestantism with the ruling Anglo-Irish minority and the Union with Britain, and Catholicism with the oppressed Irish majority and the Republican tradition. The spirit of John Knox and the Reformation was dominant both in authority and, until recently, in numbers; yet the Protestant Churches have usually tried to foster decent, and often cordial, relations with the Roman Catholic Church, the members of which formed a fairly small minority at least until the massive waves of Irish immigration in the 1840s and the early years of this century.

Such friction as there has been has had more to do with the rival abilities of Glasgow Rangers and Glasgow Celtic than with ecclesiastical differences!

For all these historical and cultural reasons, Scotland has always been far happier about her union with England than Ireland ever was: as we have seen, the two countries came together by mutual consent rather than as a result of conquest and forcible domination, and the union has continued to work to the advantage of both for 270 years. It is worth noting that the monarchy never had anything like as close a relationship with Ireland as it has with Scotland: British monarchs paid few visits to Ireland, and never had a residence there. By contrast, the Scottish House of Stewart ascended to the British throne in 1603: Balmoral remains a favourite royal residence, and the Queen Mother — a very popular figure — is still very much a Scot. There is no deep well of bitterness and resentment of the kind that existed in Ireland, merely waiting to be tapped; and it is inviting trouble to pretend that there is.

Again, it should be remembered that proposing Home Rule for Ireland in the 1880s was a far less complicated business than proposing devolution for Scotland in the 1970s. Quite apart from the fact that Ireland is geographically separated from the rest of Britain (something which also applies *vis-à-vis* the fag-end of Home Rule that was — ironically — given to the people of Ulster from 1922 to 1972), the economies of England and Ireland were nothing like as closely integrated as those of England and Scotland today; nor was government nearly so closely involved in the management of the economy. Late nineteenth-century Britain was not a land of Industrial Development Certificates, Regional Planning or huge national-ised industries, all of them intimately involved with the actions of government In. the 1880s, the standing of a Government did not rise or fall with the announcement of the monthly balance of payments or unemployment figures; nor did it occur to people that Mr Gladstone or Mr Disraeli should be responsible for a coherent employment policy, and shoulder the blame if thousands of teenagers were unable to find a job. It was far more realistic for Mr Gladstone to contemplate 'hiving off' certain domestic functions of government to Dublin than it is for a present-day government to face up to the appalling complexity

that would be entailed in breaking up the economic management of the United Kingdom.

It is, of course, impossible to say whether Ireland would have
eventually broken away from the United Kingdom even if
Home Rule had been granted: I suspect that, given the sad
history of Anglo-Irish relations, it would have done anyway.
Yet to Parnell and his followers, Home Rule was an entirely
acceptable objective in itself; and had it been granted, it would
have been given ample time in which to work itself out. The
situation is very different in Scotland today: not only is Home
Rule so very much more difficult to implement, but there exists
in the SNP — to say nothing of Jim Sillars's Scottish Labour
Party — a well-organised political body which has no interest
in working within the framework of devolution, and openly
admits that the Assembly is little more than a stage on the way
to full independence. (Incidentally, the SNP are much given to
quoting Parnell's famous edict 'No man can set a limit to the
march of a nation ... No man can say to its people "thus far and
no further".') I have argued elsewhere that if this was made
clear to those who at present support the SNP as a form of
protest against the major political parties, they would hurriedly
think again: to offer an Assembly from a misguided fear that to
do otherwise would be to risk an Irish situation is to play into
the hands of the nationalists.

Ulster and the Fear of Violence

English politicians in particular have been terrified that if the
Scots were denied devolution, political violence and near civil
war might spread from Northern Ireland to Scotland — fears
that were exacerbated by the ephemeral activities of the so-
called 'Tartan Army' in the early 1970s, and a confused
tendency to assume that the existence of Orange Lodges in
Scotland and the ritualised reflection of the Irish troubles in
Rangers versus Celtic football matches must have something to
do with an unpredictable Celtic readiness to flare up at random
provocation.

Michael Foot was the first major politician to make a lurid
parallel with Ulster, when replying to a question on Thames
Television in December 1976. Had this been an ill-considered or

off-the-cuff reply — even from so experienced a politician as the Lord President of the Council — it might not have been worthy of repetition: but he returned to the theme in a major speech to the Scottish Conference of the Labour Party at Perth in March 1977. As Neal Ascherson, the pro-devolution correspondent of the *Scotsman*, put it next day: 'Mr Foot startled delegates by twice alluding to Irish bloodshed, to explain why Scottish devolution was urgent. The guillotine defeat had reminded him of the nineteenth-century Liberal defeats over Home Rule for Ireland.' 'I hope we shall do all in our power to ensure that no such tragic events follow February 22nd, for that is the parallel,' Mr Foot went on. 'If the Labour Government and the Labour Movement cannot bring the politics of persuasion to success, then very often what we condemn our people to is the politics of violence and force, as we can see across the Irish Channel.'

At a superficial level, it is easy to see why the fear of Ulster-type violence spreading to Scotland has been so great. In 1969–71, in particular, many politicians were terrified that violence would slop over from Belfast and Londonderry into Glasgow and the West of Scotland: indeed, the then Home Secretary, Mr Callaghan, refused to take with him to Ulster his Scottish PPS, Gregor Mackenzie — the MP for Rutherglen — from a fear that Mr Mackenzie might find himself in trouble if he made any statement to the press on his return. Yet these fears had nothing to do with Scottish nationalism as such, but reflected worries that — out of sympathy with their co-religionists in Ireland — Protestants and Catholics in Glasgow in particular might come into confrontation. The fact that this did not take place serves to underline the deep differences between the Irish and Scottish situations.

Again, there is no tradition of political violence and insurrection in Scotland, such as exists in both parts of Ireland. There are two reasons why the SNP did not take to the streets after the defeat of the Scotland and Wales Bill. In the first place, they are — and claim to be — dedicated to achieving their aims by lawful means; and, even if they were not, it would have been almost impossible to muster more than derisory support. The vehement disclaimers by the SNP concerning the activities of the 'Tartan Army' should be believed. The attempt to blow up an electricity sub-station and the damage done to part of an oil pipeline near Bo'ness in 1975 were hooligan pranks rather than politically motivated acts of sabotage. News of these incidents were received with horror in Scotland. There was an overwhelming feeling in all sections of the community that the kind of tragedy afflicting Northern Ireland must at all costs be avoided; SNP leaders genuinely abhor violence, and recognise that any resort to it would do irreparable damage to their cause. Irish republicanism has flourished on myths of suffering, bloodshed and martyrdom: this is far from being the case in Scotland.

The Example of Stormont

In an interview with the Glasgow *Daily Record* of 7 May 1976, Edward Heath said:

> I don't accept that you have to have a federal system of government in order to devolve most of the functions of government, including finance and economic functions. This is shown in the Government of Ireland Act of 1921 when legislative power over a very wide field, including finance and the economy, was given to the Northern Ireland Parliament at Stormont. Northern Ireland remained, and is, a part of the United Kingdom. I see no reason why Scotland should not have these powers and remain part of the United Kingdom.

By one of the absurd ironies of history, the very part of Ireland which had most fiercely opposed Home Rule for Ireland was itself given Home Rule at the end of the day. The existence of a large Catholic minority in Northern Ireland, and the fact that it was governing only part of a larger historical entity, presented the Stormont government with unique problems which — mercifully — would not be shared by an Assembly in Edinburgh: but leaving these aside, why should Scotland not have, as Mr Heath has suggested, a Parliament of its own along the lines of that enjoyed until recently by Northern Ireland?

Certainly many Ulster people — and particularly those from the Protestant, Unionist majority — speak well of the days when Ulster had her own Prime Minister and Cabinet. Shortly before his untimely death, Lord Faulkner — the last Prime Minister but one — told me that, on balance, more industry, investment and jobs had come to Ulster under the devolved system of government than would have been the case had UK Ministries been responsible instead. He claimed that quicker results and decisions could be obtained as well. On the other hand, the uncomfortable fact remains that Ulster has had the most intransigent problems of unemployment of any part of the United Kingdom for the past half-century: and this may well be because, as we have argued elsewhere in this book, civil servants in Whitehall gave, and tend to give, priority to investment in those areas for which they, and not another Government, have responsibility. And exactly the same would apply in the event of there being an Assembly in Edinburgh.

Again, Stormont provided an awful warning that small is not always beautiful. Had Stormont not existed, and had Westminster enjoyed direct responsibility for those areas 'devolved' to it, the immediate cause of the present troubles would have been eliminated a long time ago — namely blatant bias against Catholics in the the allocation of council houses in Protestant-dominated areas. Whatever Westminster's shortcomings, it is inconceivable that British Governments with a direct responsibility — of whatever complexion — would have tolerated the behaviour of the Ulster Housing Authorities. Is it conceivable that governments which included Herbert Morrison and Chuter Ede, Harold Macmillan and Iain Macleod, would have acquiesced for one week in housing allocation bias against British citizens on account of their religion? No, it is not.

Now it could well be said that this is no reflection on devolved situations as such, and that the situation in Ulster was uniquely difficult and fraught. Up to a point, this is true: but the suspicion remains that difficulties of this kind are more likely to brew up in a small, inward-looking governmental set-up, where the various factions know one another only too well, than in a large cosmopolitan nation of 50 million people, run from an international city like London.

One final digression on the subject of Northern Ireland, since it has some relevance to the Government's most recent devolution proposals. Michael Foot has often enjoyed taunting those Ulster Unionists who want to see Stormont restored, without favouring devolution for Scotland and Wales: 'For themselves, but not for others!' as he put it earlier this year. And it is true that, since the 1920s, the twelve Ulster MPs (most of whom have, until recently, stoutly aligned themselves with the Conservatives) have been able to vote on UK matters over which, until the suspension of Stormont, the Westminster Parliament had no say in Ulster — a situation which, as we have seen, would be replete with problems if applied equally to the Scots and the Welsh following devolution, especially since each Ulster MP represents on average some 85,000 constituents, whereas the seventy-one Scottish MPs represent on average 52,000 constituents.

Ironically enough, the Labour Government seems willing to allow Scottish MPs to vote at Westminster on matters for which they would have no responsibility following the establishment of an Assembly in Edinburgh: yet between 1964 and 1966, when his Government had a precarious majority, Harold Wilson argued day in and day out that the twelve Ulster MPs should have no right to vote on issues such as the nationalisation of steel because there was no steel industry in Northern Ireland. As David Wood of *The Times* has pointed out:

> The argument seemed profoundly popular at the time with Labour ministers and backbenchers. They made a dead set at the Ulster Unionist MPs, and backbenchers were apparently encouraged or perhaps needed no encouragement, to align themselves with the civil rights campaign that eventually ran out of control and made it necessary to send in the army to restore law and order [*The Times*, 6 December 1976].

But then the moral of this chapter is that one cannot always judge the Scottish situation by what has happened, or is happening, in Ireland.

14

Some Proposals

One of the fatal temptations of senior Ministerial life is the urge
to make changes not merely because they are necessary or
desirable, but on account of a feeling that to leave things as they
are does not justify one's tenure of the high office. Besides,
senior Ministers are as human as the rest of us: preserving the
status quo is unlikely to earn a man a place in the history books
or gratify a member of the Cabinet's understandable desire for
tangible achievement; yet very often it is vastly preferable to
change largely for the sake of change. The whole devolution
saga is riddled with dispiriting examples of the ways in which
the appetite for unnecessary and ultimately unwanted change
can, self-generating, feed upon itself. However indifferent or
even hostile a member of the Cabinet may have been towards a
particular aspect of Government policy in a previous incarna-
tion, he is almost certain to change his tune should he become
the Minister responsible for the implementation of that very
thing — even the most modest and self-effacing of politicians
hopes to be remembered in some way; the chance of steering
through Parliament and on to the Statute Books a Bill which
fundamentally alters the Constitution of the United Kingdom
in a way that has not been witnessed since the Act of Union
itself can provide the opportunity for immortality, such as is
given to few of us in a lifetime or a generation.

Small wonder then, that a once cautious, balanced politician
like Edward Short should have overnight become almost messianic about devolution when Harold Wilson made him the
devolution supremo; and this in spite of his long allegiance to
and concern for the North-East of England, an area well-known

even in 1974 for its awareness of the problems caused by the special interests of the Scots; or that his successor, Michael Foot, so long the marvellously eloquent champion of the sovereignty of Parliament, should have been willing, even anxious, to perpetrate so grave an incursion into the power of Westminster, and accept his Ministerial inheritance with unanticipated enthusiasm.

A comparable itch to make one's mark in history sometimes afflicts the members of Royal Commissions. Setting up a Royal Commission is an understandable enough reaction on the part of a Prime Minister who is baffled by a particular problem or is anxious to play for time while giving the impression that he is doing something about it; or genuinely wants to establish what are the settled opinions of the people most intimately concerned before committing himself to action. The trouble is that the Commission's members then come to have a vested interest in suggesting changes to the *status quo* which may not be really necessary. Royal Commissions generally sit for months or even years like hens on broody eggs, costing the taxpayers a mounting sum in the process; as spring turns to summer and summer to autumn, their distinguished members feel almost duty bound to come up with suggestions for change, if only to justify the time and expense that has been lavished upon them, while their chairmen are sadly aware that recommending 'no change' will dash expectations, provoke ribaldry at the paucity of their effort and is unlikely to make their names echo down posterity.

And so the momentum for change builds up — with often potentially disastrous implications in the case of an issue of such fundamental importance as devolution. Two particular facets of recent Labour administrations have fortuitously hastened the process still further. Mr Wilson always took great pride at party Conferences in listing those promises in the party manifesto which his government had carried out or was in the process of carrying out — to such an extent that his being able to tick off another manifesto commitment seemed to assume more importance to him than deciding whether the issue in question was, in fact, desirable, as relevant or as feasible as it had seemed in the heady, far-off days when the manifesto was first drawn up. Surely it would not be dishonourable to point out that the offer of an Assembly in the October 1974 manifesto, if ill thought-through and hastily devised, was made in all good faith. Just as Mrs Nancy Trenaman, a member of the Kilbrandon Commission and the Principal of St Anne's College, Oxford, can publicly confess that she voted — 'just' and 'reluctantly' — for the Commission's majority recommendations but, with hindsight, would no longer do so on account of a lack of the necessary consensus essential to their implementation, so a Government can change its mind. It is only reasonable that politicians should want to honour their electoral promises, but to do so in the face of their subsequent convictions and experience partly in order to be able to chalk up a plus in the party's achievements over the preceding twelve months is carrying a narrow interpretation of honour too far.

The second fortuitous factor which has had some bearing on the devolution story is, as we have seen, the weakness of some Government Ministers for spending their time tinkering with the constitution and the machinery of government as a substitute for facing up to and tackling the real problems confronting the country. Fiddling about with the constitution may appear to be a comparatively harmless exercise; but, alas, politicians are all too often blissfully unaware of the implication of what they are up to; and once one has embarked on changes of this kind, it is very hard — indeed impossible — to go back to square one, even if that clearly becomes the right thing to do.

Mercifully, it is still not too late to stop the devolution juggernaut in its Gadarene rush, despite the 'vested interests of the mind' — to use Tawney's famous phrase — that it is now carrying along with it, and despite a vague and almost fatalistic belief that it must by now be virtually unstoppable. Public figures are understandably reluctant to change their minds too often in public or to admit that they have been mistaken or misled: yet I passionately believe that there need be no shame in Ministers admitting that, on further reflection and in the light of more recent experience, devolution now turns out to be unexpectedly costly and a threat to that which, above all else, they wish to preserve — the unity of the kingdom. Although they may not realise it, the majority of people in Scotland would not think the worse of them if Ministers blurted out the real feelings of so many of them; namely that the time had

come to think again about the whole preposterous exercise
which goes under the name of devolution. Nor is there any
need to be over-fearful about Scottish reactions to a *volte-face* of
this nature. As we have seen, many people in Scotland would
heave a sigh of relief if they never came across the word
'devolution' again; and for all the ballyhoo in political circles
and in the media, it has never rated at all highly as a priority
among the Scottish electorate, and its passing would be mourned
only by the comparatively few, who genuinely believed that
devolution would bring government closer to the people, and
by those who wanted to use the Assembly not for its own sake,
but as a tool to obtain the objectives of a separate state. However, the moment an Assembly came into being, it would be too
late to unscramble matters; even at this eleventh hour, to think,
think and think again would be neither dishonourable nor
politically disastrous.

After all the sound and fury of the past few years, is it realistic
to hope that we could return to the *status quo*? Once expectations have been aroused — however misleadingly — can they
in practice be damped down or diverted that easily? My answer
is that most of those who favour devolution have hitherto failed
to think out its full implications — apart, that is, from members
of the SNP, who rightly perceive exactly where it would lead us
— and that the time has come for us to confront the residents
of Scotland with the practical paraphernalia of becoming a
separate country: passports checked every time a businessman
takes the Glasgow-London shuttle or a family from industrial
Lanarkshire sets off down the motorway to show the kids the
Blackpool illuminations; pounds Scots and pounds sterling,
with all the chaos for industry, pensions and a host of other
everyday concerns; friends and relatives in England becoming
foreigners. We must rethink our whole approach to the problem and do certain things to meet some of the legitimate niggles
of people in Scotland *within our existing contstitutional framework*.

In Chapter 11, I argued that there are three theoretical
alternatives facing the United Kingdom: separate nation states
for Scotland and Wales, as favoured by the SNP and Plaid
Cymru, which would mean the end of Britain as we now know it
and would almost certainly prove disastrous to the people of
both countries; federalism, which is impractical since England

would so obviously dominate the federation — hardly the ideal
way of assuaging an alleged sense of grievance in Scotland and
Wales; or retaining and trying to improve the *status quo*. For all
the wild and woolly schemes of those who favour devolution,
and the glib sloganeering which accompanies them, the last of
these is the only one which is compatible with the continued
existence of the United Kingdom. What, then, can be done? My
suggestions are dull and earthy, and would command no
headlines:

(1) My first suggestion is an essentially negative one. We
must stop pandering to the nationalists and conceding that they
have a respectable case. Their proposals are crackers, and we
should say so. The gut issues which really concern the people of
Wales and Scotland are exactly the same as those which bother
their fellow-citizens in England, and — as we have argued
already — votes for the SNP and Plaid Cymru have essentially
been protest votes against the apparent inability of successive
Governments to deal satisfactorily with rising prices, unemployment or whatsoever. Only once in the entire history of the
Union have MPs voted along national rather than political
lines; it would be tragic — and unnecessary — if they were to
start doing so now. Rather than devoting time to working out
elaborate constitutional changes with which to outwit the
nationalists the Government should concentrate energies now
being diverted into devolution on those issues which caused so
many Scottish voters to turn to the SNP in the first place.
Tackle the real issues and a rampant nationalist political party
can be contained. Given a glimmer of economic success, dis-
affected voters will realise how irrelevant the SNP was to their
real interests and return to their old allegiances with a sigh of
relief.

(2) As we have seen, devolution would add yet another layer
of government to those already endured by the over-governed
people of Scotland — quite apart from the cost of the caper.
How much more rational and economical to build on the
regional reforms introduced in 1973 following the Wheatley
Report. Not only do the Regions bring government closer to
the people in a way that an Assembly would not: they are also
far more sensitive to the very different demands of the various
parts of Scotland. Both the major political parties should make a

genuine commitment to the regions, including a clear undertaking that — whatever teething troubles they have had so far
— they propose allowing them at least a decade in which to
settle down (with the possible qualification that there should be
all-party talks with Strathclyde Regional Councillors and
officials to see whether there is not some mutually acceptable
way of dividing Strathclyde into three separate regions).

Nor should the regions of England be forgotten: it is worth
remembering that according to the Attitude Survey commis-
sioned by the Kilbrandon Commission, people in Scotland
were only marginally more interested in 'devolution' (in the
sense of a super local authority rather than a legislative
Assembly) than those in the English regions (73 per cent in
Scotland, as opposed to 69 per cent in North-West England, 66
per cent in southern England, 65 per cent in the Midlands and
62 per cent in Yorkshire). Urgent talks should be held with key
councillors such as Sir Stanley Yapp of the West Midlands and
Bill Sefton of Merseyside and Michael Campbell of Tyne and
Wear about the possibilities of local government in England —
and Scotland — being given greater power in the industrial
field. A system which preserved a rough uniformity in the
relationship between industry and local authorities throughout
the United Kingdom would be essential. Considerable powers
could be devolved in this way — indeed, it might be as well to
await the outcome of such discussions before going too far with
the dismantling of Strathclyde Region.

(3)   One of the difficulties one faces when discussing local
government — at whatever level — is public scepticism about
the probity of local government officials and councillors. In the
light of the Poulson and T. Dan Smith scandals, this is hardly
surprising, though sections of the press have fanned the flames
of prejudice in a cruel manner against councillors, many of
whom sacrifice their personal and family lives to serve the
public. All too often, people seem to assume that if local
authorities aren't actually corrupt, they are likely to be self
perpetuating, complacent, insensitive and unimaginative. If we
are going to build up the regions in Scotland and Wales, it is
essential that we should try to build up trust again and to
stamp out corruption in local government. Corruption is, in
fact, far rarer than the press and the media would lead one to

believe; but I have no doubt that the running saga of alleged Labour local government corruption in Dundee has done much to swell the SNP vote throughout Scotland, and the Regions themselves cannot be presented as a feasible alternative to an Assembly in Edinburgh until the taint of corruption has been lifted from local government in general.

(4) Money must be allocated to Scottish local authorities for the specific purpose of building up their house maintenance and repair capability. Scotland has the largest proportion of state-owned houses of any country outside the Eastern bloc: failure to put through housing repairs reasonably promptly has created immense and festering dissatisfaction of the kind which reduces Labour and Conservative councillors to despair, and win far more votes for the SNP than any amount of rhetoric about Scottish independence.

(5) The Wheatley Report's recommendations that Community Councils should be established — forming the bottom layer of the governmental pyramid — should be far more widely implemented than they are at present. Such councils really would bring decision-making closer to the individual, yet whether through lethargy or lack of cash, District Councils have been extremely reluctant to accept the Wheatley proposals — with the result that local government now gives the deceptive appearance of being more remote in many parts of Scotland than it did before the Wheatley Commission reported.

(6) New towns in Scotland have always tended to be hotbeds of nationalism. To some extent, this is because of the highly undemocratic structure of a New Town Development Corporation; many voters will therefore turn to the SNP as a way of registering a protest against it. The Development Corporations should be abolished and responsibility for new towns put in the hands of Regional authorities. Such a move would also be justifiable in that it would make it more feasible for a Region to plan for an area as a whole. As it is, a new town like Livingston gobbles up educational and other resources at the expense of the surrounding area.

(7) Urgent action should be taken to advance the cause of industrial democracy. This is neither the time nor the place to argue the merits of the Bullock Report: suffice it to say, however, that the SNP has benefited very considerably from a feel-

ing common in many firms and factories on both sides of the Border that key decisions which affect the lives of those who work in them are made by remote managerial figures in distant offices without their being consulted in any way (naturally, the SNP has made much play of the fact that so many of the firms operating in Scotland have their headquarters in England). An Assembly of the kind proposed in the Scotland and Wales Bill could do little or nothing to promote industrial democracy; yet the implementation of industrial democracy would do much to reduce a particular source of grievance in Scotland.

(8)   British politicians must show themselves to be more concerned with the good government of Scotland than with the possible consequences of their views on devolution and other Scottish matters on the party line-up at Westminster and the maintenance of a particular party in power. One of the great tragedies about devolution is that it has become inextricably involved in short-term questions of political expediency; and Labour politicians are particularly — and mistakenly — vulnerable to threats that, unless devolution is introduced there will never be another Labour Government at Westminster. It is natural enough that any Government should do its utmost to remain in power, since its members are bound to believe that their remaining in office must be for the good of the country; but devolution, with its disastrous implications, is far too important and fundamental an issue to become a mere bargaining counter in the political game.

(9)   As we have seen, many often very trivial issues have contributed to the rise of Scottish nationalism — small irritants which could, with a little care and sensitivity, be very easily remedied. For example, a simple partial remedy would be to ask the broadcasting authorities to provide finance so that Scottish soccer matches could be filmed on BBC and ITV with the same standard of camera work as that employed in England. It is almost no exaggeration to say that in the early 1960s the most effective political propagandist working in favour of the SNP was Kenneth Wolstenholme of the BBC — a sports commentator whose propensity to patronise the Scots was insufferable.

Televised recording of the House of Commons is unlikely to have such electoral appeal; nevertheless, it would almost certainly counteract the Scottish feeling of being remote from the

centre of political life far more effectively than setting up an
Assembly in Edinburgh. If televised proceedings were thought
undesirable, sound broadcasting would do almost as well.

(10) The government's publicity machine should never be
used for party political purposes under normal circumstances;
but when the break-up of the United Kingdom is involved, I
seen no reason why Government Departments should not have
the right — indeed the duty — to spell out exactly what would
be involved in the event of a separate state being eventually
established following the introduction of an Assembly in Edinburgh.

For example, the Foreign Office should make it clear that
passports would be required between England and Scotland.
The cost of diplomatic Scottish representation abroad should be
made more widely known; although, as we have seen, Scotland
would not be a member of the EEC, she would need diplomatic
representation in the Community, as well as in London, at the
United Nations and in Washington, Canberra, Delhi, Islama-
bad, Ottawa, Wellington, Oslo, Stockholm, Helsinki, Reykja-
vik and elsewhere — quite an expense for a population of only
5 million to carry.

Hitherto, Ministers have been supercilious and bone idle
when asked to produce some kind of costings of separate Scottish armed forces. But costings should be done giving the extra
expense involved in naval, oil and fishery protection and the
maintenance of separate Scottish armed services.

A separate Scottish air force would involve substantial extra
costs; the maintenance problems for example of the Nimrod
squadron, based on Lossiemouth, might be almost insuperable.
And yet, without the Nimrod surveillance role, who could say
that a Scottish air force would be a viable unit? It is quite
unreal to think in terms of hiving off a segment of the RAF, and
supposing that the one-ninth or so of the British air force would
be able to fulfil its operational requirement, even inside NATO.
In an age when it costs £500,000 or more to train one pilot for
a multi-role combat aircraft, small effective air forces are something of the past. The RAF today needs many special skills,
and it is highly unlikely that these skills would be divided
so neatly, if a Scottish air force were formed, that it would have
the right proportion of particular skills in every sphere of activity.

A separate Scottish army could be formed on the nucleus of the Scottish Regiments, though many of them, such as the Royal Scots Dragoon Guards, have more English than Scots currently serving in them. Besides, there is the question as to whether regulars in the British army, albeit Scots, born in Scotland, would necessarily want to continue their career in a Scots army. When I went to Sandhurst in the summer of 1976, to give a lecture on devolution, several young officers in Scottish Infantry Regiments volunteered to me that they would resign their commission if a Scots army came into being. They averred that they would not wish to serve in a Scots army, nor be in the position of mercenaries in an English army.

Defence Ministers have a duty to bring such practical problems to the attention of the public, since the Scottish people cannot shirk an electoral judgment on a vital matter of national security.

15

The End of Britain?

It may well be said that the proposals put forward in the last
chapter hardly include any fresh or inspiring initiatives with
which to counter the appeal of the Scottish National Party or
even pro-Assembly orators. This is quite true: they do not.
They pretend to be no more than they actually are — a hotch-
potch of fairly marginal, palliative measures, designed to help
the electoral fortunes of the traditional political parties. Plans
for setting up an Edinburgh Assembly may seem, at first sight,
more plausible, more attractive and far more impressive; but to
offer instead altogether more modest, tinkering proposals of the
kind I have suggested has a better chance of helping to avert
the disintegration of the United Kingdom. Yet all the proposals
of this nature, whether negative or positive, cannot cumulatively
be of more than marginal use in underwriting the continuance
of the Union. In only one way can we hope to guarantee the
unity of the country, and that is the realisation by the people of
Scotland that they could easily bring about the break-up of
Britain. The choice is stark and cannot be evaded.

One of the most dangerous illusions of politics is that a clutch
of panaceas can be found for complex, intractable problems of
the kind I have been discussing in this book. If such magic cures
existed, they would surely have been discovered months, even
years ago by hard-working civil servants and able Ministers
groping around for solutions. Politicians, like the rest of us,
yearn for the all-embracing answer to the seemingly baffling
question; and their natural tendency to do so — to look to
devolution to resolve the challenge presented by Scottish and
Welsh nationalism, in this particular case — has been exag-

gerated in recent times by the constant pressure put upon them to produce instant answers before they have had sufficient time to ponder and reflect. And the central fact about the Government's commitment to devolution is that not since October 1974 has the issue of a Scottish Assembly in Edinburgh been properly considered *on its merits*. It has become hopelessly intertwined with personal and political issues of the kind discussed in the last chapter, most of which are short-term, extraneous and ultimately irrelevant to a matter involving the very integrity of the United Kingdom herself.

We cannot go on fudging the issue any longer, refusing to take a stand out of an unjustified fear that to resist devolution would be to create a second Ulster north of the Border or from a fatalistic belief that one would never be forgiven by one's erstwhile supporters in Scotland. The people of Scotland must be made to realise that there is not, and never can be, a tenable half-way house between remaining an integral part of the United Kingdom and opting for a Scottish state. As we have seen, one of the rocks on which the Scotland and Wales Bill foundered in the House of Commons was the realisation that one cannot have a subordinate Parliament in part — though only part — of a unitary state. The great danger is that Scotland may well stumble into independence simply because not enough people understand where devolution — which sounds so harmless and unexceptionable — will lead them: and once the School Room in Edinburgh has accrued to itself the trappings of a Parliament there will be no turning back. As they set out on the inevitable slide to independence, it will be no use devolutionists whining that they never intended to bring about the end of the Union; they merely neglected to apply their minds to the foreseeable and predictable consequences of taking the easy road. Can we reasonably imagine that England, perplexed and jilted by a divorced partner, will make no difficulties when the Scots reapply for membership of the United Kingdom as the oil reserves in the North Sea begin to drain away? Yet once an Assembly had opened in Edinburgh, the process of divorce would become inevitable. Once the machine is in motion, it cannot be put into reverse.

It could be argued that life in an independent Scotland could hardly be less agreeable and might be a good deal better for some than life in a United Kingdom racked by inflation, unemployment, rising prices and an apparently incurable economy. Yet we have seen that this is very unlikely to be the situation, and that life in a Scotland which was divorced from England and unacceptable as a separate member of the EEC to any foreseeable Government of France or Germany would be a good deal less rosy than Scottish visionaries would like us to believe. Nor can it be argued that political nationalism is one of the great liberating causes of the human spirit. National self-assertion has not done much for the cause of peace or the improvement of living standards in this century; it is out of tune with man's struggling attempts to gather himself into slightly larger groupings than before for the better use of his limited resources. Nationalism is a poor answer to the need felt by a great many people to have more control over their own affairs, for one cannot be sure that a more narrow-minded and centralised bureaucracy will not replace the one that went before, however imperfect. Feelings of pride in one's land and one's culture are both respectable and desirable, but they are perfectly compatible with membership of a somewhat wider political family; to sacrifice the benefits accrued over 270 years in order to gratify confused and ephemeral political ambitions would be tragic and unforgivably foolish. Now it is up to the people of Scotland to decide whether they really do want to dismantle the United Kingdom and bring about the end of Britain.

Index